Economic Integration and Economic Strategy

Economic Integration and Economic Strategy

Ferenc Kozma

1982

Springer-Science+Business Media, B.V.

Library of Congress Cataloging in Publication Data

Kozma, Ferenc.

Economic integration and economic strategy.

Rev. translation of: Gazdasági integráció és gazdasági stratégia.

1. Europe, Eastern—Economic integration.
2. Council for Mutual Economic Assistance.
3. European Economic Community. 4. International economic integration. 5. Hungary—Foreign economic relations. I. Title.

HC244.K6949 337.1'47 82-6383

AACR2

DOI 10.1007/978-94-017-1362-7

Revised edition of Gazdasági integráció és gazdasági stratégia
published by Közgazdasági és Jogi Könyvkiadó, Budapest

English translation by György Hajdu
Translation revised by András Bródy

Originally published by Akadémiai Kiadó, Budapest in 1982.
MyCopy version of the original edition 1982

Contents

Introduction

It was in 1967–68 that I wrote the book *Economic relations between "the two Europes" and the socialist international cooperation*, published in 1970. Its main message may be summed up as follows:

1. Between economic development and underdevelopment exists a state which stabilizes under capitalist economic—and world economic—relations and constitutes a particular peripheral zone around the developed cores of the world economy. It is a historic feat of the European socialist countries to have broken out of this peripheral situation and to move towards the complete liquidation of their historical backwardness.

2. The position of the group of European socialist countries in world economy, and within it, in Europe, is determined by the asymmetry which is at the same time the most characteristic feature of their domestic development: namely, that the "traditional" extent and manner of their participation in the international division of labour no longer corresponds to their development requirements, their having become much more developed and exacting. At the same time, their full participation in the division of labour of the highly developed countries is still hindered—beyond the deliberate and spontaneous repressive efforts of the West—by the fact that their forces of production have not yet reached an advanced state. This is what makes East–West economic relationships even more contradictory and constitutes a menace to every effort made in this direction.

3. Today, similarly to the fifties, the European socialist countries put the development of their economic cooperation at the service of eliminating the relative backwardness of their forces of production. The central issue of socialist integration is not how to solve the market problem or improve the conditions of competition with the industry of the United States of America, but to ensure collectively a high and even rate of growth—initially through industrialization, and, from the mid-sixties on increasingly through planned modernization. Therefore, the integrational efforts of the CMEA (Council of Mutual Economic Assistance) countries will necessarily focus on the collation of economic development projects, or programs. It is through the latter, among other things, that the group

of European socialist countries might achieve positions worthier of their results also in East–West economic relations.

The years since the publication of the book (1970) have been rich in events. I should like to draw the readers' attention to three in particular:

First of all, a new stage of the crisis of capitalist world economy evolved, manifesting itself in highly diversified phenomena, from the disturbances of the world monetary system and inflation—which might be called *a grave illness of the "nervous system" of world economy*—to shortages in primary energy, raw materials and basic foodstuffs—which point to *a grave disturbance in the "metabolism" of capitalist world economy*. It has become clear that, under the prevailing capitalist relations, growth and equilibrium—and, with it, a minimum of political stability—can be maintained only with the preservation and development of a distorted productive machinery. The basic conditions of the functioning of this productive machinery are: (a) the centralization of development activities in a few centres—which results in a world-wide polarization of development, and (b) the abuse of nature, the wasteful consumption of wastefully extracted natural resources and thus the pollution of human environment. In this manner capitalism is likely to become *fatal* for all mankind, even apart from the production of weapons for mass destruction and the menace of war. The explosively emerging and amassing crisis phenomena in recent years have called attention to the fact that the trend and quality of technical progress strongly bear the imprint of capitalist relations weighed down by the crisis. From this we have to draw far-reaching conclusions for the national economic strategies of the CMEA member countries, for socialist integration, as well as for East–West economic relations.

The other process evolving in recent years, by far not independently of the former, is *the destabilization of the world position of West-European capitalism*. This has taken West-European capitalism by surprise, precisely when it had the greatest momentum in its strivings to reconquer its pre-war role, and to break the political and economic domination of the USA. All this confounded and *shook in its foundations the West-European economic integration process*, too. Events rapidly followed each other also in this field. Expansion of the Common Market became only half successful and restricted after the Norwegian veto. The plans for gradually creating a monetary union failed, and so did those envisaging a common energy policy and a regional fund. The reactions of the member countries to the dollar crisis were different and they did not tolerate the enforcement of a collective solution. Attempts to coordinate industrial policies also remained on paper and finally, as a result of measures taken by the Italian government, a rift appeared in the "common market" in the narrower sense, too. We can fully agree with Mrs. Gabriella Hedri Izik, according to whom the conditions of long-term and medium-term regulations in the integration of the West-European type are missing, which could be preconditions of the harmonization of structures and technical development. Because of the sharpened conflicts, integration is forced to make short-term compromises. As a consequence, a conflict situation "stabilizes" and crisis phenomena appear more frequently and with growing force.[1] All this allows us to draw far-reaching conclusions regarding the nature of socialist cooperation as well.

The third process to be mentioned which has become perceptible in recent years, but by far not the last one as regards its importance, is the *socialist integration evolving on the basis of the Comprehensive Program.* Its development has much confirmed the signals I gave in the book quoted.[2] On the one hand, it has become clear, and the text of the Comprehensive Program itself reflects this recognition, that the mechanism of cooperation can be reformed only if the development objectives are known, and the mechanism must be made to conform to them. Practice has also proven that in the present stage of development the economic situation of the European socialist countries allows no decisive qualitative jumps either in planning or in the field of market mechanisms. It follows that a period of gradual progress through small steps follows, in which a highly differentiated system of instruments will be applied.[3] Also a tendency seems to evolve which makes integration dependent on the technical and scientific revolution which is strengthening and widening in Soviet economy.[4] The most important statement of the book, not contradicted by development up to now, but not yet fully evolved in life, was that *cooperation should be definitely concentrated on the development of an international division of labour in development projects which are of decisive importance for the Community as a whole.* In technological research there exist already some cooperation projects which are near in nature to this; multilateral cooperation in computer technology, as well as the international unions formed in our days are already reminiscent of the said principle, but they are still very far from promoting the deliberate and definite shaping of real international "development poles". They are much more motivated by efforts to solve the given tight situation, than by a well-reasoned long-term macro-economic strategy. As such, they rather demonstrate the real *necessity* of strategic concepts than the *domination* of such concepts in the integration.

In this book I intend to continue the reasoning started in the *"Two Europes".* For me it has now become even clearer that if we want to develop the economic integration of a *given* group of countries, we have nothing else to rely upon than

[1] „Az EGK válságjelenségeinek okai" (Causes of the crisis phenomena in the EEC). *Külgazdaság*, 1974, No. 5.

[2] F. Kozma: *A „két Európa" gazdasági kapcsolatai és a szocialista nemzetközi együttműködés* (Economic relations between "the two Europes" and the socialist international cooperation). Közgazdasági és Jogi Könyvkiadó, Budapest 1970.

[3] *Op. cit.*, p. 250 and pp. 267–278.

[4] *Op. cit.*, pp. 255–257 and pp. 276–278.

the needs and economic development conditions of that *given* group of countries. In other words, *there is no general model for economic integration*, or if there is, it is merely a collection of generalities that cannot be implemented in practice.

A real integration program is thus determined in space and time. When we speak about developing the integration, the further development and the plan for action for the CMEA community, we have to set out from the facts that

— the majority of the CMEA countries, those most mature for economic integration, are situated in *Eastern Europe*. Eastern Europe is meant here mainly not in the geographical, but in the historical sense;

— the pivotal problem of economic integration is the *harmonization of economic development strategies*, with regard to the internal development possibilities of this group of countries and their world economic position as well;

— the economic development of the countries associated in the CMEA is a particular *socialist* development.

Thus, the division of labour within the integration has to solve a treble task: it has to promote *in the long run* the economic development of the member countries *in the direction of socialism*, by providing real collective solutions for the particularly *East-European* development problems. I should like to stress that *the test of the success of integrational cooperation is the opening up of long-term perspectives for the national economies participating in the cooperation*. This is why the two notions selected for the title of this book: economic integration and economic strategy, are closely related.

I should like to express my thanks to my colleagues from whom I have received much help in formulating the ideas to be expounded in the following.

PART ONE

The World Economic Environment of the Socialist Economic Integration in the Early and Mid-Seventies

CHAPTER ONE

The new stage of the crisis of the capitalist world economy and the socialist alternative

It was a great historical feat of the capitalist order that it *rendered production social.* This resulted in exponential growth in four domains: the rate of specialization, the pace of production, the volume and assortment of useful goods all advanced with giant strides and, finally, obsolescence also accelerated. All that is more or less reflected in the accelerating growth of the productivity of social labour as a synthetic indicator. The growth of productivity on a social scale assumes an accelerating shift within the relative ratios of the factors of production in favour of technology, while society has to draw into production more and more human and natural resources—in absolute terms—to operate the technical machinery which is becoming ever bigger.

The deeper the specialization and the more gigantic the technologies, the greater masses of people have to cooperate with clockwork-like precision in order to operate the productive machinery—and the greater the effect of an economic decision on the growth-rate and equilibrium conditions of the reproduction process and, in the last resort, on the fate of mankind. *Within* the framework of capitalist ownership relations rational management of the available factors of production is motivated by a single criterion, that of profitability. At the same time, profitability also determines the optimal ratios in which the various factors of production are combined in technology. In an essentially anarchical market, where concentration is low and which is dominated by many capitals, the temporary relations of demand and supply and, simultaneously, the principle of private profit, are short-term regulators. The capitalist firm which is forced to adapt itself every day to the "ultra-short" business fluctuations of the unorganized market, must possess a good many possibilities of "manoeuvring" with the factors of production: the commodity must be turned quickly into money and the money into commodity, and, in order to be able to offer maximum performance when the need suddenly arises, it must also know not only how to procure low-concentration, technologically relatively primitive tools of labour, but also how to acquire the necessary labour. But *within* the enterprise the manpower-factor cannot be geared to the maximal potential, the capital power is too small. The "reserve army" of the unemployed develops. From the viewpoint of rationality—according to the logic of capital—this is an indispensable reservoir of the factors of production but this, beyond the human sufferings it causes, *means huge waste from the point of view of the whole society, wasting the most valuable force of production, man itself.* On a global social scale, capital also manages investments and natural resources wastefully, but this does not yet appear on the surface. The capital risked in the 19th century is very small, and the risk is entirely shouldered by the owner. The geographical expansion of capital is still at its beginning, large parts of the easily accessible natural resources of the earth are not yet disclosed. The smoky, unhealthy factory quarters spoil the landscape only at a few places. *It is labour that is at the focus of wastage in the 19th century.* In a considerable part of the reproduction cycle unemployment is significant. Labour is the only factor of production which capital can acquire without engaging itself for some longer time, and, for some time, it will be still abundant. Born for waste, capital fiercefully attacks this factor of production and shifts onto it every consequence of its own disorganization and imperfection.

In a capitalist society with *monopolistic* organization the amplitudes of reproduction cycles increase at an *accelerating* rate, and become less and less tolerable on a global social scale. Capitalism, which is bent on *expansion* by its nature, does everything to preserve this comfortable form of existence. The rate of mechanization is dependent on wages, and the latter, on the industrial reserve army. Technical progress slowly gives rise to the plans for complex systems of machines performing work processes, and to the technical possibilities of a radical transformation of fuels, materials and transportation. All that is rendered on the whole was ready by the end of the 1910s. But capital still does not surrender: national frontiers have been no obstacles for its spreading for some longer time already, now it reaches for the world. And, if there are no more free areas, it tries to expand the possibilities of making profit at the expense of other capitals—basically still in an extensive manner. Wars are alternating with economic crises, ever more frequently and ever more destructively. *The first half of the 20th century is the era when the cyclic development of capitalist expansion, and simultaneously, the uninhibited waste of human factors become impossible.*

In order to halt its starting dissolution, the capitalist society is compelled to apply instruments which are partly foreign to its nature, macro-economic market regulation and intensification. The growing role of the state in the economy is, from this point of view, but the sacrifice of a part of the "sovereignty" of private capital, while, from another aspect, it means the coordination, on a national macro-economic level, of the activities of private decision centres. But national and international state capitalism remains, in the final analysis, a foreign tissue within the organism of capitalist society. National-level economic policy, which would be indeed efficient if it enforced the *global* capitalist interests by coordinating all capital properties, becomes necessarily subordinated to the interests of *individual* groups. The sharper the economic situation, the greater the struggle for the hegemony of economic policy. The private nature of capital produces an "immune reaction" to the restriction of its sovereignty. This is what makes the capitalist compromise with the socialization of production temporary and relative. At the same time, at times of lull, when the forces of cohesion are gaining against centrifugal tendencies, state monopoly capitalism may actually lead to huge results, bringing about such an environment in which, *beside* the tendency of expansion (sometimes *above* it) the tendency of intensification may also assert itself.

The prime condition for the massive intensification of the forces of production is a strong dampening of the fluctuation of production. An organic part of this is the securing of full employment (or, at least, keeping unemployment at minimum), the channelling of a large part of the national income through the budget and, at the same time, its redistribution, influencing the competitive mechanisms by administrative or semi-administrative means.

Indeed, the cycle has undergone basic changes since World War II. We cannot say that it has been *liquidated,* because there are always spontaneous forces which push the capitalist national economies, and through them also world economy, towards cyclicality.

True, this had to be preceded by the use of technology in the *war industries*—its economic reason may be found in the financing of the costs of research and production organization by the state. *The costs of private capital are restricted to adapting the modern techniques to civilian needs.* The maintenance and "operation" of gigantic military machines, world-wide and local wars, the danger of armament and of a nuclear holocaust, as well as space research controlled from military viewpoints—as the necessary first stage of the modern technological revolution—again entail huge waste of the factors of production.

The present level of economic development, which is attributed with predilection to the "renaissance" of capitalism, was conceived in the womb of waste forces of production in the hot and cold wars. Its midwife was the "artificial interference" of national and international economic policies foreign to the substance of capital, and the evolution of fast development took about four decades.

In the development which is taking place in the structure of capitalist society and evolving in the wake of the changes outlined in the preceding, many qualitatively new elements may be found. Their totality results in the *general crisis* of the capitalist social order. Its present stage is characterized by the fact that the crisis phenomena appear *simultaneously* with the fast development of the forces of production. This asserts itself to such extent that a superficial or biased observer looking at the fast technical and economic progress in some periods is inclined to forget, or at least view as "difficulties of growth", those deep and fast-deepening contradictions which indeed precede and, simultaneously, *follow* development unavoidably.

The new stage of the development of the forces of production, which evolved in the middle of this century, is called "technical-scientific revolution". Undoubtedly, some changes that have taken place in technical knowledge and in the work processes are *radical* and may be said to be *qualitatively superior*, and thus our logic does not object to this name. This process, which had started in the most developed centres of the capitalist world system in the fifties and became rather widespread by the seventies, was not developed under the conditions of capitalist societies unconditionally by observing the interests of mankind as a whole. Not technology itself is to blame for that, not even the scientists and engineers who created the innovations, but the social environment which even unintentionally deforms the direction of technical progress.

I should like to draw attention to a few findings, almost unanimously accepted, of the social sciences about the development of world economy over more than two decades since the evolution of the technical-scientific revolution:

a) The fast development of the forces of production could evolve more or less proportionally *only on a smaller part of the globe*. The part comprising the so-called "developing" countries, which is the absolute majority of mankind, was *hardly* touched by the scientific revolution. The radiations of technical progress from the developed capitalist world are random, irregular and distorted, and thus they multiply all difficulties deriving from economic backwardness, instead of bringing their solution nearer. The development of the non-socialist world has become more divergent than ever. The abyss between the developed and under-developed economies is greater and is widening faster than ever in the course of history. *Fast development in the industrial-scientific centres of the capitalist world has led to an accelerating polarization of world economy.* At the same time, it has sharpened to the utmost some fundamental problems of the developing economies which originated in backwardness, such as overpopulation, hunger, the dual economies, the lack of infrastructure and dependence. On the other hand, the developed capitalist economy "infected" the developing societies with such diseases as the unsatisfiable thirst of the narrow élite for luxury, demonstrative consumption, oversized bureaucracy, militarism and nationalism. All this results in almost bursting economic and social situations within the developing countries, but also in the whole of world economy and world politics, and the long-term consequences may become unsurveyable and incalculable.

b) In the smaller part of the capitalist world, where it was born, developed and spread, the technological and scientific revolution is on the road of *prostituting itself.*

On the one hand, insofar as development is going on under the auspices of *capitalist states*, it is motivated, directly or indirectly, *by anti-social motives*, and put at the service of power objectives. The developed capitalist powers try to *monopolize* research, and use it for the consolidation and expansion of their military, political and economic power. Not *innovating, but dominating* economies and societies are born, and try to replace or, at least, counterbalance each other. Research and development activity becomes subservient to the quest for power.

On the other hand, scientific research and technical innovation carried on as a function of the competition between different power and firm interests, lead to a complete chaos of real and phoney results of actually useful and useless innovations. The producer and consumer markets are manipulated by the monopolistic enterprises to an unprecedented extent and in ways never experienced before. At the focus of the manipulating activity we find *planned obsolescence*. The rate of the technical obsolescence of productive equipment and consumer durables follows the fluctuations in fashion dictated by a huge machinery. Consumer habits have been changing for some longer time already not as a function of growing and perfecting human needs, but depending on the acceleration of the birth, flowering and dying of status symbols which emerge and change in the wake of the frantic quest directed by fashion dictators. In this wizardry, the *real* technical innovations mingle hopelessly with, and are inseparable from, *swindle*. Research and innovative activities become uncritical servants of the race for the consumer's money.

c) Both the power machinery and the productive machinery which is subject to business competition, whirling at the highest speed, are built upon waste of gigantic dimensions and reproduce all these on an expanding scale, *devour the factors of production* in huge masses: the exploitable natural resources of the earth's surface and crust, the able-bodied labour force and investments alike, without being able to secure the conditions for a rational management on a social scale nor the possibilities of reproduction.

The profit motive of private enterprise directs *the extractive activities* towards the most easily exploitable sources of primary energy, ores and agricultural products. Manufactures and the distributive networks develop on these extractive bases such technical cultures and build upon them such volumes of capital which can be recovered but in long decades. They do not make parallel provisions for exploring the natural resources which are accessible only with difficulties—including scientific and technical research—nor for the development of new technical cultures in time, nor for the possibilities of a gradual, organized transition. Therefore, the narrowing of the geological bases of a given technical culture can shake the whole production system to its foundations. As a result, the capitalist world runs from time to time into "futurological conflicts", and goes through hysterical energy- and raw-material crises. Bourgeois economists project apocalyptic visions about the inescapable decline of human civilization, one of its reasons being the depletion of natural resources.

The other side of the same coin is the pollution of human environment. In the era of the technical and scientific revolution one cannot manage the exploitable natural resources in isolation and for the short run only, nor can this be done with the waste of production and of the human life processes. The production machinery concentrated in the hands of humanity is too large, and humanity itself is too concentrated to shun the highly rational management of its own ecological relations becoming the centre of economic activity. But it would be utopistic to expect capitalist enterprise to reason and act according to interrelations beyond its own costs and revenues. This is why industry pollutes the water, the air, the soil and inundates the population with vehicles, packaging materials, chemicals which further pollute the environment. Agriculture destructs and poisons the soil, clears the forests and thus, in an effort to produce more, abolishes the long-term conditions of food production and even the regeneration of oxygen in the air. In this manner the whole technical civilization built on private enterprise—though advocating human comfort—might make our planet uninhabitable.

The ring is thus closed. In order that producers and consumers should wastefully use masses of commodities growing and becoming obsolete at an accelerating rate (because this furthers business and power interests), the society of developed capitalist countries wasted ever growing labour inputs (or, an ever greater part of the working population is used *ab ovo* for the production of products that are to be wasted). An ever growing part of productive equipment is invested *ab ovo* for such purposes, people producing for waste should do it with greater productivity, and waste in the meantime the mineral resources, the productive soil, the air and the water—the elements which are needed for human existence itself.

Under such conditions, scientific-technical research and innovation become unintentional catalysts of waste. The capitalist state and the intergovernmental economic institutions provide frameworks of organization and coordination for the world-wide and colossal waste. International trade as well as the financial system help to spread waste like an epidemic.

Thus, we have here again the basic antagonism of capitalism in its naked reality long ago formulated by Marxism; only the new phenomena built up in the second half of the 20th century have to be *recognized* as the signs of antagonism. As the socialization of production progresses—and among its components are the development of the forces of production as well as the domination of national and international enterprise-empires and the attempts at coordination of private enterprises in national or international frameworks—the organization of economic processes in the framework of private enterprises becomes more and more dangerous for the life of the whole mankind. When the fluctuation of production has become finally untenable, it has been successfully tamed. But, precisely because this happened in a *capitalist* framework, and in a capitalist manner, it has necessarily entailed an extreme world-wide polarization of development, and an extreme waste of all factors of production. All that may become the hotbed of such military, economic and even biological conflicts whose destructive effects we are still unable to assess.

What I have expounded in the preceding differs from what is contained in the book *The Limits to Growth*, sponsored by the Club of Rome. First of all, I do not believe in the possibility of zero growth, nor in its expediency.

On the one hand, the world has not yet reached a state when it can do without a quantitative growth of economy. The world average of per capita national income is still below $1000 (1964 prices), thus on a relatively low level. In order that the developing countries, which constitute two-thirds of mankind, should emerge from physical poverty, the industrialized world must provide huge material help in the future. This is impossible without continuing fast growth.

On the other hand, I do not believe either that a concept raised today and restricted *merely* to economic-policy measures could restrain the clearly perceptible tendency at upsetting the world's demographic, economic, political—and even ecological—balance. We are, so to say, within braking distance.

Thus, if I accept the forecast of the Club of Rome as realistic—for 2000, 2100 or even later—I must consider the solution of "zero growth" as utopistic. If, however, I assume that the cataclysm can be forestalled by global social, organized measures (that is, not by zero growth, since this would contradict the whole history of mankind, but by eliminating polarization and waste), I think this is realistically conceivable only through a radical change in the structure of society. In order to liquidate polarization and waste, a management of the factors of production and of the results of production at a global social level and in the interests of society as a whole has to be implemented. The basic antagonism of societies organized in a capitalist manner must be solved finally and radically. Not the future generations, not economic development, but *capitalism must be sacrificed* in order to escape the dangers menacing humanity.

We have now come to the real *punctum saliens* of our reasoning. Is the socialist reorganization of society a guaranty against those harmful—and, as regards their final outcome, maybe tragic—tendencies which endanger the modern capitalist society? During the historically short period of its existence, socialist society has already been able to achieve significant results in the fight against polarization and social waste. The introduction of planning provided a possibility for the fast development of backward regions, and planned, long-term manpower management permitted, beyond the liquidation of unemployment, the harmonization of educational and training activities with the concepts about structural transformation. Exploration and utilization of the natural resources is proceeding according to long-term plans, in productive and personal consumption the aim is to satisfy needs, not to sell at any price. Pollution is braked with the aid of strict rules concerning environment protection. All this has been achieved in the socialist countries at considerable material and financial sacrifice, frequently under highly difficult economic and foreign-policy conditions.

Let me add that, in spite of the achievements quoted, socialist power, the social ownership of the means of production and *planned economy* do not seem *in themselves*, to be satisfactory guaranties either against social polarization tendencies, or waste of the factors of production, they merely bring about qualitatively more favourable social conditions to avoid them. In other words, socialism does not establish by itself such *spontaneous* processes which act automatically in a favourable direction of social progress, but creates "only" the conditions for deliberate organized social action to fight *successfully* against the tendencies endangering the future of mankind. Thus, we cannot comfort ourselves by claiming that on the socialist one-third there is *no chance whatever* for mismanaging natural resources, labour and the means of production, or for a dangerous pollution of the environment. Nor can the nations still living today in capitalist societies delude themselves: by liquidating the private ownership of the forces of production, and *merely* by creating the skeleton of a socialist social organization they do not automatically, once and for all solve the above-outlined huge concern of mankind. But as much is true: *without* making this first revolutionary step neither individual nations nor mankind as a whole has much chance of finally avoiding cataclysms.

Socialism is the adequate form of motion for the modern society, insofar as it eliminates, radically and definitively, the discrepancy between the interests of the whole society and the micro- and macro-economic decisions concerning the factors of production and the goods produced. There is an incomparably greater possibility for a highly conscious organization of investments, production, the goods produced, for the rational management of the natural resources and of human activities than in any preceding society. If socialist society uses these possibilities well, it will always be in a position to organize scientific and technical research, education, investment and productive activities on a wide scale and with *sufficient foresight*. As a result, the chasm in development and culture between the nations will gradually diminish, sufficient food will be secured together with the raw-material supply of industry necessary for a cultured, high-standard life for a growing number of people.

Everything depends on *what way of life, what kind of welfare we make the basic pillar of the system of goals of socialist economic policy.*

I believe I need not prove in detail that *every model of technical and economic development is based on a concept of the way of life—developed either spontaneously or deliberately*. This concept for the way of life is a reflection of the development of the forces of production and, at the same time, of the mode of social order. The development level of the forces of production determines the general level at which needs can be satisfied, and offers alternatives regarding the basic structure of social consumption. The social order *chooses* from among these alternatives the one which best corresponds to the interests of the classes, strata and groups at the centre of the decision circles. This *interest* is radiated by the whole economic, political and ideological superstructure of the given society to the whole population as *life ideal*.

The way of life thus spontaneously developed, manipulated by a class or a group, or perhaps deliberately formulated on a social level enters into a particular interrelation with the productive machinery which had created its conditions. If the way of life as suggested by class interests alienates global social interests, then the state, group and private interests which evolve under their effect may strongly deform and, in the last resort, ruin the whole of the productive machinery, nature, the structure of the division of labour, and man himself. This process is evolving under our very eyes in the capitalist economy. Thus, the ruin of the productive machinery begins with the way of life, not with the possibility or impossibility to plan. *From the viewpoint of the danger it is quite immaterial whether the ruin of nature and of the productive machinery finally results from a way of life which derives from the substance of the social order, or from an ideal of life borrowed from elsewhere.*

Under conditions of the coexistence of the two social systems, particularly when the *peaks* of the capitalist sector of world economy are still on a much higher level of technico-economic development than the socialist world, an increased demonstration effect has to be reckoned with. *Copying the way of life* of a society possessing developed forces of production and securing a higher level of consumption offers itself, even without its obvious capitalistic outgrowths. Similarly, *copying the forces of production*, which are more advanced from the technical point of view, also offers itself. I would stress the *copying* separately, that is, the uncritical adoption of the elements of the way of life and techniques. All that may *introduce* into the socialist societies efforts at developing such structures of production and consumption that lead similarly to the waste of factors of production on a social scale. In an advanced stage these efforts become rigid structures and irreversible. The danger of the matter lies in the fact that society does not perceive the anti-socialistic, harmful effects of such development for a long time, since there do *not* emerge extreme differences between the living standards of nations, classes and strata, *neither* technology, *nor* society becomes militarized, there do *not* originate outrageous social injustices in the spheres of either decision or consumption. The society free from exploitation inherits from capitalism "only" the high costs of welfare. The given welfare rests on a technology which assumes the ruthless exploitation of resources and, finally, the natural field of life of mankind becomes exhausted.

It should be clear that a socialist society, whether it is organized on a national scale or in a regional international framework, must not take this road. *It is not sufficient to overcome exploitation and anarchy, it is not enough to introduce a planned economy, nor to produce a development faster than that of capitalism. Socialist societies have to shape such a new and attractive way of life on which a very comprehensive, very long-term and very rational management of the factors of production can be built.*

Today we cannot yet state that this new way of life—which differs qualitatively from the capitalist one—has fully matured in any of the socialist countries: ways are being sought and experiments are in course. But some basic criteria are already known for certain. They are:

a) At the centre of the socialist way of life stands the *useful activity* in such a form that individuals and groups are conscious of this utility. The welfare of social strata, productive groups and individuals develops depending on their own contribution to the welfare of society. A direct consequence is that *the welfare of individuals and groups shows a much smaller dispersion around the social average than in any other society hitherto.* As a matter of fact, working ability and the volume of labour exerted differs less between individuals and collectives than the amount of accumulated private wealth.

This assumes, on the one hand, a relatively much smaller difference between individual real incomes than is the case in class societies (in spite of the fact that differences in the quantity and quality of labour performed for society remain rather considerable), and, on the other hand, it requires the adaptation of the whole productive machinery to the particular structure. The increase of socialist welfare—that is, the welfare differentiated only through labour—is characterized by a production structure suited for the mass production and quick diffusion of new products and product systems satisfying higher needs. Products and product systems which *indeed* raise welfare have to spread in mass dimensions sooner so as not to exist previously for some longer or shorter period as status symbols of certain privileged strata. Clearly, such a model of living standards requires a particular production structure, investment policy and enterprise reaction system considerably different from those of capitalism, and it has a perceptible effect also on the direction of technical research and development activities.

b) The concentration of the socialist way of life on useful social activity *embraces not only the sphere of production but also that of utilization.* Man in a socialist society may spend his income deriving from useful work at his discretion, yet not without any restriction. Consumption must not cause either material or moral damage to society. The consumption habits of individuals must not disturb the health, peace, rest, or cultural activities of others, must not destruct the ecological environment. The welfare of socialist man is a wise adaptation to the conditions of the environment at the same time. It is not sure that this must happen at the expense of the *degree* of welfare: on the contrary, riches, comfort, hygiene and the cultural level can be only winners if society excludes from the very outset enjoyments at the expense of others.

This involves, at the same time, that the pattern of the supply of goods and the qualitative characteristics of products appearing on the consumer market must be developed in a direction preferred by society, and the consumer market must be influenced and educated in this direction on a social scale. The first place among social consumption preferences should be accorded to the liquidation of poverty in the physical sense and to preventing its re-emergence, which includes securing the conditions of cultured and hygienic working and housing conditions, food, clothing and transportation for every stratum of the population, independently of occupation, domicile and age. Simultaneously, first priorities include high-level education and cultural services, as well as health protection embracing the entire population. All these combined can secure a highly cultured state of the socialist way of life, which affects the relations between men and, in the last resort, reacts on the growth rate of the forces of production as well. I would stress here only that all these demand the development of special research, development and production cultures, which significantly differ from those existing at present in the United States, Western Europe, or Japan.

c) Finally, the socialist way of life—precisely because of the balanced and cultured state of human relations—makes it possible to *satisfy, in a collective manner, a considerable part of the consumption securing welfare* and that foreseeably at a higher level and much cheaper in terms of either social or individual costs than they can be met through individual solutions by a *minority* of society—not reckoning now that the individual solution of a part of them (e.g. transportation, recreation) is impossible on a mass scale or entails grave pollution of the human environment. Also, several factors are pushing the socialist society towards satisfying a part of the needs through collective means. Such is in part the factor already mentioned that owing greatly to the relatively narrow limits of differences between income levels, several needs become large-scale ones sooner. And also, in the long run, the creation of collective instruments for a high-level welfare demands much less social input, even in the central investment demands are higher initially. This is of prime importance for societies which build socialism in an environment more advanced from the technical viewpoint than themselves.

I need not particularly prove that all this entails a special national economic structure as regards either the commodity pattern of industry, or the nature and national dimensions of service activities.

Some elements of the industrial and service branches and systems necessary for the development of the socialist way of life are partly functioning already, the task now is to create a consistent and comprehensive system and to "calibrate" the whole technico-economic machinery, above all its long-term development, according to this socialist way of life.

When I expound that wastefulness at the macro-level is a condition of the existence of capitalist society, it should also be observed that the profit motive regulating economic processes in the micro-sphere commands extreme economy. It is a curious contradiction that *the result of the striving after economy of the capitalist enterprise is insane waste in national and world dimensions.*

The present practice of the socialist countries seems to exemplify the reverse of this contradiction. While the economic spheres of decision became centralized in order to prevent anarchy in the reproduction process, mechanisms have started which stimulate irrational management of both invested capital and natural resources on both enterprise and branch levels. The well-known symptoms are: surplus labour within the factories, incorrect management of qualified manpower, expensive investments, protracted implementation, competition between enterprises and industries for state investment funds, unnecessarily high consumption of materials and energy in production. The result is a perceptible loss of efficiency of the factors of production, that is, similar *waste* even if for other reasons than in the capitalist system.

It would be difficult to quantify what entails *bigger* losses: the macro-level waste which is accompanied by micro-level saving, or the micro-level waste appearing with the present methods of planned economy. I believe that the important thing is not to raise the question in this form, but to recognize that the contradictory management in the present socialist economies does not derive from the substance of the social order. The present management systems of the socialist countries cannot be considered as mature. They emerged partly under conditions of underdevelopment, and partly under strong world political and military pressure, and, finally, they came about under highly heterogeneous internal and international circumstances. All these factors favoured "rush-work", quick and temporary solutions, securing a fast-rate growth, the liquidation of century-old backwardness of the forces of production. At the same time, relatively little attention was paid to the rational management of the factors of production within a productive unit under the conditions of quick and uneven modernization. All that caused the *appearance* as if the elimination of the profit motive from among the determinants of micro-level decisions fatally linked, at the same time, the rational socialist macro-level planned economy with irrational management on enterprise level. In fact, the private profit motive is the mechanism—for lack of a better one—of the ulterior regulation of the division of labour which is unsurveyable on a social level: a mechanism which is necessary when subjective factors still have a decisive role in economic decisions, since the mechanical technology itself has still hardly delimited the operational possibilities of a productive unit. The smaller the role of subjective factors in the planning, organization and implementation of technological processes, the more technology itself determines the volume of labour, producer goods and natural resources to be utilized in the production process, the more insignificant becomes the volume of factors of production that can be wasted on the enterprise (technological) level relative to the total amount used.

However, as long as technologies do not attain this level, a temporary bridging must be secured by means of incentive systems and by forming social consciousness. These incentive systems attempt to reconcile the maximum saving of factors of production on the enterprise level with the maximum of planning of the social work process or, from another aspect, they try to minimize the irrational elements in the enterprise management of the factors of production. The most important general lesson to be drawn from these attempts at reforming the system of control has been so far that *it is possible to implement a parsimonious and flexible enterprise management under the conditions of socialist macro-level planning.*

At the same time, experience—Hungary's included—had proven that

a) an *"overrationing"* of the elements of indirect control, the overstatement of the role of the profit motive, may lead to the weakening of the central management of the factors of production. This can be averted with *ad hoc* central interventions only with low efficiency, while these interferences also disturb the mechanisms stimulating rational enterprise management;

b) the same is true also conversely: sham, superficial handling of the enterprise motivation does not exploit the reserves inherent in rational enterprise management, while it may weaken the efforts of the central planning and control agencies in managing the factors of production on a national economic level;

c) the correct *method* of amalgamating these two systems in a fortunate manner *is highly differentiated in the various branches of economy.* The big enterprises based on advanced technology, the basic-material industries and infrastructure require different methods from those to be applied to a network of fragmented small and medium-sized establishments or to the service sector. The less developed and the more heterogeneous the forces of production of a country, the more difficult it is to state the optimum of this double requirement.

Last but—unfortunately—not least, the socialist sector of world economy has to reckon, for the time being and for some longer time still, with a deliberate, unavoidable "waste" of its factors of production. This is unavoidable also because of the necessity to maintain the conditions of military defence, but also because, in the interest of accelerating technical progress, it has to make available a part of its natural resources to the capitalist production machinery as the countervalue of the imports of new technology. Finally, it must also reckon with averting the most harmful effects which would cause environmental pollution in the capitalist world on the economies and nations of the socialist countries. All that will claim a not negligible part of the forces of production of socialist societies also in the future, without having a direct effect on the development of economy and welfare. These are the "costs of coexistence" which diminish to the same extent as coexistence develops from a political and military confrontation into economic cooperation and competition, and as socialist societies become stronger.

Thus, the abstract possibility, deriving from the revolutionary change in the social order, to replace the society of waste by global social rationality and thus to avoid the cataclysms menacing mankind is *realizable in practice*, even if not without difficulties, even if internal and external counter-tendencies may brake the rate of evolution to a considerable extent. The overcoming of obstacles facing the development of society, the opening of the gates to further development will not be accomplished by any kind of fate for us and instead of us. Marxism never predicted that social progress comes automatically. Mankind has several theoretical alternatives regarding its own future. It may *leave its social relations unchanged*, and then it will follow the road of waste towards some kind of cataclysm. *It may take inconsistent steps* towards founding its own future and thus the period of decline may be deferred or brought forward. But it also has the possibility to *let*, boldly and wisely, the possibilities of history just being born, *ripen*. The economic strategy of the socialist countries has chosen this latter road and a break with every kind of wastefulness regarding the wealth of nature, human knowledge and diligence.

CHAPTER TWO

Realistic perspectives of East–West economic cooperation

In recent years there has been a growing number of indications that the more sober Western scientists, specialists—and sometimes even politicians—reasoning in terms of perspectives, believe that *cooperation between the two large social systems* is unavoidable in the interest of improving the conditions of world peace and promoting economic progress.

Socialist Eastern Europe could contribute to this by supplying its raw-material resources and primary energy to bridge over the acute difficulties in energy and raw-material supply, and by making its huge scientific machinery and its expertize in perspectivic planning available in order to promote solutions that would be effective also in the long run. "In exchange", modern technology could be massively transferred to the CMEA countries, above all to the Soviet Union, in order to reduce the still existing differences in development level.

Of course, the efforts are not always in the focus of attention of business circles. The latter invariably hope to find big sales markets for their manufactured products or cheap skilled labour, which would solve the labour-shortage problem more comfortably than the system of guest-workers, entailing many problems, or the development of industry in the developing countries involving great political risks.

There are important shifts as regards interests in cooperation, above all because of the more pronounced appearance of the Soviet Union on Western markets and the expansion of East–West trade beyond Europe.

In the sixties, the cooperation activity of the West-European developed capitalist countries was restricted mainly to the smaller Central and East-European socialist countries.

The background for this was provided by the so-called softening-up strategy, which, following the aborted counter-revolutionary attempts, hoped to weaken the political unity of the socialist countries through the forms of cooperation to be developed in the various fields. Independently of this political mental reservation, Western capital tried to exert an indirect influence, through commercial, industrial and technological cooperation schemes with the smaller socialist countries, on the Soviet market which, already at that time, was its sole interest.

The seventies have been characterized more and more by direct relations. Soviet economy established direct relations with the Western countries in an ever wider scope and in diversified ways. The *importance of the smaller European socialist countries as economic springboards ceased for Western capital.* As a consequence, in the relations between Western firms and the smaller socialist economies, business interests in the stricter sense of the word come increasingly to the fore.

At the same time, West-European capital is faced on the *Soviet market*, by more competitive adversaries: American and Japanese capital. The key to the competitiveness of American capital is, on the one hand, its supply of equipments fully corresponding to the particular features of Soviet economy, and, on the other hand, its essentially more favourable credit terms. At the same time, the American equipments are substantially more expensive than the European ones. But this is little comfort to Western Europe, since the Japanese offers are even more favourable than theirs. American and Japanese competition hits the West-European capital badly not only on the sales and credit market. There is a competition among the three developed capitalist cores for the countervalue of exports, for the raw materials and energy sources of basic importance as well. He who can supply technologies better conforming to the Soviet conditions will have access to Soviet ore, oil, gas, etc., cheaply and/or at better terms of credit. This factor must not be underestimated. Beyond that, there are strong aspirations in Western Europe to gain access to the results of the Soviet natural-science research which is of gigantic dimensions. Basic research is, namely a bottleneck in all West-European countries, while they can hardly manage to keep pace with technical progress, and to develop, from "a reproductive society", into an "innovative society" with a weak basic-research basis. Soviet relations thus have a multiple role in West-European development concepts: market for equipment, source of raw materials, and basis of technological basic research. This is why it is of extreme importance for Western Europe to hold its own in the competition with the USA and Japan.

For the smaller European socialist countries, however, it is still Western Europe which seems to be the most realistic partner. This is justified not only by traditional relations, but also because, in the majority of cases, their forces of production are better suited for adapting West-European technologies than American ones.

Beyond that, the relations among the smaller East-European countries and Western Europe continue to be characterized by the "traditional" asymmetry of interests. The Western countries and firms are interested, as before, in selling to the small East-European socialist countries, including machinery and equipment. Regarding the standards of their manufacturing industries, the smaller socialist countries are, in most cases, not competitive in the West-European markets, or only at a very low wage level. They appear as sellers generally in those industries in which competition is sharp also on the West-European markets, supply is rich (clothing and textiles, leather industry, simpler household gadgets, metal mass products, fruit, vegetables, poultry meat, etc.), and the dominating form of production is the small and medium-sized plant, whose protection is, to a certain extent, in the political interest of the Western governments. Therefore, the smaller socialist countries cannot expand their exports to the extent they would need by their inclination to import even in the future.

It is similarly a new feature that in the future the smaller East-European socialist countries will be increasingly compelled to import raw materials and primary energy from the convertible currency areas, than was the case in the last ten years. On the one hand, this increases their import needs in absolute terms, and on the other hand, it also increases the unit import costs because of the rising prices of materials and energy. In respect of the import of materials and energy necessary for the functioning of the national economies, the governments may easily get into a squeeze. This factor increases their debts, while, on the other hand, it narrows the possibilities for the import of technology slowing down the development of their forces of production (thus delaying the evolution of their export capacities to the West), and also reducing their attraction in the eyes of Western partners as importers of equipment.

As regards Soviet–Western relations, the easing of the political atmosphere is an essential condition of their smooth development from two respects. Soviet economy is incapable of covering its needs of Western imports with current exports, since its export capacity in industrially processed products for end use is rather limited—similarly to any other East-European socialist country. The Soviet products which are, for the time being, most attractive for the West, are ores, hydrocarbons and wood, that is, products of the extractive industries. In order that the Soviet economy—whose European regions are also struggling with a shortage of raw materials—should possess a sufficient exportable commodity fund in these products, investments exceeding its financial powers are needed, above all in Asia, where the direct costs of opening up the sites of exploitation are weighed down by colossal expenses of infrastructure and where wage costs are three- and four-fold of those in Europe.

However, to advance the costs of exploring the large raw-material deposits in Siberia, Kazakhstan and the Far East, the West needs a major and lasting world political détente. The evolution of this détente is hindered, on the one hand, by the behaviour of China and, on the other, by the fact that the necessity of a radical policy of détente lasting for several decades has not yet become a definite conviction in the strategic and political circles of the Western great powers. Therefore, any success of the peace policy of the Soviet Union and the other socialist countries also considerably expands the perspectives of East–West economic relations. Nevertheless, in the present situation the great Western business circles are still reluctant to undertake long-term engagements in the interest of increasing the extraction of raw material in the USSR *to such an extent* as would be needed for a major and final shift in Soviet–Western relations relative to the situation in the past.

Modern technology imported against exports of raw materials is indeed useful for the Soviet economy if the conditions for its adaptation and relatively quick spreading are secured. The Soviet Union does not want simply *to use* Western technology. Nor does it purchase equipment with the main aim to produce commodities which are competitive on the world market and then export them. The Soviet leadership buys Western equipment, technologies and systems of organization first of all as factors accelerating the development of the domestic forces of production, and spurring the imagination of designers, even if after a few years or decades Soviet industry will appear on the Western markets with modern finished products as well. Without understanding this basic concept it is impossible to understand the nature of the Soviet "opening up", nor to project its development.

The primary condition of spreading the purchased technology is speed, that is, that adequate human factors and productive capacities should be available which can use, multiply and further develop the imported technology. Soviet economy already possesses such human and plant capacities in several fields. Thus, massive imports of Western technology into Soviet economy will become a factor in the development of the forces of production which the Soviet leadership can *reckon* with and which is *worth* the sacrifices to be made in its interest, if it can be concentrated on the strategic points of Soviet economic development and has the time to spread therefrom to other sectors of economy.

It is apparent from the preceding that stabilization of East–West relations has—beside all its possibilities—two uncertain points:

a) The development of economic relations sensitively reacts *on the easing or sharpening of the world political and military situation—in the medium and long perspective perhaps even more than in day-to-day relations.* In the present situation the expansion of economic relations in itself is insufficient to give a big push to political détente for the latter to become irreversible. The case is rather the reverse. Interest in developing economic relations remains moderate both in the West and in the USSR as long as political détente does not become irreversible.

b) *The Western interest experienced in the development of economic relations is, for the time being, still rather one-sidedly related to the exploitation of Soviet raw-material resources.* This makes the Western inclination to cooperate in part dependent on the circumstances of the raw-material and energy crisis. Furthermore, such an interest makes cooperation so capital-intensive that it may be relatively easily preceded by other possibilities of solution if such arise (exploration of new sources of primary energy, agreement with the Arab world, etc.).

What, then, are the realities concerning development possibilities for the socialist countries?

In my opinion, despite all contradictions and difficulties, *the world political situation has considerably increased the possibility that East–West cooperation may yield gains for us.* But all that can be realized only if our economic policy regarding East–West relations is based on more realistic and sound judgements than before. The most expedient direction seems to be if in our short-term policies we put together *"the most earth-bound" pragmatic measures* as building stones according to a clear *strategy constructed on the basis of class principles,* in the following manner:

a) "Earthbound pragmatism" demands that we should favourably react to the inclination of the West to cooperate, owing to its grave economic and other concerns, that is,

— that we should make efforts to draw additional financial funds into accelerating the economic growth of the socialist countries, either in the form of credit or—within certain limits—as operating capital;

— that we should expand trade and cooperation in the interest of an absolute increase in solvency and in order to liquidate the dichotomy of our commodity trade.

This means that we have to increase the turnover with every means available in the interest of further development and of learning those elements of advanced Western technology and organization which can be utilized in our countries.

Nevertheless, we should beware of fitting ourselves in the division of labour of the capitalist world according to our present economic performance. It would do immeasurable harm to the cause of socialism if the developed capitalist countries could built out, in the next decades, in the European socialist community a base of raw-material supply, food supply and of cheap, moderately qualified "subsidiary" labour, which would *one-sidedly* depend on Western capital and technology.

It would be a mistake to believe that a mere multiplication of the East–West trade or cooperation relations could make the dependence mutual. At present the total East–West trade, inclusive of Soviet trade, makes but 3 or 4 per cent of the total foreign trade of the West-European countries, while it reaches about the maximum of the export capacity of the CMEA countries as regards Western markets. Exports could be substantially increased—by orders of magnitude—only at the expense of the raw-material and food supply within the CMEA, which has its close limits because of the growing tensions on the CMEA market. Massive exports of manufactured articles to the West will not be competitive for a long time to come, and this because the products are not so *new* that the "extra profit" to be included in their price could bear the relatively high social costs of labour. On the other hand, the manufactured commodities that could be otherwise sold in the West, *are not introduced* to the Western markets. The costs of marketing which emerge in convertible currencies are, however, much higher than what could be borne by the particular socialist countries. It follows that the *expansion of relations has, from the aspect of socialist export capacities, clearly delineated possibilities in the long run.* It is not likely that in a perspective of a few decades the absorptive capacity of the West-European market in regard to socialist commodities will grow much faster than its imports in general. It is thus hardly likely that, *with the maintenance or slow closing of the present development lag*, trade with the socialist countries will become a realization or—from the point of view of raw materials—a supply problem of prime importance for the West.

Since the export potential of the small socialist countries follows their growth in import needs but with difficulties, *their equilibrium may soon become dependent on Western imports*, that is, these economies may become increasingly *incapable of functioning* if Western imports fall out or even if only the *increment* is missing. If the small East-European countries were compelled to import a growing part of their basic-material needs from the convertible-currency area, this would make the one-sided dependence complete.

In such a situation credits allow a respite of some years. But the credits needed for maintaining the day-to-day equilibrium of the economy do not provide a basis, even in the long run, for the fast development of the forces of production, for increasing competitivity on the market. *Thus, an indebtedness related to the "daily" deficit in the balance of trade is only good to make the country's economic policy improvident in taking the road to dependence.* Short-term indebtedness does not amount to additional resources drawn into the building of socialism, but mainly serves as a cover for the *overspending of national income.* The price of the "help" may be *dependence.*

One of the ways of becoming released from this dependence is to work hard and assiduously in order to pay back these short-term debts. This requires resolute, far-sighted economic-policy decisions, great discipline in investments, material management and production, but frequently also in personal consumption. The government that does not make this decision will be compelled to escape from the squeeze of dependence due to equilibrium problems into *structural dependence.* It will be compelled to transform the structure of the economy in favour of the activities which are, for the moment, attractive, — i.e. which being foreign currency from the Western markets, practically in favour of agriculture, the extractive and the primary manufacturing industries and the production of semi-finished products and parts not requiring higher production culture.

All this would be, of course, in sharp contradiction with everything the East-European socialist countries have done under the title of socialist industrialization during the last quarter of a century. In spite of all its deficiencies and exaggerations, this economic strategy had two basic starting points which are correct even today, namely, that the development of the economy should rely on developing the intellectual capacity and technical skills of the population and that the highly important specialization should be implemented *within* the socialist community. The abandonment of these two principles would amount historically to *abandoning the efforts at true development* in Eastern Europe. Such a subjugation to the Western division of labour as dictated by the West—either deliberately, or through its economic mechanism—could have been attained by any peripheral Mediterranean country even without socialist transformation. I set out from the realistic assumption that the East-European socialist countries continue to be determined to radically eliminate economic backwardness, to maintain their economic and political independence of the centres of the capitalist world, and to establish a development level and way of life corresponding to socialist society. Therefore, I can assume for the future decades only such forms, extent and mechanism of East–West economic relations which *do not subject* the development of any socialistic country to the equilibrium and structural requirements of the capitalist world market.

For such development, however, as has already been stressed, a very clear East–West economic strategy collated on CMEA level is needed, whose main elements are the following:

— The economic development of the socialist countries and of the CMEA community takes place on the basis of *their own laws.* These demand, on the one hand, fast growth, modernization of the economy and the approximation of development levels both within and among the countries, without fast development leading to wasteful management of factors of production or to the pollution of human environment. Insofar as the effects of Western connections promote and accelerate this in both the short and the long run, and serve the creation of a politically favourable medium, the socialist community is interested in developing these relations.

— The socialist countries and the Community must also reckon with the fact that the Western relations relay also impulses opposing their basic economic development and social objectives. Economic policies and control systems have to eliminate and neutralize such harmful impulses by all means.

In other words, the above means in terms of economic policy: *a sound balance has to be maintained at any time between business ventures promising gains in the short run and the assertion of our long-term economic development and political interests.*

A few examples:

a) At present the *production cooperations* appear, on the basis of a narrow terminological approach, to be deceivingly homogeneous. Everything qualifies as production cooperation—thus also as a desirable East–West deal—that brings about inter-firm relations aimed at a lasting division of production or products, joint appearance on markets, etc. *The criterion is the existence of the division of labour, not its quality.* In reality, the division of labour between two industries or enterprises may rely

— on the complete technological hegemony of the Western firm or on one that cannot be changed in the framework of the given cooperation;

— on a gradual rapprochement of the technical and economic standards between the Western firm and our cooperating unit;

— on the technical and economic "equivalence" of the two partners.

If we do not take into account these *qualitative* criteria which can be evaluated only in the long run, we may easily end up by choosing the first group (that is, simple commission work, sub-contracting, mass production of parts not requiring any particular special training), since they are easier and more comfortable to bring about, and the momentary interests of the Western partner push development rather towards such ventures. Economic policy, therefore, should prefer the types listed as second and third.

At the same time, strategy must bend before the argument of "earthbound pragmatism" that industrial exports may grow best through primitive types of cooperation, even their momentary efficiency is much greater than that of "traditional" exports. The two viewpoints should not be seen as antitheses, but rather the notion of cooperation should be split into two in the dictionary of our economic policy: the first of the above types could be called—for lack of a better expression—*F* cooperation (meaning the acquisition of foreign currency) and the second and third *T* cooperation (meaning the acquisition of technology). I would immediately stress that they occur in "pure" form but in very rare cases. It is up to economic policy to decide whether the *F* or the *T* elements are preponderant in a given cooperation or cooperation opportunity and to *take care that the* F *element should not suppress on a national scale the* T *effect to be acquired.*

b) The need for acquiring convertible foreign currency pushes the *trade* of the socialist countries in the direction of selling possibly every product in the West which can be exported thereto. This leads to such a harmful phenomenon that the domestically developed modern machines and equipment, the high-quality industrial consumer articles produced and high-quality domestic basic materials are exported to the West and thus, on the one hand, put a brake on domestic technological progress and on the further expansion of the export capacity and, on the other hand, draw away commodities from the mutual trade among socialist countries. This phenomenon shows characteristically how East–West trade becomes an end in itself, caused by short-term shortage of foreign currency whose effects are extremely harmful in the long run.

When coordinating plans, the CMEA countries should pay increased attention to the production and exchange of commodities which can be placed on each other's markets, satisfy each other's needs and mutually save convertible foreign currency. This also means that the increased development possibilities of East–West cooperation must act as a catalyst to the further development of socialist economic cooperation, on the efforts at economic integration.

PART TWO

Contributions to the Theory of the International Division of Labour

CHAPTER ONE

Internationalization of economic processes

The development of the forces of production includes the evolution of human knowledge, demanding organizational ability and love of work as well as the perfection of individual tools and of more or less complex systems of tools, and also the changes in the use of the materials provided by nature, depending on the former two factors. The development of the forces of production increases in itself the volume of social production and the expansion of the relations in the division of labour. From the aspect of our investigation it is this wider social effect of the development of the forces of production that is important, and this is why it has to be discussed in greater detail.

Society is capable of producing use values in an ever greater volume, in ever wider assortments and in ever richer composition. Parallel with this, the demands of society are growing concerning the quantity, use value and diversity of the commodities. That is, for a smooth social production, productive and personal consumption, more products and many more kinds of products are needed; as a consequence, more and more kinds of technologies are invented. These technologies enable the appearance of new products on the market. Thus, needs and production have growing mutual effects on each other as regards both volume and diversity. The final result is the increased expansion of the world of commodities, and this in a double sense: on the one hand, the technology of the different kinds of commodities proceeds from individual to mass production and, on the other hand, the diversity of technologies producing different use values increases.

With the development of the forces of production certain commodities which yesterday fully satisfied needs, become obsolete together with the technologies attached to them, and are replaced by new commodities turned out with new technologies, which satisfy the existing needs according to the prevailing tastes. Furthermore, the ever-growing requirement of efficiency soon makes the technologies producing the same product obsolete, the use of a new technology becomes necessary and spreads in production. This in turn makes products obsolete on the market of producer goods and demands the appearance of new products, affecting the pattern of products thereby. In the final analysis, the development of the forces of production accelerates the obsolescence of the individual commodities and results in the obsolete products (means of production and consumer articles) being replaced by new ones.

Products satisfying some given needs of production and consumption are related from two aspects. In part the demands of mass production bring about such technologies which derive certain commodities, parts and finished products from a common root. Therefore, the development of the production of some commodity, its appearance and spreading on the producer and consumer market, is not independent of those of other commodities, and the rate of their obsolescence and their replacement by new ones cannot be judged in itself either, but only in the context of the related technologies. *The productive machinery is growing more and more into an interrelated network, bringing about interrelated systems of producer goods and consumer articles. On the other hand, productive and personal consumption is increasingly made up of the use of products which are turned out by this interrelated system. Needs are not satisfied individually, but a complex system of certain use values is called upon to fulfil this task.* Individual use values are increasingly replaced by extensive *networks*, system which are uniform also as regards the "technology" of utilization. Thus the world of commodities is growing ever more complex from the aspects of both production and consumption.

The rate of development outlined in the preceding sections can be satisfied only by such productive machinery in which the social division of labour also becomes more detailed and refined. Industries which were independent only a few decades ago, have become split up unto several dozens or even hundreds of "independent" technologies. At the same time, this process integrates the technologies which developed earlier independently, and realizes a very close mutual dependence among them. The development of the forces of production is becoming a unified process, including technical development and, in a certain sense, even basic research.

Qualified knowledge, technology and production growing steadily and multiplying as if by bipartition drive society partly towards specialization of the forces of production and partly towards extreme requirements as regards the organization of research, development and production. Work processes, which a few decades or only a few years ago could be surveyed, organized and developed in a workshop, now require complicated macro-economic coordination. Traditional scientific disciplines become specialized to the extreme, while fields of research which were very far apart meet and amalgamate in the course of this specialization. The same process takes place also in the field of productive processes. In the last analysis, the social division of labour assumes quite new forms, and an intricate web of specialization and amalgamation develops which simultaneously calls for huge social organizational and control measures.

The specialization process outlined above takes place simultaneously with the uninterrupted growth of the necessary research, development and productive capacities. In the more and more specialized productive process ever larger productive collectives constitute the basic nuclei of society and their supply with means of production is growing faster than the human collectives themselves.

The development indicated may be discovered, as a matter of fact, throughout the history of the whole mankind. The fact that we have attained a clear recognition of this development tendency in the 20th century may be attributed mainly to the chain-reaction nature of the process. It was in the 20th century that mankind came to such a stage of this chain reaction where development causes humanity to face, several times even during the activity of a single generation, radical changes in the whole productive and organizational process and the concomitant requirements of reorganization. We may add that the process indicated, the chain reaction, is not developing at an even rate. There are relatively slow phases (preparing the explosions, collecting the conditions of fast development) and phases when the quick changes suddenly take place. The periodicity is quite sufficiently explained by the Marxian general theory of social development, based on the dialectical mutual effects of the forces of production and the production relations.

Up to this point there is no need to include the international economic factors. Insofar as the process indicated takes place within a country, its rules can be explained and understood through the interrelations of general economics. The international problems come in when this chain reaction conflicts with a particular organizational form of society developed under capitalism: the autonomous national economy.

In its most abstract and most sterile (autarkic) form, national economy is a complete sphere of producing use values. At the same time, it is the forum where individual and group work is valued, that is, the market where the works of individuals and groups dividing the labour establish a relationship with each other, where it is decided whether the individual or the group fits fortunately or unfortunately into the blood circulation of the whole society. At the same time, the national economy is also an "averaging unit", where the interaction of individual productive activities takes place, and through this the development level of the national forces of production, the average productivity (efficiency) of national labour and, simultaneously, the national value and the national market develop as real categories.

The chain reaction reviewed collides sooner or later with the potential energies of this particular social macro-economic unit. When it collides and where this collision takes place, is determined partly by the size of the historically developed national economy, and partly by the unequal development of the individual productive activities within this historical unity. (The latter is again influenced by several factors, e.g. natural circumstances, relations of production, the historical traditions of society and the degree of its general culture, as well as the relative state of these.)

In the long run the needs of the forces of production always emerge victoriously from the confrontation between these needs and the national–social frameworks of organization. The first such "victory" is the emergence of exchange of commodities with other national units and the international division of labour evolving as a result of the former becoming regular.

The international division of labour developed as a kind of specialization between or within productive activities which had come about and developed relatively independently of each other. As soon as the different products, technologies and, in their wake, consumption, become integrated into a uniform and interrelated *system*, the international division of labour also undergoes a radical change. Therefore, we speak today not only of industries, groups of products or priority development projects joining the international division of labour, but also of *"technical cultures"* joining it. By technical culture I mean the many-sided suitability of the forces of production to satisfy a certain social need at a high level. Thus, technical culture is not identical with the state of development of the forces of production in some narrower field of production, with the technical state of fixed assets, with labour productivity, etc., though all these have their part in it. Technical culture is always a product of the special historical development of the country.

Economic development concentrated around the "technical cultures" requires a new way of reasoning both in economic guidance and in planning, as well as in the control mechanism. This clusters, on the one hand, the main related fields around complex tasks—mainly modernization problems—of high importance, which reach into the development of several industries, entailing ramifying cooperation and foreign-trade relations but also touching more or less extra-economic fields, such as education, health, veterinary practice, environmental problems, defence, etc. For example, health and hygienic culture includes building, engineering and electronics, the food industry, the chemical industry, but its core is the high tradition of medical science and the health service developed in the country in question. Its intellectual products, its educational and organizational parts affect the domestic and external economic relations of development just like trade in antibiotics or cooperation in the production of instruments. It is expedient to concentrate research, development, planning and production highly both financially and as regards administration and to carry on an efficient export drive.

These technical cultures are playing an increasing role also in international cooperation. It is, namely, much more attractive if a country's readiness to cooperate includes the development of complete *systems* and their implantation into the economies of the partners. This relieves the partner not only from production, but also from a major part of these. If the products are sold or offered for cooperation individually, their fast moral obsolescence will always burden the "hardness" of the pattern of trade. But the "selling" of technical structures may raise the efficiency of its elements to manyfold, whether the whole culture or some of its major interrelated parts are "sold". It is attractive precisely because it frees the importing partner from the concerns of internal organization and adaptation, and also because there is a safer guaranty that the exporting country will be able to develop it with concentrated forces according to the needs.

Naturally, the world economic relationships of a country cannot get exhausted by the exclusive production and export of technical cultures. An exclusive approach through technical cultures might results in a one-sidedness similar to any other such approach. The second level where a country may join the international division of labour consists of those fields *where domestic conditions for an independent modern technical development are missing* (e.g. lack of domestic raw materials, insufficiency of development and production traditions, high capital intensity and large scale of production necessary in the branch concerned, etc.), but where, because of full employment and export needs in manufacturing it is not expedient to suppress production entirely. In this case it will be expedient for the country either to put up with "follow-up" techniques, that is, to produce the finished products on the basis of foreign production technologies, or to cooperate on a sub-contracting basis with the industries of other countries. The industry of the country may keep pace—or almost keep pace—with the development of world technology also in these branches: but the bulk of development activity will be done abroad.

In the course of implementing development policy, first of all research and development should be stopped in the fields "dropping out" from the centre. The existing capacities, insofar as they can be converted, should be channelled towards the priority technical cultures, and if they are inconvertible, they should be used for sub-contracting work if they otherwise conform to international standards. Productive capacities in such fields should be linked first of all to high-standard production in other countries through cooperation or sub-contracting agreements.

Of course, these levels and sectors cannot be found in pure form either in space or time. It should also be taken into consideration that areas now belonging to the "follow-up" sectors *may in time develop into areas of primary importance*. Also the reverse may occur, but, desirably, rarely. For this, however, the direction of the world's technical progress must be well known and prognosticated, and from among the cultures to be developed those technical activities should be excluded at the outset in respect of which the capital input per unit of output, or the scale of production, or its research requirements will foreseeably exceed the capacity of the economy during the period while the capital invested is recovered, or the world market becomes saturated, and technical culture starts to decline, etc.

The *ratios between the different "levels"* are also important for the countries fitting into the division of labour. If a country attempts to concentrate "technical cultures" in the economy on a too wide scale, the whole development strategy may fail and the whole national economy may be pushed to a lower level, wherefrom it is increasingly difficult to "bring up" any industry. The same effect is produced if selection has not been fortunate, if e.g. such complexes are selected from the technological and production traditions are missing, or where the scale of efficient production exceeds the possibilities of the efforts. If, however, the economy is too cautious, if it does not take risks, or if it accords one-sided preference to advantages that can be realized in the short run against those to be reaped in the long run and draws, on this account, the limits of the technical cultures to be developed too narrowly, it may irreparably slide to the periphery of development.

In a world economy where the basis of the division of labour is the linking of technical cultures across the frontiers, a division of labour which is not regulated by anything else but the exchange of commodities based on the laws of demand and supply cannot be called either organic or stable. The national economies (and their parts, e.g. enterprises or trade) feel the need to rely on another definite productive capacity beyond the country's frontiers. Without their participation not even domestic reproduction takes place. That is, they have not surpluses and shortages in *general*, which they try to clear by relying on sources or markets abroad, but the volume of work expended *for foreign countries* becomes increasingly important relative to the volume of national labour, both as regards its entirety and its details. The deeper the *direct* dependence in reproduction on the foreign partners, the stronger the objective effort *at stabilizing the economic relations with foreign countries*. At a certain stage of development this already amounts to the need of coordinating the reproduction process internationally.

At the same time, the more the particular national economies feel the imperfections in the coordination of reproduction processes going on in the different countries, and *the impossibility of its being perfected*, the greater efforts they will make to assure (or over-assure) both their markets and their procurement sources abroad. This is, however, a factor which works against the stabilization of relations, since it leads to the "spreading" of both export and import connections, which dampens the importance of the division of labour "by pairs" or "by groups" for the reproduction process of the given national economy (or industry, enterprise, etc.). The world-economic development which preceded the efforts at integration was the resultant of these two opposing tendencies. All that was much influenced and distorted partly by the efforts of the colonial empires and partly by the protectionism of some countries. In this respect, the internationalization of the forces of production advances under the crossfire of different opposing effects, extremely inconsistently and at a rate much slower than would be possible otherwise.

CHAPTER TWO

Limitations to the measurement of intertwining

The process of the internationalization of the forces of production is very difficult to quantify and to measure exactly on this basis. The relatively most reliable yardstick is the ratio of the volume of internationally exchanged commodities to the national income expressing the volume of national labour. Depending on the extent to which an economy is compelled to resort to national exchange, these ratios differ along a wide scale. The huge economies which, although developed as regards their forces of production, are less dependent on extending their productive processes beyond their frontiers (or on introducing the productive processes of other countries into their own economies), as e.g. the USA or the USSR, exchange less than 10 per cent of the national income they produce with other countries of the world. Those, otherwise small, countries whose forces of production are not sufficiently developed to hold their own in the international division of labour, also exchange a relatively small percentage of their national income on the world market, Greece e.g. only 12 per cent. At the same time, medium-sized countries with developed forces of production, as e.g. the German Federal Republic, France, Italy, or the United Kingdom, are intertwined with the other parts of the world economy to the extent of 25–35 per cent of their national income. Such smaller economies which are strongly dependent on the international intertwining of productive processes as e.g. Hungary, Czechoslovakia, Bulgaria, Norway, Denmark, Belgium and the Netherlands, participate in the more or less stabilized international division of labour to the extent of 40–75 per cent of their national income.

Thus, the ratio of the commodity trade between countries to the volume of the national product depends mainly on the country's size (exceptions in this respect are less developed countries with highly monocultural structures, which offer for exchange a much higher proportion of their national income than would be otherwise warranted either by their size or by their development level).

Commodity flows are not distributed in the world economy evenly between the different countries. The regions consisting of many countries with smaller area and smaller economic potential exchange, naturally, a greater part of their

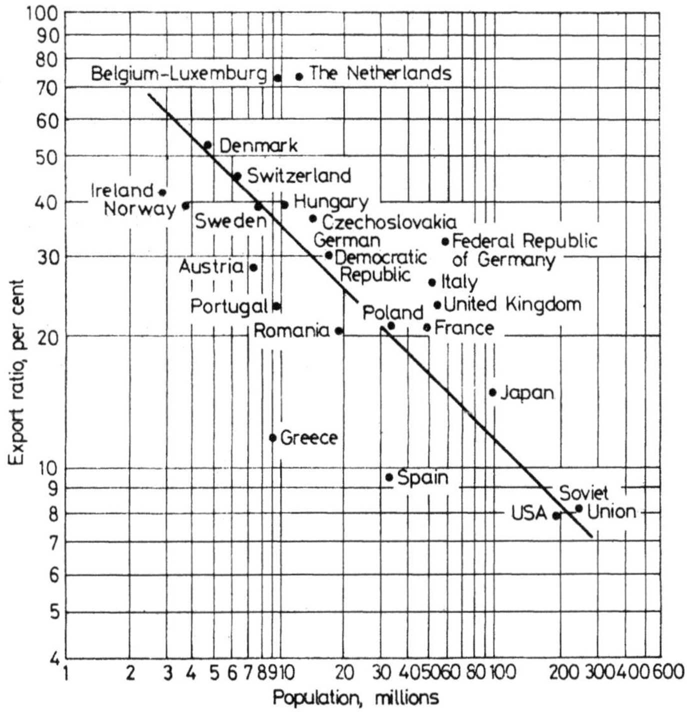

Fig. 1. Interrelation between the size of the countries and the ratio of exports to national income in 1968. (In the case of industrialized countries national income converted to net material product.)

national income among each other than the regions where fewer countries can be found or which comprise a huge country. It becomes understandable on this basis why the developed European capitalist countries exchange among each other almost 20 per cent of their national incomes, while the similar indicator of the CMEA countries does not exceed 5 per cent. If, namely, we form in Western Europe seven imaginary countries whose population is distributed on the whole in a ratio similar to that in the CMEA,[5] and consider the trade among each other of those "aggregated" as "home trade", then, by deducting the latter from the

[5] I used the following method for the "aggregation": from the German Federal Republic, France, Great Britain, Italy, the Benelux states and Denmark I made a conglomerate whose population (251 million) is to the total population of Western Europe (358 million) as that of the Soviet Union is to the whole of the CMEA. In addition, from Sweden, Norway and Switzerland I made a "German Democratic Republic". The result is the trade among seven "countries" which can already be compared with trade within the CMEA, since the same amount of foreign trade is measured among "national"units of the same size and proportion.

European regional trade, the volume of 93 billion dollars will fall to 29 billion (1970), that is, to 5.9 per cent of West-European national income summed up. The commodity flows in Western Europe are not much more intensive than those in the CMEA, but, on the one hand, their composition is different (this will be discussed yet) and, on the other, they pass more customs frontiers.

World economy does not consists, thus, of evenly intensive spheres of commodities, and of the divisions of labour behind them, but has "density points", such as the North-American continent, Western Europe and the group of East-European socialist countries.

The developed countries exchange significant volumes of products within the group also relative to the volume of social labour: they have established an intensive division of labour in their own region.

Exports as percentage of national income or net material product

North-American countries among each other:	3.3
West-European countries among each other:	19.0
CMEA countries among each other:	4.6

At the same time, the mass of commodities exchanged—in interregional trade—shows an essentially smaller ratio to national income in the countries of the two

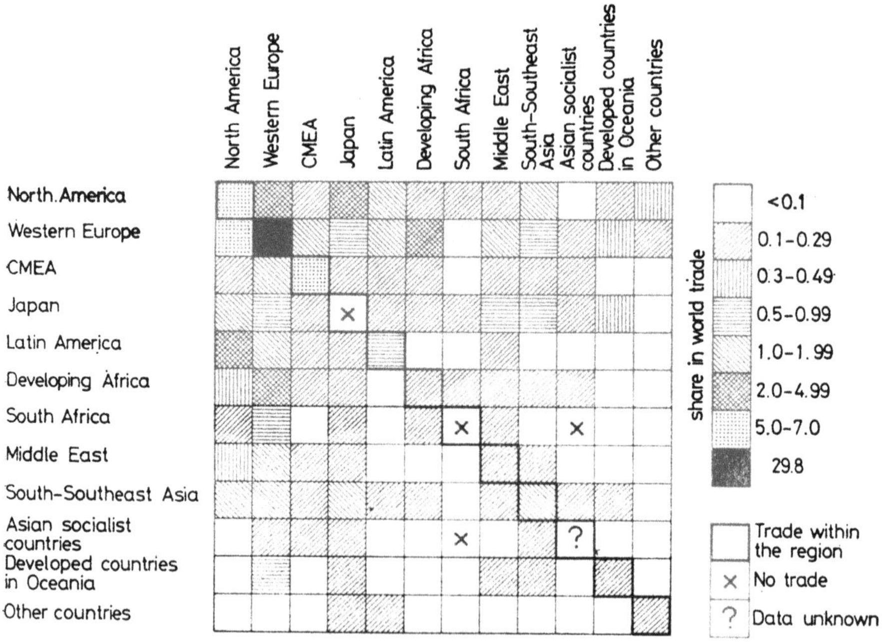

Fig. 2. Distribution of world trade in 1970. (World-trade total = 100)

Source: **UN Statistical Yearbook 1971**

European groups, than the trade within the group. About 2 per cent of the national income of the developed European capitalist countries and less than 3 per cent of that of the East-European countries goes into the channels of East–West trade.

This condensation process can also be shown dynamically. Between 1958 and 1970, world trade increased to about threefold. The North-American and East-European "nodes" kept pace with this rate, the West-European one exceeded it. Nor did relations among the three lag behind the average rate. In the other geographical units of the world the growth rate of trade did not attain the average (see the diagonal quadrants in Figure 3). At the same time, we can observe the above-average export–import dynamism of Japan and the generally slow growth of trade among the geographical units formed from the developing countries. For the groups of developing countries it is the developed cores that are the centres which attract trade.

The internationalization of productive processes cannot be described merely with the relation between commodity flows and national income. This is, namely, only the final result of internationalization expressed in the movement of commodities and—as indicated above—not every movement of commodities is backed

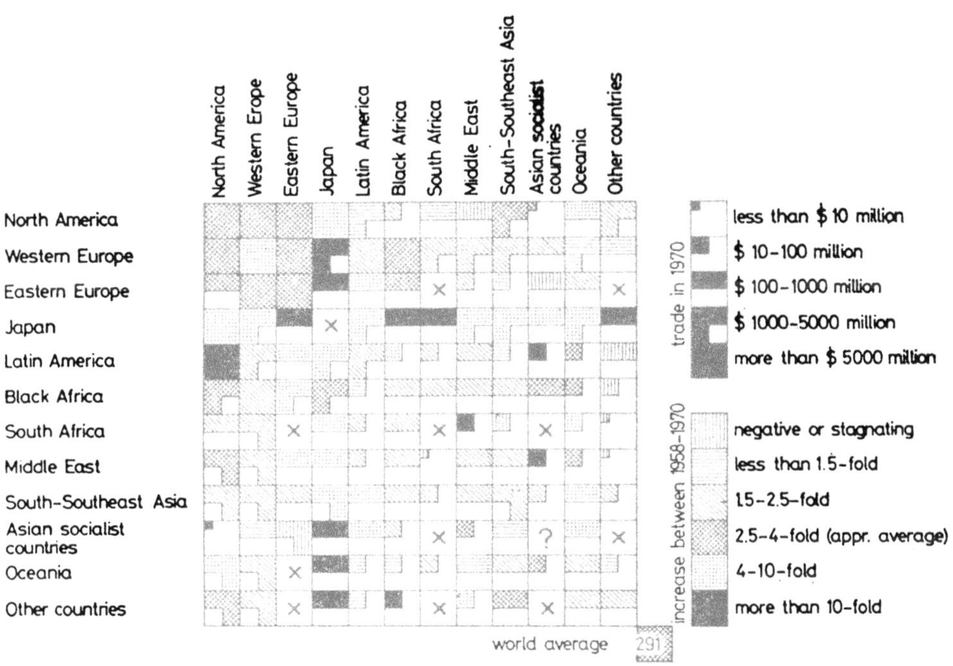

Fig. 3. Dynamics of world trade in the sixties (1970 data relative to 1958)

Source: UN Statistical Yearbook 1972

simultaneously by a stable, consolidated international division of labour. A considerable part of these commodity movements is the result of unstable and temporary division of labour, and the volume of those commodities which are moved as a result of occasional individual deals, and which are not backed even by an unstable, temporary division of labour is not negligible. At any rate, the intensity indicators of commodity flows indicate, on the whole, the deepening of the division of labour. A more reliable and more accurate picture could be obtained about the extent of the division of labour if those decisions could be mapped and quantified, together with their secondary national economic effects, which are taken partly or entirely on the basis of criteria of some internationally coordinated decision centre: e.g. the extent, directions, nodal points of the international intertwining of capital, the degree of efficiency of intergovernmental bilateral and multilateral economic coordination, as an ordering principle of international structure and development for the whole of the economy. But we have rather scanty data for such surveys. Therefore, we can estimate the tendency only on the basis of sources of varying quality, quantity and reliability and only tentatively. We know, e.g., that between 1961 and 1969 more than 15,000 acts of capital mergers took place in the six Common-Market countries, and only 20 per cent of these took place within the particular member countries, about one quarter were acts between the member countries and more than half, between Common Market and third countries. We also know that the multinational companies of mainly American origin possess a decisive portion of productive capacities in some West-European industries, thus of about 80–90 per cent in the industries producing electronic equipment and the necessary components.

American investment into European industry increased from 32 billion dollars in 1960 to 78 in 1970 (according to the so-called Rey report of the OECD). It is also known that some international giants extend to several countries and various industries. All these data are fragmentary and, though indicating the directions of regional or of an even wider division of labour, they do not provide a reliable hold for a synthetic measurement.

At any rate, as much can be deduced from the relevant sources of data and from studies that the internationalization of decision processes takes place basically on two planes. One is the breaking of national economic frameworks which have become narrow for the development of the forces of production by the economic policies of the state, i.e. the coordination of macro-economic activities. This takes place in the forms of collating and harmonizing governmental economic policy activities through bilateral trade, cooperation, technical and aid agreements, as well as through coordinating activities in various international organizations as the World Trade Organization, the Economic Commission for Europe, the OECD, the IMF, the GATT, but also the activities of the EEC and the CMEA may be classified as such.

The other is the "enterprise plane", the dimension of the international intertwining of ownership and capital, which result on micro-economic level, in decision centres reaching beyond national economies, which coordinate certain research, production and marketing activities.

World economy after the emergence of the efforts at integration is struggling with the contradictions caused by the fact that the two dimensions of this decision-coordinating network developed simultaneously. This is better observable in Western Europe, where the international micro-economic intertwinings have already historical traditions—through the industrial and bank capital's becoming cosmopolitan. It is less observable in Eastern Europe, where, although the necessity of micro-economic integration is similarly felt, the historical traditions are missing and the economic conditions for the creation and proliferation of international enterprises are just beginning to mature.

The other cross-section in which the internationalization of production might be examined is reaching back to the technological processes. The needs of the development of the forces of production crush the frontiers of national economies above all along the great technological faults: what we have in mind is the division of labour between the extracting and the manufacturing activities. The typical division of labour in the 19th and in the first half of the 20th century developed between the national economies carrying on basically extractive activities (agriculture, mining) and those characteristically manufacturing. More exactly: the groups of countries which were more advanced in developing the forces of production made efforts to get rid of the extractive activities requiring less skill and engaging greater masses, and to concentrate the forces of production on "more intelligent" activities and those securing a quicker return of capital. This division of labour has essentially persisted to our very days between the developed and the developing countries.

As manufacturing activities became more capital intensive and started differentiating explosion-like through chain reactions, it also became indispensable that the international division of labour among manufacturing activities should also accelerate to an unbelievable extent. We are witnessed to this process in the second half of the 20th century. This division of labour has emerged above all between the industrially more advanced countries and seems to develop in basically two directions: one is the international separation of consecutive technological processes, that is, the kind of division of labour where the various phases of working a basic material to be processed reach beyond the frontiers of two or more countries and the materials become products ready for final consumption in the *n*-th country. The other is the scattering of concentrically concurring technologies in different countries. Usually this means the production of articles consisting of many complicated parts, the economical scale of production of which is not identical, and the optimal series of each differs from that of the assembled end product. Finally, the third direction is the scattering of the production of the various individual products and assortments of the world of commodities proliferating through bipartition all over the world. The first two trends are commonly called cooperation, the latter specialization. In an actual venture usually the elements of all three directions can be found, thus their "classification" in any of the categories seems wilful in the actual cases.

The division of labour mushrooming within manufacturing also brings about its hierarchy. Neither the phases of technology, nor the parts, nor the specialized end products are equal from the viewpoints of the research background, the quantity and quality of qualified labour, the size of the technological basis they require, nor in respect of the rate at which world demand increases for them. The smaller the country joining this division of labour, the less developed its forces of production and the less definite its development policy, the smaller the realistic possibilities and chances for it to acquire within the manufacturing division of labour those phases and areas which secure a more dynamic quantitative development. Thus, the internationalization of manufacturing activities does not automatically entail equal chances for every participant to enjoy the fruits of scientific progress.

Potential and acquired advantages should be reckoned with also in this respect. This bears new protectionistic tendencies, partly in the national economies, partly in the nodal points of the regional division of labour. Internationalization is thus not an unambiguous process even in this sense. Strong resistance on the part of national and regional economies is accompanying the internationalization process of production, partly braking and partly hindering the economies, with the greatest advantages, to derive from their position and their history one-sided advantages.

The modern social division of labour has been organized on three levels. All three—national, regional and international—are equally objective realities: they constitute such relatively autonomous centres of forces, structures which are palpable and measurable even if their frontiers are not always sharply drawn and permeate each other. World economy is a galaxy whose density regions are the regional economies and its elements the national economies. From these three, national and world economies need no definition. Regional economy is a product of the past few decades. It will not be, therefore, useless to attempt a notional definition.

By regional economy we mean such a group of national economies in which the particular national economies

a) are in a palpably closer production and trade relationship with each other than with other countries;

b) the valuation of products and activities exchanged among each other shows particular features, deviating from those of the environment;

c) characteristic normatives, "rules of the game" have developed in the mutual economic contacts and, as a consequence:

d) the closer than average cooperation implemented with particular tools entails mutual advantages of mutual extent for the members of the region.

I do not think that the institutionalization of cooperation is an absolute criterion of regional economy, though in some regions the activity of the cooperating organizations plays an important role.

As a matter of fact, three sharply distinct regions can be found in world economy: the North-American, comprising the United States and Canada, the West-European, consisting of the EEC countries and the non-member advanced and peripheral capitalist countries, and the East-European, comprising the European socialist countries and, from outside Europe, Mongolia and Cuba.

In 1970, 67 per cent of the exports of the affected countries were sold within the West-European region, the CMEA countries transacted 61 per cent of their trade among themselves, and the trade between the USA and Canada was 33 per cent of the total trade of these two countries. As a contrast, this indicator was 22 per cent in the case of the developing South-East Asian countries, 22 per cent for those in Latin America and 6 per cent each in the Middle East and in East Africa. Japan is not integrated into any of the regions. Its relations are most intensive with the USA. The trade between them amounted in 1970 to 17 per cent of the combined exports of the two countries. Thus, the intensity of the intertwining of the USA with Japan, which has 100 million inhabitants, is half as strong as with Canada, which has a population of 20 million.

I do *not* consider the EEC as an autonomous region, independent of Western Europe, but as its most solid, institutionally also supported core. The trade within the EEC was, in 1970, 49 per cent of the combined exports of the member countries, that is, of a lower intensity than in the whole of Western Europe. At the same time, exchange within the EEC amounted to almost half of the trade within Western Europe. Thus, the West-European region is a *wider* notion than the Common Market (though much narrower than the OECD). Neither do I regard as a region the preferential area of the British Commonwealth of Nations, this fading memory of the British colonial empire, nor the still existing systems of relations between the colonies and the earlier mother countries which are in the process of dissolution. *The regions are thus the condensation nodes of the world economy, the centres in which the process of the social division of labour takes place at a rate faster than the average.* Regionalization of the economies is a synonym for international economic integration.

Owing to the fact that the regions are emergent formations which are products of the condensation of the cooperation relations among independent, though ever less independent, national economies within the uniform, though not homogeneous, world economy, it follows that the situation and relation of the particular national economies to the various regions may be highly different and may develop in many ways: the *regions are formations, fast changing in space and time, and possess highly heterogeneous features.* Nor have been their frontiers quite stabilized, nor can their internal structure and their equilibrium position within the whole of the world economy be considered as settled. There are several national economies *outside* the regions or in the space around the regions, linked to a minor or major extent to the regionalized spheres or to some of the economies belonging to the latter. These economies, depending on their development level, size, and dynamics, may augment the already existing nodes, may form new ones, become cores or parts of such. The regional spheres of condensation come about because of power effects in the international economic relations. Attracting and repelling forces are operative. In world economy, similarly to the universe, the principle of *gravitation* prevails. The power that attracts the different national economies towards establishing links with each other, or towards integration or which, in other cases, repels them, is nothing else than the extent of advantages to be derived from the foreign economic relations.

CHAPTER THREE

Advantages deriving from the division of labour

By advantages to be derived from the foreign economic relations I mean such consequences of the division of labour which create more favourable conditions for the national economy in question to develop its forces of production and to utilize more rationally its factors of production. *The advantage is thus an improvement of the efficiency of the national economy induced by foreign economic relations.* I should like to stress that I am speaking about national economy and wish to analyse the individual elements of the division of labour, too, from the viewpoint of the national economy. Namely, the efficiency of foreign economic relations on the national level does not automatically coincide with profitability on the enterprise level. An enterprise may transact foreign trade at high profit, it may isolate itself from forming economic relations in the interest of higher profit, or may shift them from one external partner to the other, while the national economy suffers.

The same may be imagined also conversely. But this is again another problem: the problem of adapting the internal exchange relations and income relations to the optimum requirements of fitting the national economy into the world market, that is, the general problem of the economic mechanism, which, however, cannot be satisfactorily solved without clarifying the conditions of the general orientation of the national economy—with the external conditions among them. Every economy endeavours to orientate its foreign relations in those directions which offer the most advantageous conditions in the division of labour for its further development.

In the following I shall attempt decomposing the effects of the world market on the national economy into its major elements. I wanted to carry the analysis up to the threshold of quantification. However, in lack of suitable statistical data systems, for the time being only a part of the quantitative relationships worked out can be filled with data. Nevertheless, I am convinced that the various kinds of advantages to be derived from the international division of labour will sooner or later become separable in quantitative terms and an opportunity will be given to analyse them one by one.

Since I believe there is not much sense in giving separate names to the elements of the effects, for an easier handling, and in order to avoid complicated formulations, I will denote them with capital letters.

a) Comparative advantages (*A* effect)

If the national economy is in relatively initial stage of joining world economy (or one of its regions), i.e. when it is just being industrialized or has a diversified economic structure mainly adapted to satisfying domestic needs, the simplest way of adaptation to the world market is to develop (or emphasize) such productive activities for regular export in which the annual labour of the common producer contributing to the exported product is valued by the world-market exchange relations higher than the average. It is self-explanatory that the economy will not develop or will even suppress those branches where the annual performance of a producer is valued relatively low by the world market. In the final analysis, we have here the effect of comparative costs relying on the Ricardian principle; we are conscious of the determining influence which given world-market price relations have on the decisions of the particular national economies regarding the mode of their joining the international division of labour.

The comparative costs may be worked out as follows:

First the efficiency indicators of the domestic productive activity are determined. Efficiency is expressed as the total labour input necessary for attaining a unit of price receipts from foreign trade:

$$E^n = l^n X$$

where

E^n = the national economic efficiency of the domestic productive activity n,

l^n = labour input into the end product of the given productive activity n, per one unit of foreign-trade sales receipts attainable, that is:

$$l^n = \frac{L^n \text{ (total man-years, in units of skilled labour)}}{P_s^n \text{ (value of the end products in a year in activity } n\text{, at foreign-trade prices)}}$$

X = the inverse matrix of the input–output table.

The efficiency indicators of the different productive activities are weighted according to the commodity pattern of exports and imports to different areas:

a) $E_{ex}^{a} = \sum_{a=1}^{n} e^{a} E$

where

E^{α}_{ex} = average efficiency of the country in export production, according to the commodity pattern of exports to the partner α,

$a = (1, \ldots, n)$ = sectors (productive activities) of the internal quadrant of the input–output table,

e^{α} = commodity pattern of exports to partner α,

E = efficiency of productive activity.

b) $E^{\alpha}_{im} = \sum_{a=1}^{n} i^{\alpha}E$

where

E^{α}_{im} = virtual efficiency of import substitution, that is, the average efficiency with which the product pattern imported from partner α could be produced at home,

i^{α} = commodity pattern of imports from partner α.

The comparative saving of costs (A)—or additional cost—is the quotient of the export efficiency and the import saving efficiency:

$$A^{\alpha} = \frac{E^{\alpha}_{ex}}{E^{\alpha}_{im}}$$

In view of the fact that a growing value of the basic indicator E signals the deterioration of efficiency and its diminishing value, an improvement in efficiency (the more man-years are needed to produce 1 dollar of foreign-trade sales receipts, the less efficient the productive activity, and the fewer are needed, the more efficient it is), $A < l$ means a comparative saving of costs, and $A > l$ involves additional costs.

The A effect may be strongly modified by the differences between domestic and internationally acknowledged inputs. Maybe some industry "pays well" on the world market for those who produce at least with average productivity (inclusive of the phase releasing the product to be exported), but it may happen that the same "does not pay" for the given economy because of the high social domestic input, and conversely, a product which "does not pay" on international average, might be efficiently exported because of fortunate or well-developed domestic production conditions.

Thus, the A effect is itself the resultant of two factors: of the terms of trade on the world market, and of the domestic input (i.e. input acknowledged in the world-market prices). That is, with its system of value judgements the world market generally rewards or punishes productive activities. And both the "reward" and the "punishment" may multiply or vanish as a consequence of the efficiency of domestic labour. At any rate, this effect stimulates the countries searching for fitting organically into the world economy to make structural changes. At the same time, in the case of free price movements, the world market revenges itself after a while for the "structural pickings" of the national economies, through the price-changing effect of supply and demand. Therefore, a lasting improvement in the efficiency of the domestic structure can be attained in this manner only in a monopolistic situation, or in the framework of a regional "defensive alliance" developed expressly with the aim of collectively promoting a given type of industrialization.

For more advanced economies with greater economic potential, this favourable structural effect concerning their relations with the less developed and weaker world around them is usually given, precisely owing to the world-market power relations. The fewer the restrictions imposed on the market mechanism, the more their economic superiority becomes pronounced. Of less developed and weaker economies which desire to break away from backwardness, and of their regional groups, rather a protectionistic economic policy is characteristic—and, in addition, its introvert type, which keeps in view not the world-market competitivity of some product, but the maximum utilization of the domestic forces of production available, full employment, the raising of the technical culture of the population to the minimum level, the processing to a higher degree of the raw material available, the increase of the technical equipment, the supply with assets of social production, etc. This economic policy puts into the centre of the criteria of decision the comparison of the productive activities within the country. Its first concern is not whether domestic mining or agriculture is competitive with mining and agriculture in other countries, but whether—considering the given international structure of prices—it can better utilize the investment and labour available in the textile or the engineering industry than in the extracting industries. Of course, we haste to add, the given price structure must be relatively rigid (in consequence of monopolistic situation or regional agreement), and also marketing possibilities have to be secure (similarly because of monopolistic situation or regional preferences). Otherwise, the competition on foreign markets will strangle these new industries in their embryonic state. It is not immaterial even in what form the input or engagement of a factor of production for a unit of sales receipts on the world market appears. The developing countries usually abound in—not very qualified—labour and are short of capital, frequently even of natural resources. Accordingly, "picking" from among the productive activities with similar indicators is aimed at minimizing the engagement of capital as long as there are labour reserves. For example, if a unit of sales receipts demands greater engagement of resources in agriculture than in mining, but within that mining requires more embodied labour than living labour, the country will presumably prefer agriculture—after manufacturing—for development for exports. Thus, the A effect will be the following: the higher the proportion of highly processed products in exports, and of raw materials in imports, the more efficiently the economy operates, since it saves social labour, with special regard to advancing embodied labour.

Insofar as the given economy has no more unutilized labour, it will rank agriculture first in its imports, and, e.g. the primarily processed products in its exports: namely, their exchange will maximize for it the saving of living labour.

b) Dynamic advantages (B effect)

In the above I have tacitly assumed that the different products are neutral as to their market absorption. The A effect reckons exclusively with the world-market "price position". In reality, the dynamism of demand should be reckoned with. The growth rate of a national economy which is highly integrated with the international division of labour is necessarily affected by the dynamism of its export pattern—in direct proportion to the degree of "openness"—as well as by extent to which its import structure supports the dynamism of exports and, through that, the dynamism of the whole economy.

Therefore, the structural policy of the national economies also has to further the share of those articles for which demand on the world market is increasing, and to import instead such articles whose use promotes the development of its dynamic industries. The B effect is related to the A effect, but cannot be identified with it. It increases the efficiency of the domestic economy not through the high external price of the commodity, but through the increasing volume to be sold on the world market and thus through the increasing foreign-exchange receipts of the national economy and, as a consequence, through a higher rate of growth.

The division of labour of the country with the partner country α is called advantageous from the viewpoint of B, if the sales possibilities of the assortment of exports to partner α; (e^α) increase faster than the sales possibilities of the commodity assortment produced for the domestic market (g^α). The difference in rates is:

$$B^\alpha = \frac{e^\alpha}{g^\alpha}$$

Those countries aim at achieving the B effect which much depend on world economy and whose growth rate considerably depends on the absorptive capacity of the external markets. This policy assumes a diversified structure, the possibility of the economic policy to choose from among the productive activities which should be more or less developed. Confrontation of exports with imports appears here from the viewpoint of efficiency not necessarily as a confrontation of dynamic articles with those having lost their dynamism. This, too, exists: if a country strives after exports of machine tools, it will be more advantageous for it to import metal mass products and to convert its released capacities for the production of machine-tool parts, if reliance on a lasting investment boom supports its growth rate more safely than reliance on a more slowly growing demand for consumer articles. But this can become the main line of economic policy only if the national economy is able to be in a creditor position for some longer time. Otherwise it is necessary to have a roughly balanced dynamism of the export and import patterns on the whole world market. With multilateral settlement this balanced state may fluctuate—this is allowed with multilateralism. In a bilateral system the dynamism of structures must tend towards a balanced state also in bilateral relations.

It is in such cases that the flexibility of machine and human capacities producing for export, that is, their fast convertibility to the production of those products, which are more in demand, comes to the fore. For smaller countries and those short of capital, if two export possibilities with equal dynamism are available, it is more worthwhile to choose the one whose technology is less "committed" to the production of a given kind of use value. This also explains why smaller countries prefer engineering to heavy chemical industry and why smaller countries arrange for the production of relatively smaller batches of machines which can be competitively produced, against mass production, or why they rather produce pharmaceuticals instead of petrochemical products.

Thus, for countries with small internal markets joining the international division of labour is the more advantageous:

— the greater the share of dynamically developing articles in exports,

— the better their imports "serve" these industries with raw materials, parts, investments goods,

— the more flexible their export capacities and the more they import from products turned out with "rigid" technologies. Large economies are less sensitive to the latter effect, they rather keep in view the utilization of the advantages of mass production.

c) Adaptation advantages (*C* effect)

In the next step I will try to resolve further the abstraction applied. In the foregoing I have tacitly assumed that the degree of usability of identical products is also identical, regardless of the country they are produced in. With raw materials, foodstuffs, primarily processed products this is a more or less acceptable assumption. (Only more or less, since natural conditions, the quality of the technology applied, etc., produce palpable differences also in this respect.)

However, there may arise considerable differences in quality as regards highly processed products, between the products of the earlier and the more recently developed industrial countries. It is not at all the same whether, say, a radio set is produced and sold by a body of specialists having thirty or three years of experience. It may thus happen that, in order to develop the forces of production more quickly, some country imports investment goods in exchange for agricultural products or those of the extracting industries, even if the annual output of those working in its home industry producing investment goods is generally valued higher by the international market than the output of its workers employed in the extracting industries. In this case, when judging the advantageous or disadvantageous nature of the relationship, the efficiency of the domestic production (expressed on the scale of values of the world market) is confronted not with the efficiency of import-substituting production, but with the improvement in efficiency achieved by using the imported articles.

Of course, the increase of efficiency asserts itself not only direct in the industry which imports the equipment, licence, know-how, etc., but—in a correctly planned economy—in all industries where the imported force of production may be adapted (where the technology is similar, or the imported knowledge may fertilize other technologies as well). Therefore, we distinguish primary, secondary (tertiary, etc.) C effects. The formula of the primary C effect exerted in industry r is very simple: the acceleration of the growth of efficiency relative to the period preceding the import:

$$C_I^{\alpha,r} = \frac{\sum_{0}^{n} E_r^{\alpha}}{\sum_{-n}^{0} E_r^{\alpha}}$$

where

E_r^{α} = efficiency of industry r importing from country α,

$0 \rightarrow n = n$ years after the import,

$(-n) \rightarrow 0 = n$ years prior to the import.

On a national economic scale:

$$C_I^{\alpha} = \sum_{a=1}^{n} C_I^{\alpha}$$

where

$a = 1, \ldots, n$ denotes the industries importing technology from country α.

In practice, of course, it is very difficult to distinguish the improvement in efficiency originating *expressly* in imported technology, particularly those derived from country α, in those very frequent cases when the imports of several countries participate in the reconstruction of the industry (or enterprise). Therefore, it is very difficult to find data for this formula.

The situation is even more difficult in the case of reckoning with the secondary (C_2^α), tertiary (C_3^α), etc., effects. Considering the present state of data collection and analysis, we have to rest satisfied with a theoretical formula serving only the purposes of illustration:

$$C^\alpha = \sum_1^n C^\alpha$$

where 1, 2, ..., n denote the primary, secondary, etc., effects.

The most widespread form of the effect denoted by C is related to the import of investment goods. This system of investment policy is characteristic of those countries whose economy is in a process of transformation from exporting agrarian products and raw materials to exporting manufactured goods. If we judged their international exchange pattern merely on grounds of the A and B effects, we would find some quite incomprehensible phenomena: with their considerable and visibly export-oriented manufacturing industries they import machinery in exchange for raw materials and food. This creates additional growth resources if the increase in efficiency due to putting into operation the imported equipment exceeds (by its primary and secondary, etc. effects) the loss in efficiency owing to the fact that they maintained and even developed their extracting industries at the expense of the import-substituting manufacturing industries. Thus, the exchange with country α involves advantages for the country if

$$C^\alpha \geqq \frac{1}{A^\alpha}$$

With a domestic price system which reflects the differences in inputs between the various fields and phases of the productive process in a relatively reliable manner, the measurement of the C effect may be approached by confronting the additional comparative cost in relation to country α with the additional profit arising through the imported technology, or with the cost savings at points where the effect of the imported technology may be felt most markedly. This is not necessarily the area of primary use. If, e.g., technology has been purchased with the aim of import substitution, it may happen that at the place of direct adaptation and production additional costs will emerge relative to imports for a few years, but they might be richly returned in the fields where the purchased technology is used—produced with domestic forces already. In this case the C effect is a function of the increase in secondary profit (or efficiency) less the increase in primary cost. (Of course, such increase in efficiency may be achieved only if the imported technology may be adapted to the domestic forces of production.)

A similar effect may be attained also with the import of consumer articles —against basic materials which can be less efficiently extracted with domestic labour—if the increase of the domestic production of consumer goods required, particularly in a short time, a change of such extent in the whole investment policy which would lead to a deterioration in efficiency in the other industries, and, at the same time, putting off the satisfaction of demand for consumer goods would endanger the otherwise attainable rate of growth of the economy from the side of the human factor. In this case it will pay not to break the investment trend of the raw-material and food-producing sector, but import the necessary consumer goods against the articles of the extracting industry or against primarily processed goods.

d) Cooperation advantages (*D* effect)

The first two effects (*A* and *B*) are, as a matter of fact, results of the adaptation of the export–import, and through that, of the production pattern of the economy to the world market's value judgements. I have ventured to use the expression "structural picking" for the characterization of this adaptation, in order to underline that there is nothing else in it but adaptation to medium- or long-term world-market demand. In principle, both may be attained even without developing the aggregate of the forces of production, merely by regrouping among or within industries. In practice, of course, specialization alone affords possibilities for technical progress, and this is usually exploited by economies establishing a deeper division of labour.

The effect shown in the third (*C*) is not the result of domestic technical development either, but the confrontation of the future productivity-increasing effect of technological imports with the present productivity of domestic labour producing exportable commodities.

The substance of the next effect, to be denoted by *D*, is that the development of the division of labour, particularly the development of specialization and cooperation in manifacturing, allows a faster development of the domestic forces of production through the concentration and more efficient use of the growth resources available even independently of the efficiency determined by the world economic price relations. In principle, the effect *D* can be measured in the same manner as *C*. The difference is that productive activity r figures here not as an importing branch, but as a specializing or cooperating one. The increase in efficiency E_r^α is the result not of a foreign equipment, licence or know-how entering as *deus ex machina*, but of the increase in the domestic efficiency deriving from the greater concentration of research, investment and production activities, of the reduction of costs and improvement in the price position of the commodities in question. If specialization or cooperation are related to the purchase of foreign equipment or intellectual product, the C and D effects appear inseparably linked. Accordingly:

$$D_I^\alpha = \sum_a^n \frac{\sum_0^n E^\alpha}{\sum_r^n E^\alpha}$$

where $a \to n$ denotes the industries participating in the specialization.

The D effect may occur also with such export-oriented productive activities which are judged unfavourably by the world-market exchange relations (the A effect is negative, that is, it involves disadvantages) and, in, general it must occur unless the country or enterprise participating in the division of labour leaves the development possibilities deriving from the division of labour unutilized (e.g. if it "neglects" the technological development of the product, if it does not meet its delivery obligations, if it produces too small batches, etc.). The national economy may also lose in the division of labour if the price relations of the divided production undertaken are very unfavourable (the gain to be realized on foreign markets or a large part of it is realized not in the product or technical phase undertaken) and this cannot be compensated even with the saving in costs to be attained through the division of labour. Thus, it is not certain that the increase in efficiency, made possible by the division of labour, is attained, nor that it can be realized even if attained.

At the same time, the D effect appears not only in the fields where specialization has *de facto* taken place, but secondarily also in those fields where development is spreading from the fields directly affected. Therefore, the primary, secondary, tertiary, etc. effects should be distinguished and taken into account when establishing the division of labour. The primary effect asserts itself in the growing efficiency of the industry (plant, production process) directly participating in the specialization, and may manifest itself in cost reduction, in the rising world market and domestic sales prices of the product, and in widening sales possibilities:

$$D^\alpha = \sum_{i=1}^n D_i^\alpha.$$

The measure of this increase in efficiency may be the efficiency in comparison to similar foreign production, that is, competitivity.

The secondary, tertiary, etc. effects may assume several forms. The production method (organization, technology) developed with the aid of specialization may have a fertilizing effect also in fields where the experience can be adapted. Productive equipment produced in cooperation may accelerate the modernization of other industries. Cooperation may create new possibilities for the economy to earn foreign currency and thus the maintenance or increase of low-efficiency exports may become superfluous. It is not at all immaterial for the economy what speed and radius the primary effect induces in the secondary and tertiary, etc. ones. Nor is it immaterial in what interrelated points of the development process of the whole economy the primary effect induces outstanding development and how these affect each other.

It is expedient for economic policy to deepen the division of labour first of all at those points where the most intensive secondary, etc. effects may be expected and where the separately induced development effects strengthen and accelerate each other.

e) Cumulative effects

Up to now I have discussed the four most important effects in "chemically pure" form. In reality, these are only components of the actual reaction of the economy to external market impulses. They may strengthen or weaken each other, add up, and appear in the last resort in the medium- and long-term trends of the balance of payments and in the growth rate of the economy. It is, for the time being, a hopeless undertaking to distinguish them in the general movement of processes with the tools of traditional statistics.

Until economic cybernetics develops reliable methods of computation, we have to be content with decisions, in our internal and external structural policies, and in the regulation system serving their implementation, that are correct merely in their tendencies.

In combining the different effects, the combination of *A* and *B* with *C* within the same act of division of labour should be excluded from the outset, owing to the basic nature of the *C* effect. At the same time, their combination is highly realistic in a simultaneous examination of the different acts of the division of labour.

The division of labour may come about so that the given economy specializes in the export of products that "pay well" on the world market, against the import of products that "pay worse". If the products "paying better" happen to be also more dynamic, the imports of those "paying worse" provide foundations for the exports. In this case the *A* and *B* effects support each other. By acquiring the exports of products which are highly valued and increasingly demanded by the world market (and by simultaneously getting rid of the production of low-valued products), the economy can secure, e.g. by raw-material deliveries, supply of parts, etc., also the conditions of growth, and can increase its income and sources of growth through the volume of commodities sold. Insofar as the economy obtains, through the division of labour, the possibility for concentrating its material and intellectual resources, this may start vivid technical progress in the successfully "acquired" fields. The *A* and/or *B* effects may be complemented by *D*. It is clear that economic policy should prefer those alternatives of the division of labour in which the greatest number of positive effects, and which are also otherwise the most marked, add up.

The decision is more complicated if the emergence of effects of different directions is expectable, e.g., when cooperation extends to dynamic productive activities ($B>1$), but the division of labour does not promise possibilities of considerable technological development, while it demands important national economic investments ($D<1$). In such cases the economy has to assess the short- and long-term loss in efficiency due to the lack of technical progress and compare it with the additional growth resources deriving from the expansion of realization possibilities. The economy faces a similar dilemma when it has to choose between specializing in products releasing a momentary *A* effect (involving a static comparative advantage) and arranging for the imports of dynamic products ($B<1$). In this case the high valuation of domestic social labour per unit of product (*A*) is confronted with the negative dynamic effect to be weighted in choosing from alternatives.

International economic relations are developing in several industries of the national economy and with several partners simultaneously. In the final analysis the individual effects are summarized as

$$\varepsilon^{\alpha} = A^{\alpha}+B^{\alpha}+C^{\alpha}+D^{\alpha}$$

where ε^{α} is the resultant of the four basic effects in relation with country α.

The fitting of the *whole* of the national economy into the *whole* of the international or regional division of labour may also be conceived of as the sum of advantages and disadvantages of relations with its partners and also as the sum of its basic advantages and disadvantages:

$$\varepsilon = \sum_{\alpha}^{v} \varepsilon = \left(\sum_{\alpha}^{v} A+\sum_{\alpha}^{v} B+\sum_{\alpha}^{v} C+\sum_{\alpha}^{v} D\right)$$

where $\alpha^{\alpha} \rightarrow v$ denote the partners of the country in cooperation.

The former concept comes to the fore in economic policy in the case of *bilateral* relations, while the latter is characteristic in the case of fitting into a multilaterally organized market.

In themselves, the various effects (*A*, *B*, *C*, *D*) may be conceived also as the resultant of the division of labour with different countries. For example, if a country maintains relations with 100 countries, a part of these has positive, another part negative *A* effects; thus, the *A* effect of total trade may have a positive or negative effect (that is, the domestic difference in efficiency between the structures of exports and imports will be positive or negative) depending on whether the relations saving social labour are preponderant or those where the exchange of domestic labour for foreign labour impairs the efficiency of domestic labour. In the case of a uniform world-market price system this depends exclusively on the pattern of bilateral exports and imports. If the country trades with different regions (or in bilateral relations) with different price structures, the resultant of the *A* effects is modified also by the differences in the price systems.

The fitting of the given national economy into world economy can be surveyed in its complexity if we confront the effects of varying kind, size and sign. If the conditions for quantified measurement exist, quantification of these effects may be highly instructive. (For example, what size of negative *A* effect in relation with one country stands against a positive *C* effect in relation with another country and against the positive *B* effect induced by the *D* effect in relation with a third country, etc.). In analysing the external economic relations of some country, the causal relationship among various effects may be traced at least in their tendencies. We know of many national economies which concentrate their cooperation policies with certain regions expressly on attaining the *C* effect, because this is the condition of their being able to shape their export and import patterns in the trade with another region in the interest of maximizing *A* and *B* effects. In other cases, they attempt to combine the *C* and *D* effects in one region in order to attain steady *A*, *B* and *D* effects in another region.

Both types are characteristic of the foreign economic policy of countries which are in close cooperation relationship with more advanced regions than themselves and thus, *nolens-volens* become propagators of the forces of production of more advanced regions in less advanced ones. In the first of the two above-mentioned cases, the country in question is still moderately or even less developed. In the second case, however, it is capable of fitting its own manufacturing industry into this "transmission" activity, and of absorbing more advanced technology not only through the import of equipment but also through cooperation. Thus it can transmit the advantages to the less developed partners not only through the export of manufactured products but also through cooperation.

In any case, the foreign economic policy of a national economy crystallizes from the alternative combinations of the four effects by industries and by partner countries.

f) Mutual advantages

The economic policy of a country participating in the international division of labour cannot reckon only with its own advantages. Even countries with large economies are compelled—in their own interest—to adapt themselves to their environment, even if otherwise their behaviour is dominant in world economy or for particular regions. The behaviour of small countries is characterized rather by adaptation, partly to the big economies, partly to each other. Therefore, it is a rather short-sighted policy to expect that the confrontation of concepts and measures based on one-sided national interests will develop mutual advantages by itself. Prognostication and mutual consideration of the advantages to be derived from cooperation is, therefore, an unalienable part of every sound foreign economic policy, which the countries cannot shift completely onto the international economic organizations.

Mutual advantages are most evident in the case denoted by *D*. Namely, in these cases the division of labour usually comes about in technologically related areas which are judged equally "efficient" or "less efficient" in every country by the world-market valuation. It may happen, of course, that some product which is valued low in general by world-market terms of trade, is produced in some country under exceptionally fortunate conditions. Or, conversely, the production of goods which are in a generally advantageous position may have in some country indicators which are weaker than the national average. The division of labour usually improves the conditions of production, and thus the participating countries fare well in the final analysis, whether their actual efficiency relations are similar to or dissimilar from the majority.

The situation is similar—at least in the long run—in case *C*. With some equipment or article the country intending to develop may obtain what is necessary for increasing the efficiency of its economy, while the country supplying the equipment achieves with its exportation the *A* or *B* effect, or both. The balance of mutual advantages is upset only if the new industry, which emerges following the importation of the means of production and the domestic development efforts, reduces the export of raw and intermediary goods as an internal consumer, or if the efficiency of manufacturing is far ahead of that of extraction, and the market of the country supplying the equipment does not absorb the product manufactured with the equipment but continues to demand from its partner an export structure (the traditional one) where unprocessed goods are predominant. The disequilibrium develops particularly fast if the manufacturing industry of the country importing the equipment with a negative *A* effect is coming close to the exporting country in respect of the technical performance of the products. Namely, by importing equipments producing means of production, the difference between the efficiency of the domestic equipment and that of the imported equipment sooner or later diminishes. With a diminishing positive *C* effect, the negative *A* and *B* effects of the division of labour will come to the fore. Mutuality of the advantages is particularly accidental with the *A* and *B* effects.

The engagement of domestic factors of production necessary for producing a unit of commodity, computed at world-market prices, is dispersed around the national average in every economy depending on industries and productive activities. Measurements have shown that the higher and more evenly developed an economy, the smaller this dispersion, and the lower and less evenly developed it is, the greater the dispersion; because, among other things, the latter economies scrapped their less efficient processes already in earlier stages of their development. This is also influenced by the natural circumstances as well (extraction, climatic conditions, etc.), particularly as regards the basic materials. It is conceivable that, even if measured in a uniform world-market price system, two countries may be found which obtain mutual advantages if one of them supplies mainly raw materials, food and intermediary products to the other against more highly processed articles. But this is an exception. In general, precisely owing to the nature of the world-market terms of trade, this relationship entails losses through the *A* effect for the country which exports unprocessed goods in exchange for machinery, chemical articles and finished goods. This tendency is at times interrupted by a "price revolution", and may even be reversed for some time. But the century-old tendencies show that *in the long run* it is the technically more advanced countries that reap the main advantages in world-market exchange and not those which are in a natural monopoly situation.

The situation is similar with the *B* effect. If in an economy exports become more dynamic than imports, or if it turns into a structural creditor (in which case a part of the additional dynamism is drawn off by its debtors), it is compelled to restrict the development of its most dynamic industries—this, too, puts a brake on its dynamism—or has to shift from the unstable *B* effect to methods releasing the *D* effect.

If we do not consider now the political forces, which, no doubt, very greatly contribute to the formation of regions, and focus our attention on the economic forces which form a region, it may be stated that *regions emerge where the particular national economies derive greater advantages from a division of labour among themselves than by spreading their international economic relations evenly over the whole of the world economy.* This may happen if the advantages deriving from the division of labour within a given sphere exceed those from outside this sphere by orders of magnitude, or if relying on the advantages and safety of division of labour within the region, the participating countries improve their positions towards the "outer world", taken in a wider sense. As regards the three developed regions, both viewpoints seem to be in the foreground in the case of the East- and the West-European integrations, while the force holding together the North-American region is above all the first-mentioned "internal" factor. An above-average extent of mutual advantages, whether it comes about in a natural or an artificial way (through protectionism), is in any case one of the main explanations for a growing intensity of the division of labour.

With this, of course, we have not yet done more than repeat the ancient laws of nature: the sunflower turns toward the sun, the root strives after the soil rich in nutrients, and all the symbiosis of living beings is based on maximum mutual advantages. The fact that human societies also strive after the maximum advantages to be derived from the division of labour, and that the symbiotic relationship among nations is based on such principles, is so self-evident that it is almost a commonplace. We have to probe deeper and clarify which, from among the nations with different endowments, particularly attract each other.

CHAPTER FOUR

Character of the national economies and the field of gravitation

The productive, trading and technical potentials of the national economies which are in mutual relationship (or want to enter into such), and, as a consequence, their internal dynamism, as well as their financial performance and their power to affect the world economic environment, differ. This asymmetry is a product of historical development and will act as long as the whole of the world economy does not integrate on a very high and even level of development. Since science does not yet discuss global integration, a problem of the far future, the differentiation of the forces of national economies must be reckoned with as a real fact. In this respect, realistically reasoning economists have to agree with the views of François Perroux.[6]

The extent to which two or more national economies attract or repulse each other in their economic relations is influenced by

a) the *geographical distance* between the economies, to be measured *in terms of transport costs*;

b) the relative *size of the economies, expressed in their national incomes* measured at foreign-trade prices;

c) the degree of macro-economic *complementarity* of the economies (to be quantified by comparing the sectoral patterns of utilization in the particular countries with that of the summarized production of the group of countries: the nearer the two the greater the mutual attraction);

d) the degree of the *micro-economic complementarity* of the economies, which is determined by the ratio of the output of the sectors producing "regularly" intermediary products within the economy to the social final product; and finally,

e) the *"technical throughput"* ability of the economies, to be measured by the export share of the industries which are carriers of technical progress and the per capita annual final product (per person employed) in these industries.

[6] François Perroux: *Indépendance de l'économie nationale et interdépendance des nations.* Aubier Montaigne, Paris 1969.

Accordingly, the regional attractive power is directly proportionate to the volume of national income to the degree of micro- and macro-economic complementarity, as well as to the size of technical throughput ability, and inversely proportionate to the transport costs.

If national incomes are small (either because the economic units are small, or because the national economies in question are underdeveloped), the possibility for mutual transfer of technology is also small, and transport cost is great, the mutual attraction will also be low. If complementarity is lacking on either macro- or micro-level, this does not simply reduce attraction, but appears as a repellant.

Examining the dynamics: the big and quickly-developing national economies with expanding import markets and with growing capacities to export materials and technology attract those living close to them. Weakening macro-economic complementarity (equal industrial structures) may make the division of labour indifferent, unless micro-economic complementarity increases in parallel (phase-level specialization in products, parts, partial units). Should the reduction of macro- and micro-level complementarity take place parallel, at some point the mutual attraction will turn into a repulsive force, since the advantages deriving from cooperation (ε) cease and may even end up in disadvantages. The danger of a repulsive force is increased by the mutual weakness of the throughput of technology.

a) Large economy and the field of gravitation

If, within a set of countries possessing the basic possibilities for developing into a region, one or several national economies have productive and market capacities which are bigger by orders of magnitude than those of others (they have a population manyfold of the others, and a development level at least as high as that of the others), their dynamism is not lagging behind the environment, and they also possess technical transfer capacity in at least a few important areas and contribute much to the macro- and micro-economic complementarity of the set of countries, *they will necessarily become points of crystallization of regional development, the centres of the region to be established.*

The attraction of the national economy will be enhanced if it is capable of contributing to the growth of the smaller and/or less developed partner economies by ceding material forces to them (credits, aids, investments, favourable terms of trade).

Unlike the gravitation acting in the universe, the world economic attraction is not automatic. The above-listed properties of a big economy *attract* the potential partners in its environment, but only if the big economy "allows" it itself, that is, if it pursues an economic policy which "offers" the possibilities of a division of labour—and thus its advantages—to the other countries. *In general, the field of gravitation of a big economy is controlled.* It allows its force of attraction to prevail first of all towards those partner economies which promise to be the most suited for establishing a division of labour that will support their own internal or external goals of economic strategy and whose joining the international division of labour will entail—*ceteris paribus*—the least amount of advanced resources in terms of finances. There are, however, smaller economies which are incapable of adapting themselves to the needs of the bigger economy, e.g. they are too underdeveloped to adopt its technology, and their structure as well as their financial resources are too scattered to attain adequate concentration in specialization and cooperation. Here belong those economies whose synchronization with the big economy would demand a regrouping of capital too big, too slowly returning, or perhaps too risky, which thus lose their interest for the big economy. Gravitation diminishes or ceases.

At present there are two big economies which exert considerable attraction towards their environment: the USA and the Soviet Union. The USA is the centre of the North-American region, the USSR, that of the East-European one. The field of gravitation of both affects the whole of world economy, among other things also the West-European region. It is impossible to understand the nature of the West-European region without taking into account the gravitational field of the two huge economies.

b) Medium-sized and small economies and the field of gravitation

The medium-sized and small economies look first of all for complementarity in the international division of labour. The greater the differentiation in the world of commodities consumed by production, infrastructure and the population, the greater the acceleration of the obsolescence of particular products (be they means of production or consumer goods), and the greater research and investment efforts are needed for society to recognize the labour participating in a given production process to be of full value, the greater will be the dependence of smaller economies on the international division of labour, and the greater will be the number of countries which are swept by the current from the group of "big" ones to that of the medium-sized and small ones. The more a country is reckoned to be medium-sized or small, relative to the given requirements of the forces of production, the greater the risk factor in its decisions on specialization. Under such conditions, the smaller economies become inclined to prefer the safety factor in their own foreign economic policies, that is, to build their relations in the division of labour with a huge economy rather than with countries of their size.

True, no division of labour in the classical sense can be established with a big economy, that is, it cannot be made dependent on specialization to the same *extent* to which the structure of a small economy becomes deformed and dependent. For its major partner, the smaller economy will always remain a complementary source for meeting its needs. If this production for complementary needs can become stable, the asymmetry of mutual dependence is of no importance for the small economy. If, however, the big economy is highly prone to business fluctuations, the complementary needs become *marginal* needs, which will go unsatisfied in periods of slack business. In this case the force of attraction of the big economy considerably diminishes.

A big economy where technical progress is on the upswing, is similarly highly attractive for the smaller economies. Any "undersized" national economy would like to join the productive forces of a big economy rather than those of countries of its own size, since this is the simplest way to counterbalance its disadvantages deriving from the insufficiency of its resources. If, however, the development lag between the forces of production of the two is so big that the smaller partner *can no more (or not yet) keep pace*, or the bigger partner monopolizes all those advantages in efficiency which it may call its own, owing to its size and development level, the gravitational attraction for the smaller economy may quickly diminish.

In other words, in its relationship with a big economy, the small economy strives first of all to compensate the disadvantages of being "undersized" from the viewpoints of business booms and technology. If it succeeds in finding this compensation—as is the case, e.g. in the relations between the smaller CMEA countries and the USSR—the power of attraction which concentrates the forces of international cooperation around a big economy may be particularly strong—relying mainly on bilateral division of labour. In such cases gravitation develops such regions whose core and, simultaneously, main force of cohesion is a huge economy. If, however, the positional disadvantage of the smaller economies does not diminish, or even increases in such an intertwining, a repellant force will appear on part of their economies. If the necessary conditions of a division of labour otherwise exist *among* the smaller economies in question, or they can be brought about, they will turn towards each other. In this case, too, a strong field of gravitation will develop and a region will come about. But the *cohesive force* of the region will be not the gravitational attraction of a big economy, but precisely the elementary need of the minor economies that the "energy of escape" from the undesired field of gravitation be created only by summing up the individual economic potentials. This is necessary, among other things, also for establishing such a regional protectionistic system which allows an escape from the pressure of the big economy. The region thus coming about has to create in some time its own "core" to become stabilized—not around the big economy, but outside it and as a defence against its effects. In the case of Western Europe, the "core" has come about gradually. First the Common Market of the Six became established—which the initiative of the EFTA tried to double, though with modest results—and then the Six expanded into the Nine, linking to themselves the outsiders with special preferential arrangements.

CHAPTER ONE

Eastern Europe before the socialist revolutions—the peripheral belt of the advanced West

Every economic process carries in itself *general* and *particular* features, and integration processes are no exceptions to the rule. Whichever feature we lose sight of, we get into a blind alley, whether it is a question of economic clearsight or economic policy action.

In the case of the socialist integration we cannot neglect the fact that the process of *integration* is determined historically by its being *socialist* and *East European*. I believe the particular features are as follows:

a) Prior to the period of building socialism most of the countries integrating in the CMEA belonged to the East-European periphery of the advanced capitalist world.

b) A very fast liquidation of this peripheral position demanded special economic policies in the particular countries concerned and, as a consequence, developed a special kind of cooperation among these countries.

c) Cooperation has been realized among *socialist* societies and this pushed into the fore the active fight against polarization from the very outset.

Economic history has shown that the development of modern industrial forces of production started not simultaneously, but in three consecutive waves. The first wave of industrialization took place in some Western countries of Europe —mainly in England—in the second half of the 18th century. A second group of countries started the upswing by the end of the first half of the 19th century, and came into full swing in the last third of the century (USA, Germany, Italy, Japan). The third wave emerged towards the end of the 19th century and at the beginning of the 20th in Eastern and Southern Europe, and somewhat later in South Africa, as well as in some countries of Latin America. This historical "starting position" influences the relative situation of the economic spheres in the world to a considerable extent to this very day, though, as it will be explained later, two important "outbreaks" occurred—that of the United States and of the European socialist countries.

The historical situation in which the second wave took place was highly favourable for accelerating the development process of the forces of production. In his writings about imperialism Lenin clearly explained that this was a fortunate outcome of the intertwining of two processes. The first was the fast upswing of the internal energies of the countries in question (the German, Japanese and Italian national integrations: the end of the American Civil War accelerated accumulation), while the second, the fast-emerging need of the countries of the "first wave" for capital exports, directed partly precisely towards the countries in question. The two processes combined made a fast accumulation possible concentrating first of all on the dynamic industries and the industrial structure coming about reflected the most modern standards of the age. (The differences in concentration and technology between the two groups of countries had not yet brought about a chasm, so that fast industrialization—which was automatically a modern type for latecomers—also entailed certain advantages.) The meeting of these circumstances finally ended in a levelling tendency, and became the hotbed of world-wide economic, political and military conflicts. At this point the levelling turned into its own opposite, i.e. polarization. The most favourable conditions of transition from extensive development to the intensive one of the technical revolution were present in the United States (the size of the area, a wide framework for national integration, the labour shortage forcing large-scale mechanization, etc.). As this transition evolved, the camp of those industrializing in the first and the second wave and becoming levelled in the first decades of the century, got split into two types again in the middle of the century: the North-American one and the others lagging behind.

The above may have illuminated why the world economic position of the countries industrializing in the "third wave" has become very difficult:

— their appearance in the arena of industrialization falls to a period when the gap regarding concentration and technology between them and the countries earlier industrialized was deeper by orders of magnitude than in the case of those "arriving on time";

— their accumulated internal capital and the educational standards of the population did not reach even the degree attained by the second group at the time when they started their upswing;

— as a consequence, the foreign capital that could be profitably invested was not sufficient to act with its volume towards levelling, nor could the pattern of investments by industries be so dynamic as to induce an internal development at a rate exceeding that of the capital-exporting countries;

— thus the capital imported flowed mostly into industries that had lost their dynamism and become amalgamated with the domestic capital so that their products became competitive on the world market. Thus, the industry of the "latecomer" countries was dominated by non-dynamic products, creating in this way an imbalance between exports and the development possibilities of imports;

— the earlier industrialized nations exported capital also to the dynamic industries of the "latecomer" countries. These became mostly "auxiliary workshops" of the dynamic industries in the capital-exporting countries: they arranged for the manufacture of products or parts which were simpler and required less investment and skill; the research and development basis usually remained in the capital's country of origin;

— the backward socio-political relations frequently hindered industrialization.

Thus, the same phenomenon—the meeting of accelerated internal accumulation and capital imports—in an unfavourable world economic environment (that is, under qualitatively different circumstances of concentration and technological gap) instead of levelling, produces the conservation of differences in development level and the emergence of world economic dependence. Both the development gap deriving from the half-developed state, which is almost impossible to make up for, and the particular dependence on the developed regions belong to the characteristics of the development type discussed.

The "third wave" gets industrialized under the pressing competition of the earlier industrialized countries and the circumstances of capital dependence, and this causes distortions in the development of the economy. Industry cannot become the leading sector, the industries carrying the technical progress (engineering, chemical industry) remain embryonic, mechanization of production proceeds with halts and unevenly, the backwardness of agriculture, aggravated by feudal remnants, hardly changes, living conditions are miserable. The periphery is a "take-off" region which cannot bloom under the world economic pressure.

This situation, full of tensions, resulted in the fact that, although the countries of the "third wave" had awakened from the dormant slumber of economic backwardness, they had no possibility to become really developed economies. Although modern industries started to develop, they could not evolve. Though organically linked to world economy, they were incapable of actively shaping its development. The isolation of the countries from each other, due to the artificially instigated nationalism in Eastern Europe between the two world wars, was a special hindrance to development which was added to the disadvantages of the unfavourable "starting position", and increased the dependence of the countries of the region on the West-European development centre. This is why it was justified to call this group of countries, too, the periphery of the advanced world in the period prior to the socialist revolutions.

It is also necessary to delimit this sector of the world economy called "periphery" from the economically underdeveloped countries. The most palpable symptom is again the global social productivity, that is, the indicator of per capita national income, which showed a difference of 200–300 dollars in 1968 between the periphery and the backward countries in the stricter sense. This difference is important again because it covers qualitative differences in the degree of industrialization, in the mechanization of productive work, etc. In the countries of the periphery, industrialization, i.e. the radical transformation of the structure of production—the hitherto biggest technical transformation in the history of mankind—has started. Industry has become, if not the overwhelming portion of the economy, but a part with important effects. The sectoral structure within industry is not dynamic though, but the existing industry is sufficient for being able to develop a more dynamic structure of industry in an adequate socio-political medium. All these circumstances either do not exist in the backward countries, or are at a much lower degree of maturity and their development is hardly possible through internal inducements, and even external interference can exert its effect but very slowly.

The majority of the now quickly developing socialist countries of Eastern Europe constituted the economic and political periphery of Western Europe. The most conspicuous signs of this were their backward economic development, the underdevelopment of their industries producing means of production, the agrarian relationships burdened by feudal remnants, the low standards of living, and the unstable political constructions. But the relative backwardness of society was not only a phenomenon but also a cause of this peripheral situation. Economic and political development of Eastern Europe was extremely hindered in modern times by the circumstance that it fell outside the scope of both the earlier Mediterranean commercial centres and later of the Atlantic ones which determined development from the 16th century on, and, in addition, because of the constant state of war over centuries it could not adopt either the developed forces of production or the socio-economic achievements emanating from these centres. Following the decline of the powers of the Osman Empire, multinational empires organized on feudal basis developed in the Eastern Europe of the 18th century, whose instability, becoming more and more conspicuous in the 19th century, again provided unfavourable grounds for the elimination of the then already considerable technical and social backwardness, particularly for the non-leading nations of these empires. In the first World War these empires broke to pieces. This is how the bases of the state organization in present-day Eastern Europe came about, in the form of relatively small-size countries, organized more or less on a national basis and politically sharply opposed to each other. The result corresponds to the notion used in the journalism of the beginning of the century i.e., "balkanization". Eastern Europe became a conglomerate of mostly backward countries with distorted economic structures, and with primitive and highly reactionary political superstructures, which were poor in capital, had a narrow internal market and were very weak in competition—in spite of their low wage level—and, as a consequence, the conditions of their autonomous industrial development might be called anything but favourable.

I do not wish to enter into an analysis of the nature and depth of economic history and will, therefore, sum up only the outlines of industrial development which are on the whole well known.

Above all, development started *hopelessly late*. "Late", because industry left the framework of the guilds about a hundred years later than in the West-European countries, and "hopelessly", because by that time the world market had become established, dominated by the advanced West-European countries. Thus, *industry could not be built up independently of world-market competition*, and the East-European industry was weak to compete. In the industries, namely, which would have been of key importance for development in the given world economic situation, competitiveness demanded essentially more accumulated capital and technical experience, an essentially wider internal market and a more complete division of labour than was available to these countries. Thus, a particular situation developed in Eastern Europe: the development of forces of production, of capital accumulation and of market expansion starting with a historical delay could bear only poor fruit, since these countries had become organic parts of the world economy, more concretely of the then established European division of labour, too soon to be able to develop into strong partners with equal opportunities.

Further, this development was *distorted* from every respect. Industry became an important but not determinant sector of the national economy. Industrial employment amounted to 1/5–1/4 of the population of working age, while agriculture engaged the majority in absolute terms. Within industry, the extracting branches had a great importance, differing by countries, and in manufacturing the industries transforming agricultural products, above all the food industry, were dominating. Infrastructure was also built out according to the requirements of the latifundia.[7]

Particular mention should be made of the features of the engineering and chemical industries. Some of the East-European socialist countries of today —e.g. Hungary—had a considerable engineering or chemical industry. Their importance cannot be measured primarily with their role in the structure of the economy. But they exported a part of their products, even to the West-European countries, among others. Some of them, as, e.g., the Hungarian Tungsram Co., were recorded among the known European firms. The most important characteristic feature of these industries was the lack of complementarity and the mixed, uneven technological level. In the chemical industry the production of classical basic materials was dominating (sulphuric acid, caustic soda), agrochemistry was rudimentary (fertilizers, plant protectives), and the "pulling" industries were almost missing (paints and dyes, chemicals, detergents). Perhaps the only, though not characteristic, exception was the Hungarian pharmaceutical industry. Char-

[7] In Hungary for instance, a considerable part of the main railway lines avoided the more important industrial areas, sometimes even the centres of administration. Railway building conformed to the transport needs of the latifundia and the lines observed in many cases even the pattern of land use of the latifundia.

acteristic branches of engineering using domestic capital were the production of railway equipment, food-industry equipment and simpler agricultural machinery. These enterprises supplied the underdeveloped domestic production structure with investment goods, their technology was primitive and they were short of capital as well.

Thirdly: in every country one could find a few factories much more developed than the general level of the country, which produced—mostly with foreign capital and by relying on foreign research and development bases—products which conformed to the then prevailing requirements of the world level. The bases on which these enterprises relied for materials and parts, their markets, i.e. their intra- and interindustrial relations mostly reached beyond the frontiers of the country. Today we would say that they were East-European extensions of the great "multinational" corporations, at that time they were simply called affiliates of branches of foreign companies. They were not organic parts of the national economic structures, or were only losely related to them. They did not contribute to technical transfer in the other sectors of the national economies, or to a limited extent only, domestic centres of decision disposed of their accumulated capital only to a restricted extent, and the effect of their operations on the balance of payments of the country could be influenced also only to a limited extent.

These East-European economies could be called neither colonies nor backward countries. Their accumulated forces of production, the cultural level of the whole society, as well as their socio-political systems were qualitatively more up-to-date than those of the backward countries in the stricter sense of the word. Their dependence on the developed European core was of different nature than in the case of either the actual colonies or the half-colonies (e.g. in Latin America). At the same time, at least as marked were the qualitative features which separated them from the developed countries, even from the less developed ones (e.g. Austria). With the aid of statistical indicators it is, of course, difficult to draw the line. (In Figure 4, relying on computations by Éva Ehrlich, I try to show the qualitative coherence of these countries.) But the ensemble of economic, social and political features on the whole shows that we have here not the "most developed backward countries", nor the "least developed advanced countries", but a separate group. Some people call this group "moderately developed countries"; I believe it is more correct to apply the denomination "periphery of the developed world", since this indicates not only the level of economic development but also the relationship to the whole of the world economy.

This relationship was characterized by a more or less one-sided linkage and dependence on economic cooperation with the developed countries. Exports of the countries of the periphery consisted mostly of products highly sensitive to business fluctuations in the capitalist world, while their imports comprised much

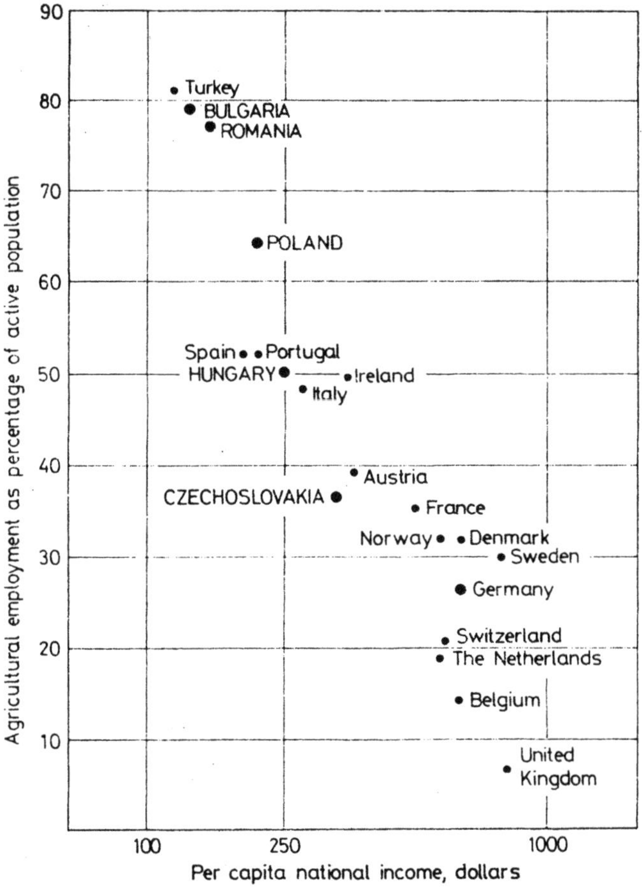

Fig. 4. Two characteristics of the peripheric situation of the East-European group of countries: per capita national income and the ratio of agricultural employment in 1937

Source: Computations by Éva Ehrlich

more dynamic products. Therefore, they became chronically indebted and the fluctuations of economic life strongly affected their export capacities. All of them were importers of capital, so much so that a considerable part or even the bulk of shares of their relatively modern industries were in the hands of the business circles of the developed countries. As a consequence, *as regards their role in world economy, the countries of the East-European periphery were rather passive than active.* Their initiatives were restricted mostly to manoeuvring between the interests of particular advanced powers. This was a non-negligible factor from the point of view of the independence of their economy and policy. We might say that the course of their efforts to fight against falling into a colonial or half-colonial state was made realistic precisely by their manoeuvring opportunities, as long as a balance of powers existed between the developed countries. With the balance of powers upset, they fell into unequivocal dependence from the power in whose field of force they were: into that of Hitler's Germany in the second half of the thirties. For them, the most important item of this situation was to maintain passive relations to world economy and one-sided dependence on the advanced West-European countries. The drawback of these two factors was that they were not versed in world economic initiatives, their foreign economic policies were oriented towards the short run, and they failed to build out closer relations among each other.

The reasoning has been restricted up to now to the general characteristics of the East-European region as a whole. It is natural that they do not fully apply to any actual country, since each of them had its own characteristics. There is no place to discuss these in detail. Nevertheless, a short digression is needed in respect of the most particular exceptions: the Soviet Union and the two present-day CMEA countries which cannot, or only with big reservations, be considered to belong to the periphery of the developed world, i.e. the GDR and Czechoslovakia.

As regards its socio-economic nature, the Russian Empire also belonged to the periphery of the developed world,[8] but it occupied a particular place within it. Its particular position is explained not only by its size, but above all by the growth disturbances of its socio-economic system, which comprised huge internal development contrasts, and an extreme seclusion from the outer world, which resulted in scarce international relations. Relations were particularly scarce with the countries which now constitute the CMEA. Partial exceptions were Germany and Poland—part of the latter belonged to the Russian empire—and Bulgaria, which had traditional, but mostly political, relations with the Russian state. Even these scarce ties were almost completely broken after the Great October Revolution.

In the interwar period a fast-rate economic and political upswing started in the Soviet Union. Until the East-European countries took the road of socialism, however, this had no effect on the economic relations between the USSR and

[8] "If we compare the precapitalist epoch in Russia with the capitalist epoch (and this is precisely the comparison that should be made if a correct solution to the problem is to be found) then we will have to admit that the development of social economy under capitalism is extremely rapid. If, however, we compare the present rate of development with the rate that would have been possible at the modern level of technique and culture generally, then we would have to admit the present rate of development of capitalism in Russia is really slow." (V. I. Lenin: *Selected Works.* Vol. 1, Lawrence and Wishart Ltd., London 1944, p. 385.)

Eastern Europe, in spite of the fact that the structural possibilities for the later evolving close economic cooperation already existed at that time. Already then the Soviet Union was a huge, stable absorptive market for industrial articles, mainly machinery and equipment, thus it could have provided a safe basis for the industrialization policy of any East-European country. With economic relations built out with the Soviet Union, these countries could have solved one of their most pressing economic and social problem, chronic underemployment, too, they could have eased their raw-material concerns, and might have attained considerable independence from the advanced capitalist powers. But all this can be mentioned only under the title of "what might have happened". The political structure of Eastern Europe was organized by the Western powers in the treaties concluded around Paris and also later in such manner that any approach to the Soviet Union was precluded. *The potential advantages of cooperation with the Soviet Union could not materialize.*

This also involved that until the Liberation no traditional relations, initial division of labour, commercial and industrial cooperation could develop on part of either the Soviet Union or the East-European countries. The Soviet Union and the countries of Eastern Europe developed in a complementary way in many respects, without being able to reap advantages therefrom in the division of labour or in trade.

Czechoslovakia was no part of the periphery, on the contrary, it was considered as belonging to the developed world. True, this cannot be told about the Slovak areas of the country. Slovakia, between the two world wars, was a kind of "mezzogiorno" of the Czechoslovak economy. But the Bohemian basin itself was considered as one of the most industrialized areas of Europe, even in the times of the monarchy, although the structure and productivity of its industry were lagging behind those of the earliest industrialized countries. Nevertheless, in the interwar period the Czech industry could not establish considerable division of labour with the East-European countries. Beyond the political causes mentioned, the most palpable reason was that the Czechoslovak national economy, as one of the countries deriving from the monarchy, was too young to be able to export capital constantly. Almost all energies necessary to hold their own in the European competition were absorbed by the internal integration of the new state, as well as by the structural changes accompanying autonomy. Thus, between the two world wars, Czechoslovakia could neither become a centre which could have played the role of initiator in the development of the East-European conglomerate into an economic region with established division of labour. On the contrary, it was looking for support to Western capital in order to improve its competitivity and thus—though under different conditions from the peripheral countries—it became itself oriented towards the West-European economies.

The German Democratic Republic—as part of Germany of those times—is the only CMEA country today which may be said to have had labour-division relations with the East-European countries.[9] But this is of limited importance from the viewpoint of the prehistory of the present-day socialist integration, since in the situation after the war, because of war damages and the division of the country, and because of having lost the former German interests, the German economic power lines became so entangled themselves that the young socialist German state had to start with a *tabula rasa* as regards her international economic relations. True, beginning with 1950 and relying on the traditional East-European relationships, the young GDR established economic cooperation with the CMEA countries much faster than any other country, with the exception of the USSR.

Thus, the traditions of a closer international division of labour, and even of regular and considerable trade started in Eastern Europe essentially with the socialist transformation following the Liberation. This created partly an advantageous situation, as the division of labour could be established on new bases from the outset. It followed that they did not take over traditional structures which did not correspond to the needs of socialist development, nor such forms or institutions of economic contact which would have been in conflict with the requirements of the new type of relationships. Nevertheless, the same traditions also meant a hindrance in many respects.

It was disadvantageous above all, that the countries *did not sufficiently know* each other's economies and, therefore, could not reckon in their own industrialization with the size and composition of the resources of the others, with the possibility of joint efforts. Information of satisfactory depth and detail, as well as a clear idea of the internal operational laws of the partners' economies is of extreme importance for international economic cooperation. This can be established even in a relatively homogeneous economic and political medium only through practical relations and economic research over long decades. All this had to be started in Eastern Europe on the road to socialism at the end of the forties, and that in a medium which was extremely heterogeneous in every respect. In addition to the efforts at socialist transformation, general isolation from the advanced capitalist world, and historical backwardness in respect of the development of the forces of production, there could hardly be found any common feature among these national economies which could have brought a deeper understanding of each other's problems, realistic on the basis of the analogy of *internal* economic relations.

[9] Whether she really had, could be decided only if we knew whether the *enterprises* operating in the territory of today's GDR had relations amounting to division of labour or capital interests in the East-European countries.

Beyond the scarce foreign-trade relations, *the lack of mutual capital relations* was an extreme disadvantage. In manufacturing, the social division of labour makes its way above all through breaking up the technological processes among several enterprises. All that requires the very fine and detailed coordination of production processes in space and time, which we cannot achieve even with our present knowledge and technical equipment in any other manner than by creating joint decision centres comprising several enterprises. The internationalization of manufacturing capital is a particular capitalist form of the micro-economic coordination of industrial activity through national frontiers. Eastern Europe was not in possession of such experience. More exactly, through the capital interests of the big Western firms a part of production *was coordinated* with that of other countries, but on the one hand, as has been indicated above, the role of the socialist countries of today was passive in this coordination and, on the other hand, the coordination itself came about in such relations which fell outside the frontiers of the new region emerging after the socialist transformation. The socialist countries nationalized the Western capitalist interests, that is, they rendered themselves independent of the foreign, *capitalist* decision centres. *In this manner and in this field they made their socialist production relations unequivocally national.* The situation would have been quite different if, when organizing the socialist ownership relations, the individual countries had been faced on a mass scale with the industrial or banking interests of other socialist countries.[10] Such a situation would have had a coercive effect as to clarifying the nature of the international socialist ownership of the means of production and, to experimenting its ways of operation. This remark can, of course, only stop at this point. The historical fact is that such intertwining of ownership never existed (or only in a very loose form and temporarily). As a consequence, no micro-level international decision centres came about in Eastern Europe. The reason for all this may be found exclusively in the presocialist economic physiology of Eastern Europe. All further speculations belong to the realm of dreams and not to that of analysis.

[10] This was the situation in Hungary with the enterprises in Soviet ownership. These were not affected by nationalization, they remained the property of the socialist Soviet State and became as such, for some time, organic parts of the Hungarian planned economy. It is a pity that this form of cooperation faded away with time, because the enterprises derived from German interests and were but accidental as regards the interests of the Soviet economy. Under more propitious circumstances they might have become "model workshops" of socialist micro-integration.

CHAPTER TWO

Prehistory of the West–European economic region

Since the purpose of this reasoning is to disclose the particular features of the socialist integration, it will be expedient to outline—as if for comparison—the circumstances under which the West-European economic region emerged.

It is important to see above all that the present West-European integrational core is composed of the earlier industrialized economies. This industrialization flourished in relatively small national units. Relative to the *then* prevailing requirements of the forces of production, these units were fully viable. The *extensive* expansion of industry, and with it, of capital, transgressed the national frontiers though. One of the main directions of this expansion was toward the developed countries which started industrialization but a step later, and this created there the conditions for fast development and, simultaneously, for "catching up", and also helped the development of economic, political and military conflicts within the capitalist world.[11]

Thus, in a particular manner, the international movement of capital was the main carrier of the historical process determining the world economic appearance of today's Western Europe which resulted in two phenomena particularly important for us:

a) The first is *the emergence of two characteristic groups of West-European economies*. The first group comprises the countries industrializing in the "first wave", the centres of the classical colonial empires. These are at the same time the economies which developed earliest, and their characteristic feature—even today—is their orientation towards exploiting the colonial empire. Their ruling industrial circles "got used" to dealing with economies less developed than themselves by orders of magnitude, to the monopolistic situation, secured also through power, and to the relatively high profit yielded under relatively comfortable circumstances of investment. Their industrial structure and technological level therefore settled down for a relatively low internal rate of development and a

[11] The other main direction was towards the underdeveloped areas, thus bringing about the classical colonial empires.

very wide sectoral pattern. At the centre of the colonial empire the continual transformation of the sectoral structure and the quick introduction and spreading of the dynamic products was rather an internal problem than one of world-market competition from the outset.

The second group is that of the countries which developed in the "second wave" and were deprived of the possibility to create colonial empires. The characteristic feature of the capitalist circles in these countries was an orientation towards world-market competition. Having no or hardly any colonies where they could have enjoyed a monopoly situation, they succeeded in expanding their markets mainly by increasing their competitiveness, either in the well-defended colonies of others, or in the centres of the colonial empires, or in areas questionable from the viewpoint of spheres of interest (thus, e.g. in the countries belonging to the periphery of the developed world)—at any rate on markets where the competitors, the earlier industrialized countries supported also by the profits of their colonial empires, were also present. The most important member of this group in Europe was Germany, whose unique capacity for economic expansion turned into political and military aggression more than once in the course of the 19th and 20th centuries.

The *characteristic* difference between the two groups did not quite cease even in the years following World War II, though it was eased, as, in the course of the dissolution of the classical colonial empires, the members of the first group, Great Britain, France, the Netherlands, and Belgium, were also compelled to turn towards holding their own on the markets of the developed capitalist countries. If we want to understand the nature and motivating forces of the West-European integration, we cannot neglect the fact that *here also we have a search for the common interests of the colony-oriented and competition-oriented countries, a compromising form of motion for their conflict of interests.* This motivates the power relations in the Common Market (the Franco–German power balance), but also shows in the extension of institutional integration in Western Europe (the Commonwealth-complex of Great Britain on entering the Common Market). It was the different size and direction of the world-market power fields of national capitalism, the defence and attack of the established spheres of interest that gave birth to the nationalistic governmental economic policies in Western Europe at the end of the last and in the first half of the present century. The most important objective task of today's West-European integration is to amalgamate these different nationalist policies into "a European nationalism".

b) The other phenomenon is the *historical process* whereby capital ownership and, as a consequence, the inter-enterprise production and market relations become international. The capitals invested into the countries industrializing a stage later and performing their national integration in the middle of the 19th century promised high profit. And that, in addition, in such productive activities which required the employment of masses of relatively cheap but skilled manpower, and where, by completing the already accumulated domestic capital, huge power could be developed with relatively modest investment. In Europe, such countries were Germany, Italy, Sweden and Denmark, and overseas the United States of America. The domestic and the imported capital mutually strengthened each other, and helped the new capitalist powers wishing to catch up to develop fast. The capital flows between the developed industrial countries soon made capital ownership international. The initially uni-directional capital flows were later replaced by multidirectional ones. By the middle of the 20th century it was already difficult to establish in certain industries what "nationality" was the capital that brought production and market activities into motion. The network of ownership interests was accompanied by the development of institutions, international pools, cartels, sometimes trusts. The process first evolved in the basic industries (e.g. in ferrous metallurgy), and it was following the rearrangement of power relations after the end of World War II and the period of reconstruction that it extended to manufacturing to a larger degree—on the initiative and with the strong participation of the already consolidated American capital which had obtained technological hegemony.

This is the other factor of decisive importance for the prehistory of the West-European integration. As a matter of fact, institutional integration served a double purpose: on the one hand, it was to secure propitious conditions for the further intertwining of the micro-sphere and for a change in the nature of the intertwinings (transfer from bank and equity interests into the directly productive enterprise units); on the other hand, the purpose of the integration was that the decision centre of the international enterprise networks in Europe should be transferred as far as possible to Europe itself.

From the viewpoint of our analysis the interesting aspects of the complicated process are (a) that *West-European economy was very rich in capital intertwinings,* (b) that the developed West-European countries were very experienced in world economic activities—though the direction and nature of their effect was different, and (c) that the need for regional integration appeared in the form of a *need to break the nationalist economic policies* (this was supported by the big capital that had become international), to accelerate the further intertwining of capitals and promote the change in their nature, to increase the power on a European scale of the capitals, and, last but not least, to counterbalance the world hegemony of American economy and technology.

It may be safely stated that *Western Europe was a world economic region in the functional sense even prior to the Treaty of Rome*, and though its character was weakened by the Great Depression and the period of seclusion between the two world wars and after the second, the conditions of its rebirth could not be eliminated. This region was never free from antagonisms at times sharpening into economic and military conflicts. But, embedded into the whole historical process, the disintegrational phenomenon may be conceived of merely as an "intermezzo". The functioning of the group of developed West-European countries as a region of world economy is not necessarily limited to mutual trade and cannot be measured by its intensity. The internationalization of capital ownership and, through it, of direct production relationships, is much more important in this respect. It is not only the need for further commercial intertwining, but above all the urge to increase the world economic power of capital that today pushes Western Europe towards gradually eliminating economic nationalism. They try to promote this, of course, through innumerable obstacles and amidst not negligible countervailing tendencies.

The determining role of the economic policy of socialist industrialization in developing the present integrational requirements of Eastern Europe

It is no mere coincidence that the conditions for socialist revolution were born first precisely in the countries characterized in the preceding chapters as the periphery of the developed world. It is both a natural and a social law that in a heterogeneous system qualitative changes start where the internal tensions and contradictions of the system are most intensive. In the first half of the 20th century we may already speak about capitalism as a world system. Locally, the internal tensions of this world system became most felt in the marginal zones between the developed and backward regions. When this started to be recognized, it materialized into a *policy* in the revolutionary workers' movements, that is, into such mass organization and activity alternatives which aimed to eliminate backwardness, *hopeless* under capitalist relations, and to attain a change in the peripheral position occupied in the world economy—a similarly hopeless aim under capitalism.

The building of the socialist power system was put at the service of this basic goal. *Objectively,* this meant competition with the advanced capitalist countries even if the declared political concept set as its objective *only* fast economic development and the strengthening of military defence. (Economic competition as a conscious political objective came to the fore only towards the end of the first stage of industrialization.)

In the hostile environment which surrounded first the Soviet Union and later the whole of socialist Eastern Europe, the evolution of industrial development and its keeping on a high level demanded from national economic policies particularly: (a) a highly selective internal development policy based on centralized planned economy, (b) central control and sifting of the effects arriving from the world economic environment. These requirements brought about such internal economic control systems which, in their methods, too, basically differed from the West-European ones and thus also channelled their *cooperation among each other* in a different direction from that of the West-European cooperation. Furthermore, they necessitated in each country a system which protected the socialist economies from the harmful economic effects of the developed capitalist countries. Thanks to this, it was possible to hinder the direct influence of Western market effects on the internal economies of the CMEA countries and their cooperation at the time when East–West economic cooperation was revived.

It is not my purpose to describe in detail the differences between the functional models established in the countries of Eastern and Western Europe. From the aspect of this book it is their effect on the international economic relations that is of decisive importance. The West-European division of labour was built upon an internationalized micro-economic structure, backed in each country by nationalist macro-economic policies of the business circles. But today this economic nationalism is useful only for the small and medium-sized capitals. Giant enterprising demands "regional" nationalism. Thus, the narrow national frameworks of protectionistic policies have to burst and expand into regional dimensions. Clearly, the *intra*regional functional model of the international division of labour corresponding to the requirements of big capital can be only the freest assertion of the market and money relationships allowed by the circumstances. The West-European region comprising only developed capitalist countries encounters but rarely the differences in development level as cardinal problems to be solved in the cooperation among nations. The development problem of Southern Italy, Schleswig-Holstein or Brittany is not a problem of *poor countries* but of backward *areas* within the generally rich countries. It is not the integrating region which is mainly responsible for their development, but the country to which they belong. And should the market mechanism work against the development of these backward areas, the country itself which belongs to the region may still develop fast because its more developed areas will prosper on the united market even under competitive conditions. If, therefore, in every country of the region there are industries, industrial areas, capital interests which are competitive or capable of development from the viewpoint of world economy, then the murderous competition released by market liberalism may even stimulate the development of economic units which are *at the margin* of viability. Who would be against economic liberalism under such conditions—except the appointed victims whose influence on "big" economic policy is very restricted and is transmitted with difficulty in the majority of cases.[12]

This situation, therefore, leads to an attack of the internationalizing micro-economic level against the conservative nationalist policies of the macro-economic level, because the elimination or "regionalization" of separate state protectionism favours the big, dynamic corporations and accelerates the liquidation of the unviable, small and non-dynamic elements of the economy.

No similar phenomena can be experienced in Eastern Europe. The bulk of

[12] Where this influence is considerable, as in the case of the French peasant masses, it distorts even the integrational policy towards restricting competition.

the East-European industry did not pass through the whole arduous process of concentration and centralization in which the weak die and their flesh and blood feed the stronger ones as the latter advance. This industry came about and grew up in the shade of state protectionism, under conditions when new big enterprises were created in quick succession, not waiting for the existing ones to gather strength, nor leaving enough means for their production to attain the competitivity standards of the world market. In other words: socialist industrialization created industry with extreme speed, and preferred spreading it—willy-nilly, in lack of sufficient means—at the expense of world-market competitivity. In the course of industrialization the socialist countries in Eastern Europe created large productive units from the very outset.

The number of small- and medium-sized enterprises dwindled—frequently more than it would have been necessary. Further, owing to planning and the central handling of means earmarked for development, in the socialist countries the concentration process takes place not through bankruptcy and liquidation but through the purposeful mergers and the regrouping of assets.

It is thus not the unviable and ailing small plant which needs a protectionistic economic policy. The particular problem in the development of East-European socialist economies is not the conflict between the efforts of big enterprises, which are competitive on the world market, aiming at internationalization and the efforts of small plants, demanding protectionism. *For the time being, in the socialist countries it is first of all the large enterprises that need protectionism in order to survive and develop.*

True, the lack of competition not only protects industry born in the form of big enterprises, but also increasingly hinders the intensification of the development of these enterprises. Protection of the CMEA as a whole would not in itself exclude competition. To be able to explain the limitations of competition within the region, two further circumstances should be reckoned with. One is that the absolute and specific performance of the new industries in East-European countries is extremely variegated. It was not possible to make the performance of the newly created large-scale industry independent of the size and general development level of the given country which constitute the socio-economic environment influencing it. The other is that if some major enterprise or industry did not hold its own in the international competition—even if on a regional level only—and if this influenced the ability of the enterprise to function (its current payments, investments, etc.) without any transmission, this would cause extremely great disturbances in the functioning of the *whole* economy, above all in the countries which became industrialized last. *Thus, a too fast creation of competitive conditions in Eastern Europe, the radical "regionalization" of national protectionism would endanger the development not only of single enterprises or areas, but of entire national economies as well.*

Finally, the conditions given within the socio-political structure for the spreading of the advanced forces and factors of production across frontiers are quite different in Eastern Europe from those in the West. As I have mentioned above, capital in Western Europe once it becomes international, will try to break the nationalism of governments. In Eastern Europe the historical situation has brought about pure national forms of the socialist ownership. However internationalist they may be, this fact must always be reflected in the internal and external policies, the economic relations and the *economic policies* of these countries. The purely national forms of ownership deprive the individual countries, on the one hand, of the traditional forms and instruments of managing the factors of production on a regional level, of income, regrouping and of international coordination on micro-level, which would otherwise offer themselves. On the other hand, the exclusive national character of socialist ownership makes, on national level, economic efficiency and incomes dependent on each other. Thus, *in Eastern Europe there exists no such internationalized network of ownership relations that would demand breaking up the national frameworks of economic policy.* On the contrary, the short-term national interests—particularly in view of the highly consistent protectionism—strongly resist internationalization. *Therefore, economic integration has no driving forces of elementary power that would have developed from the micro-sphere. The integration process breaks its way mostly by relying on the consciousness of political internationalism and on intertwinings developed in the macro-sphere.* It relies exactly on the power which is most deficient in Western Europe, or is the most passive factor of the efforts at integration there.

One of the most important results of industrialization was a considerable growth in the productivity of labour. The other basic result was a shift in the productive activities of society towards industries which demand more complex human labour requiring higher development, and whose end products simultaneously contribute to increasing productivity. The two factors assert themselves in a synthetic form in the value indicators, almost inseparably from each other. Both the growth in productivity and the structural shift towards activities demanding more qualified labour are expressed in the growth of the per capita output. The reason is that the per capita annual net output is indeed higher in these industries than in the traditional branches of the periphery. The labour spent on the products most necessary for the evolution of industrialization was recognized by the domestic and community markets of the socialist countries as more valuable. On the internal markets this did not always assert itself directly: with the two-level price system, little of the surplus product was realized in the prices of the means of production. Nevertheless, the value of net output per worker was generally higher in industry than in agriculture, and in the sectors producing means of production it exceeded the industrial average. The prices applied in the international trade between the CMEA countries also tend in this direction. As a steady deflection from the European main-market prices, which serve as a basis of price relations, we may mention the disproportionate rise in the prices of machines—at the expense partly of the basic materials and partly (mainly) of foodstuffs. Thus, the societies building socialism honoured in an exceptional manner every national and international effort which worked in the direction of accelerating industrialization. This should be stressed all the more because the direction and rate of industrialization was *fundamentally* determined by the preferences of the national economic plans and not by stimulating market impulses. It seems that either the tendencies of the terms of trade instinctively followed the plan preferences or a more or less conscious stimulation of market relations took place on the part of economic policy which made efforts to secure the implementation of its preferences also from this aspect. At any rate, a shift in the structural pattern towards industries where the net output per worker is higher than the average is clearly observable. This process was parallel with the increase in productivity in the stricter sense, that is, with the rise in the net output per worker within a given productive activity. All this was complemented by growing employment, the liquidation of unemployment, the drawing of women into the labour

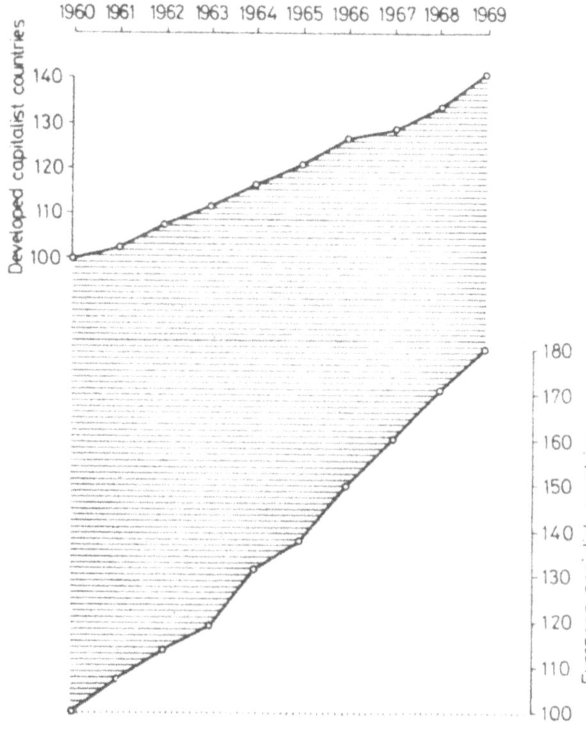

Fig. 5. Differences in the growth rates of per capita national income in the developed capitalist and the European socialist countries, 1960–1969

(The shaded area is intended to show orders of magnitude of the differences in development level.)

Source: Yearbook of National Accounts Statistics, 1970, Vol. II (UN, New York 1972)

force, as well as by quickly rising educational and qualification standards of the population. The synthetic expression of the whole process was the fast growth of per capita national incomes which generally exceed that in the developed Western capitalist countries and also those of the Mediterranean periphery.

The East-European socialist countries, taking the road to socialism, broke out of the periphery in a quarter of a century. The most conspicuous sign of this, the one which can be measured with the most general indicator, is per capita national income. In Table 1 the unweighted average of per capita national income in the industrialized West-European capitalist countries was taken for basis. Beside this average, the five countries with the lowest per capita income are separately shown in order to indicate the situation of the European periphery and the shift of individual countries as compared to the lowest level of the advanced capitalist countries.

Table 1

Relation of the development level in Eastern Europe and in the Mediterranean periphery to the West-European average

Country	If the average of per capita national income in			
	13 developed European*		5 developed European**	
	capitalist countries is taken for 100			
	1937***	1970****	1937***	1970****
Czechoslovakia	58	84	96	114
GDR	—	88	—	118
a) The other countries of the present CMEA (the earlier "East-European periphery")				
Soviet Union	36	81	59	109
Hungary	41	59	65	80
Poland	34	54	56	73
Bulgaria	26	58	42	78
Romania	28	52	46	71
b) Countries of the Mediterranean periphery				
Greece	32	45	52	61
Spain	33	43	54	58
Portugal	32	32	53	43

* German Federal Republic, France, UK, Belgium, Luxemburg, The Netherlands, Switzerland, Austria Italy, Denmark, Sweden, Norway, Finland, Ireland

** in 1937: Italy, Ireland, Finland, Austria, Czechoslovakia, in 1970: Italy, UK, Ireland, Denmark, Austria.

*** Computations by Éva Ehrlich

**** Computations of the CMEA working group of the Institute of Economics of the Hungarian Academy of Sciences and the author's own computations

Table 1, though it was compiled only on the basis of rough computations expressing but the orders of magnitude, calls attention to some tendencies, even if every possible limitation to the accuracy of the data is considered:

a) In the last peace year before the war, there was no considerable difference in per capita national income as yet between the "East European" and the "Mediterranean" periphery. As regards the general productivity of social labour, not even the Soviet Union had broken out of this zone, although its peripheral position was done away with by the socialist revolution. At the same time, Czechoslovakia did not belong to the periphery, but stood at the level of the "Five", which roughly meant about a little more than half of the more advanced West-European level and the double of that of the periphery.

b) Between 1937 and 1970 the movements were highly complex. It will not treat the conspicuous changes within the group of the "Thirteen", as e.g. the slide of Great Britain and Denmark down to the group of the "Five", or Finland's slight rise from the latter category, and will concentrate on the development of the situation of the periphery between the two world wars.

The first conspicuous change is that Czechoslovakia and the Soviet Union attained and exceeded the level of the "Five", reducing their lag behind the "Thirteen" to 10 to 20 per cent. Thus, inclusive of the GDR, three European socialist countries entered the category of highly industrialized economies.

The second change that strikes the eye is that the countries taking the road to socialism from among those that had belonged to the periphery approached the level of the "Five" to 70 to 80 per cent and that of the "Thirteen" to 50 to 60 per cent. This is an essentially faster progress than what was achieved by the Mediterranean countries.

The fact that the East-European countries did not simply develop "somewhat faster" than the Mediterranean periphery, but have *broken out* of this category of world economy, will become even clearer if—as far as it is allowed by the scarce statistical data which are comparable only with reservation—we look into the basic structural changes behind the development. At this point I considerably expanded the scope of the examination with the data of non-European countries in order to make the tendency even more conspicuous (see Figure 6).

Figure 6 compares the share of agriculturally employed population with per capita national income. The share of the agricultural population may be conceived as a primary indicator of industrialization. The less industrialized a country, the greater portion of its population is employed in agriculture. Interestingly, the figure shows a break. The very backward countries are situated, on the whole, around one line, and the highly developed ones around another, but the two trends do not meet. In the "central zone" there is a great "mess". If we lengthen the trend line of the developing countries *upwards*, the countries we have categorized as peripheries of different developed cores will be placed around it, with some dispersion. If we follow the trend line of the developed countries *downwards*, those CMEA countries can be attached to it which constituted the East-European periphery of the developed world prior to the socialist revolutions. *This allows the conclusion that the transgression of the limit between developed and underdeveloped state means first of all the regrouping of the bulk of the agricultural population into industrial and similar occupations.*

The periphery is thus a type with uncertain characteristics, and the fact whether development stops at a relatively lower level depends not so much on the extent to which the population abandons agriculture, but rather on the direction of the flow of the population released by agriculture, i.e. the sectors they flow into (see Table 2).

A similar picture is obtained if we examine manufacturing industry separately, for the simple reason that the latter comprises all non-extracting activities, from

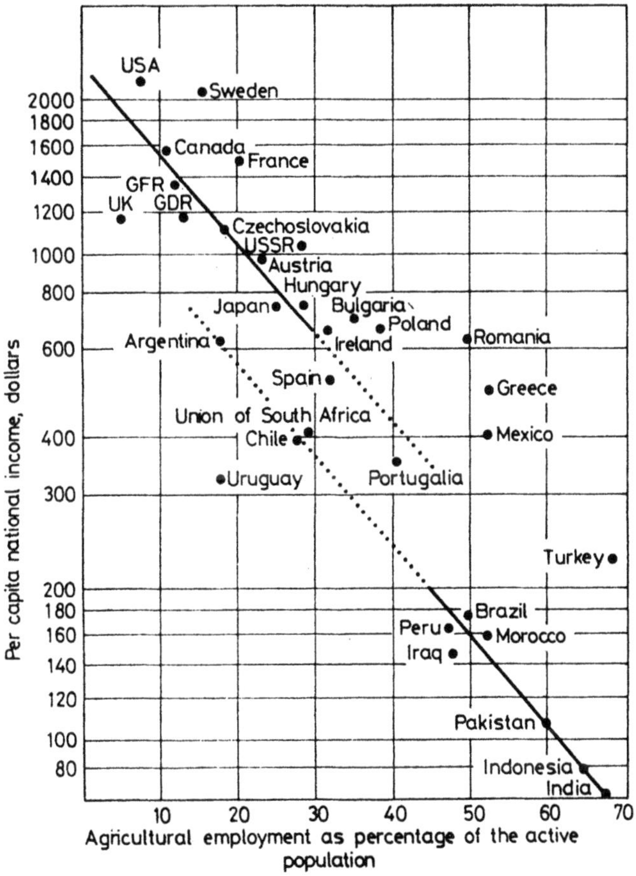

Fig. 6. Relationship between per capita national income and the ratio of the active population engaged in agriculture at the end of the 1960s.

Table 2
Distribution of the active population, total = 100

Country	Year	Agriculture	Industry and construction	Services
USA	1964	6.6	32.4	61.0
France	1965	19.8	36.7	3.5
United Kingdom	1951	5.1	47.4	47.5
German Federal Republic	1964	11.3	48.0	40.7
Austria	1961	22.8	40.0	37.2
Italy	1964	24.9	39.8	35.3
Japan	1964	27.4	31.0	41.6
German Democratic Republic	1969	13.2	49.9	36.9
Czechoslovakia	1969	18.3	46.4	34.8
Soviet Union	1968	28.7	36.4	34.9
Hungary	1969	29.1	41.2	29.7
Poland	1969	37.4	35.1	27.5
Bulgaria	1969	37.6	37.6	24.8
Romania	1969	51.2	29.2	19.6
Spain	1964	34.6	34.1	31.3
Ireland	1964	35.2	24.5	40.3
Argentina	1960	19.2	31.4	48.4
Greece	1961	53.9	18.6	27.5
Chile	1960	27.7	27.5	44.8
Mexico	1960	54.2	18.5	27.3
Portugal	1960	42.3	27.8	29.9
Union of South Africa	1960	30.0	27.3	42.7
Brazil	1960	51.6	14.9	33.7
Peru	1961	49.7	18.7	31.6
Turkey	1960	75.0	9.6	15.4

Source: ILO Yearbook 1965, and CMEA Statistical Yearbooks 1970, 1971

the primary processing of mining products and the preserving of food to pharmaceutics and electronics. The computations of Zsuzsa Bekker relating to the metal-working industries already reveal a closer relationship between development level and the weight of these industries in the economy (see Fig. 7).

In addition, export statistics allow us to separate clearly those countries which turn out and export products requiring little skill and rely on simple work processes, from those in whose structure complicated articles requiring greater skill and complex technology are dominant. This is indicated by the figures in Table 3.

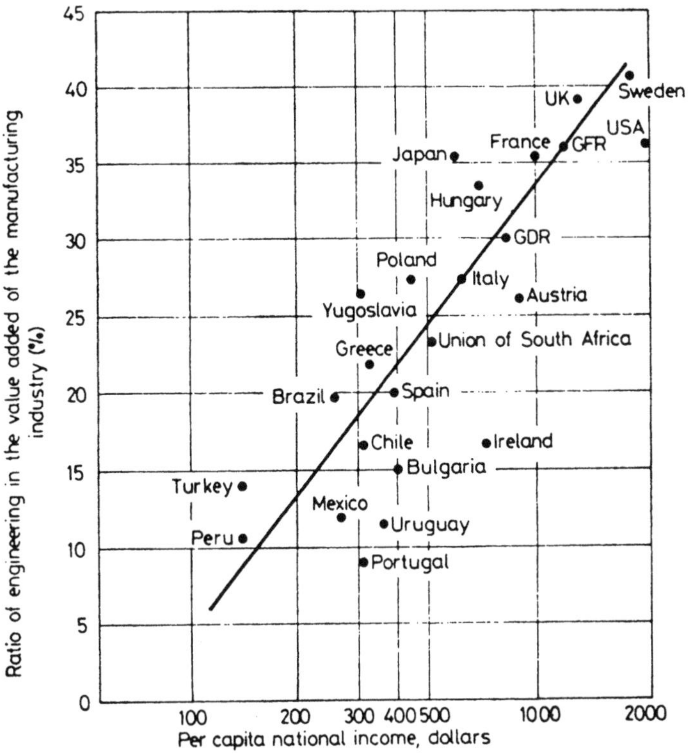

Fig. 7. Interrelation between the ratio of engineering production and the level of per capita national income, 1968

Table 3

Pattern of exports in 1968, total export = 100

Countries	Food	Raw materials	Metallurgical products	Other semis	Chemicals	Machinery	Other manufactures
Argentina	72	15	2	2	4	3	2
Chile	2	24	68	—	—	—	6
Mexico	42	29	11	6	5	3	4
Republic of South Africa	28	26	15	17	3	4	7
Greece	53	20	9	8	7	1	2
Ireland	53	8	1	12	4	6	16
Portugal	24	13	2	37	6	6	12
Spain	37	13	5	12	6	14	13
Italy	11	9	5	17	8	35	15
Austria	5	14	15	24	6	22	14
Japan	3	2	14	21	6	38	16
Hungary	21	7	6	9	8	34	15

Source: UN Yearbook of International Trade Statistics, 1968

The data render the hypothesis at least probable that the dividing line between the periphery and the sphere of the industrially developed countries can be transgressed by developing the industries requiring higher technology and skills. It was the socialist countries which took a decisive step in this field (see Table 4).

Table 4

Combined ratio of engineering, chemical and electric-energy production in industrial output, per cent

Countries	1950	1969
Bulgaria	13.7	28.8
Hungary	27.2	42.2
GDR	38.3	47.8
Poland	14.4	43.5
Romania	21.2	37.0
Czechoslovakia	18.7	38.2

Source: Computed on the basis of CMEA Statistical Yearbooks

We may state without exaggeration that the development of the dynamic industries producing means of production had a decisive role in that the socialist East-European countries have emerged from the periphery.

CHAPTER FOUR

The deviating character of the "Western" and the "Eastern" types of economic integration (the EEC and the CMEA)

The East- and the West-European integration processes show highly deviating, dissimilar features. Above all, both have different political and social backgrounds, motives and systems of goals. The West-European integration is the product of the "second flowering" of capitalism, and, at the same time, an expression of the contradictory nature of the capitalist world system, insofar as its most important functions are to protect the interests of European capitalism against the efforts of the competitive American capital. The integration of the socialist countries associated in the CMEA is free of defensive and aggressive features. Its only task is to improve the conditions for the development of the forces of production in the member countries.

Accordingly, the basic mechanisms of the two integrations also differ. The core of the West-European integration, the European Economic Community, popularly called the Common Market, tries above all to remove the national protectionistic hindrances from the way of private enterprise activities and to create a uniform regional market which may serve as a favourable framework for the rearrangement of the West-European forces of production over half a continent. The CMEA tries first of all to accelerate the development of the forces of production in the East-European socialist countries to conform to the increased requirements, by synchronizing the planned economies of the member countries. Thus, the "Western" integration tries to create a framework for accelerating the "natural selection" of competing enterprises, while in the "Eastern" integration prefers the less painful "artificial selection" through the deliberate coordination of socio-economic activities.

Is it indeed necessary for the two integration processes to differ so much from each other in character and methods? Putting the question this way does not serve merely theoretical purposes. I think it is highly important to know the conditions of integration thoroughly in order to be able to move safely within our own possibilities. Nothing is more paralysing than if we try to approach a given objective with instruments tested elsewhere and to fail, either because the conditions for using the instrument in question are missing, or because a method which is effective under given conditions, becomes blunt in a different medium. *If we do not promote the international integration by relying on our own endowments, and evaluate the experiences of others only from this aspect—this paralysing effect may occur at any moment.*

This does not contradict the necessity of observing also the integrational efforts of other regions, their motives and results with keen eyes. Not only because integration in the outer regions affects the development of the foreign economic relations of the socialist countries, but also because we can measure our own realities through comparison with others. This is the advantage of comparative approach over introspection.

a) The West-European integration with several cores[13]

If we examine the direction of the flows of trade within Western Europe, it seems as if, in the sixties, the masses of commodities had been situated around two poles (like iron filings around the poles of a magnet). One of the points of condensation was no doubt the Common Market of the Six, but not the only one. A much more vague, but still remarkable condensation took place in the trade among of the countries left outside the Common Market. These are mostly EFTA members, yet I do not venture to characterize the second pole by the name EFTA, since the biggest economy of the EFTA conglomerate, Great Britain, remained outside the condensation.

The Six were attractive mainly within their own sphere. First the Belgian–Luxemburg economies opened their import markets to the West-European outsiders, and a strong West-German and Dutch export drive was felt towards Great Britain. One of the most spectacular phenomena in the Common Market of the Six was the opening of the French market with its autarkic traditions to the commodity flows of its Common-Market partners, as well as the great extent of the export expansion of Italy and the Benelux countries. The considerable export drive of the partners reduced the importance of the GFR in the commodity turnover within the community by a few percentage points. At any rate, on

[13] I regard as belonging to the West-European region the following economies: the German Federal Republic, France, Belgium and Luxemburg, the Netherlands, Italy, the United Kingdom, Sweden, Norway, Denmark, Austria, and Switzerland. The moderately developed countries of the Mediterranean and Ireland belong to the periphery of this region. Therefore, although their economic relations with the region are very close, I neglected them to show the plasticity of the characteristic processes. At the same time Finland and Yugoslavia were omitted, since these two economies are situated in an "interregional space", their movement is thus not characteristic of the region as a whole. The West-European region will be treated as the division of labour of highly developed capitalist economies.

West-European average, we do not find within the Six, with the exception of the intensive internal Benelux relations, any bilateral relation whose development would be slower than average.

A similar intertwining, though at a slower rate, is perceivable in the case of the smaller countries left outside the Common Market. Apart from a few negligible exceptions (as the mutual Norwegian–Austrian trade), the rate of growth of trade relations attains or exceeds the general West-European average.

The relatively declining commodity channels of Western Europe are made up of the relations among the Common Market countries and those that remained outside in the 1960s. The "introverted" tendency of the integration of the Six may thus be measured also from this aspect. The uneven development of foreign commodity flows can be shown also in the relations outside Western Europe.

The majority of the 11 countries examined developed their trade with the USA and Japan at a rate equal to or *exceeding* the rate of growth of their mutual exchange, and this also applies to the majority of the Common Market countries in their trade with the CMEA countries. Otherwise, the Common Market increased its export expansion efforts towards this "doubly external" industrialized world more than towards the other countries of Western Europe. Similar

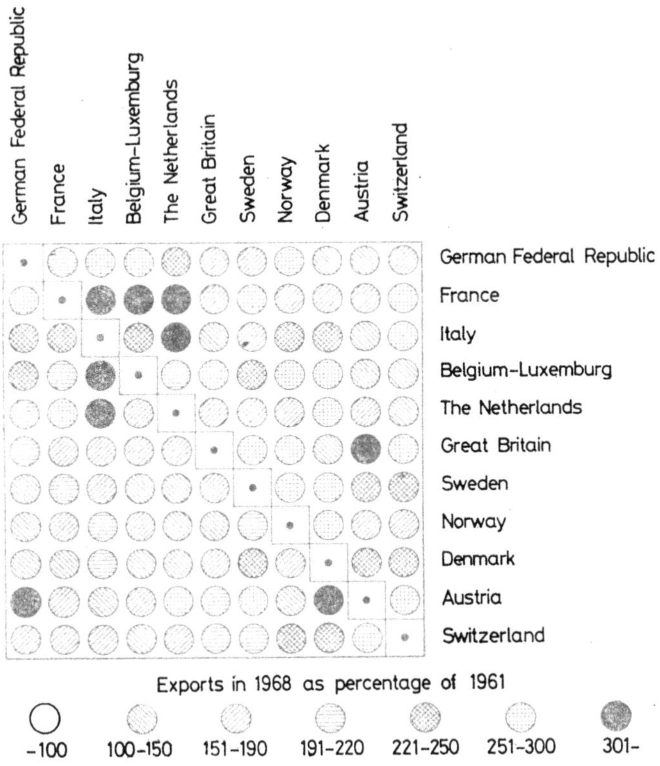

Fig. 8.
Changes in commodity flows between 1961 and 1968 in Western Europe. (The index number of the mutual trade between the developed West-European countries in 1968 relative to 1961 = 207.6 per cent)

Source: UN Statistical Yearbook 1972 and author's computations

efforts made by the smaller countries of the "rest of Europe" also seem to be stronger than those towards the Common Market. Trade with the developing countries increased, almost without exception, much faster than the total West-European trade. In the period examined, only Japan had important export achievements in the developed West-European countries. In the final analysis, the advanced European countries increased their exports to the rest of the world economy neither faster nor slower than their mutual exchange: but the growth

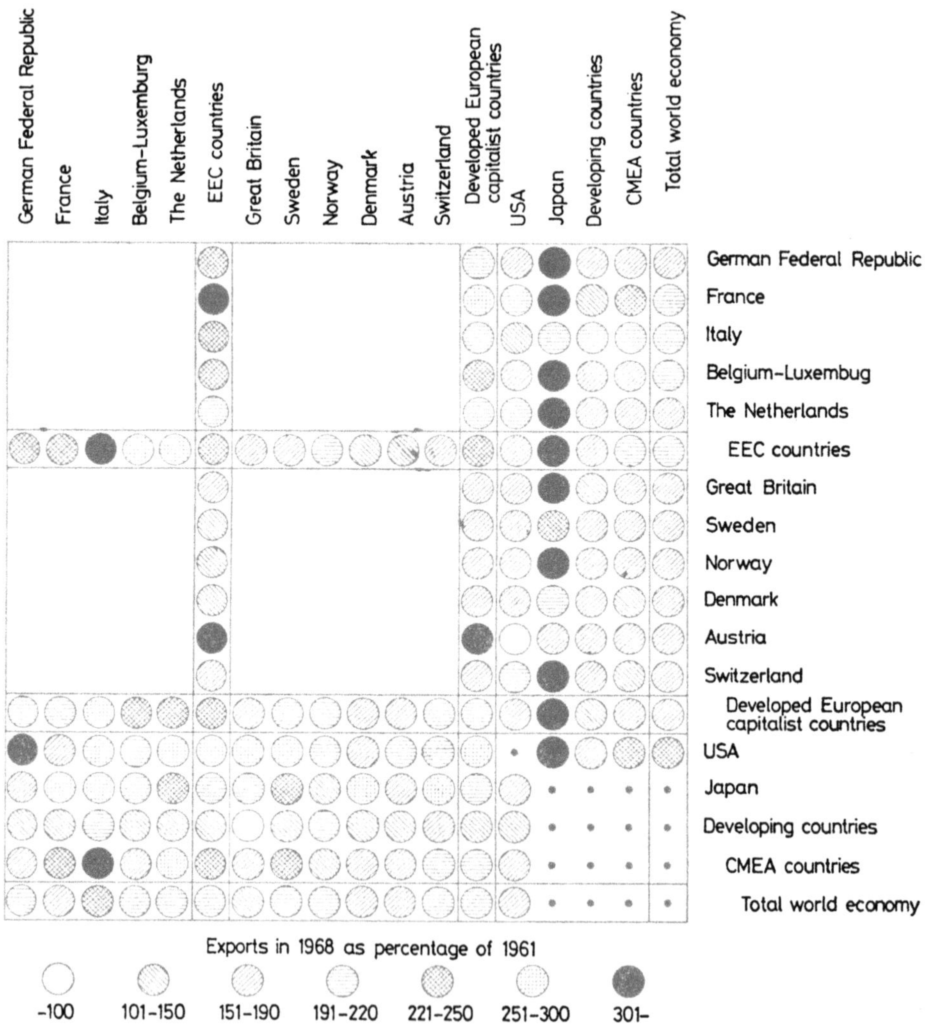

Fig. 9. **Interregional changes in the commodity flows between 1961 and 1968**

Source: **The author's computations**

of their imports was lagging behind this rate—except for imports from Japan. Thus, the "introversion" mentioned above in connection with the Common Market, may also apply to for the whole of Western Europe, and is the most manifest in the dynamics of relations with the developing countries.

Following the above, the "switchboard scheme" of the division of labour in Western Europe may be outlined. The bulk of the commodities realized in foreign trade within Western Europe appears mostly in the export and import market of the German Federal Republic and in the mutual trade of the Common Market countries. The bilateral processes *which attain or exceed 2 per cent of total West-European trade* are all realized within the Common Market or are sales of the GFR to Austria or Switzerland. These "broad" flows somewhat exceed *half* of the volume of goods to be exchanged within Western Europe. A further 20 per cent is made up of those "middling" flows which, taken separately, attain 1 per cent of the total trade. These are, for the most part, the most important export and import connections of Great Britain. The bilateral relations which, taken separately, do not attain half per cent of the total trade (comprising about half of the relations) make up only one tenth of the total trade within Western Europe.

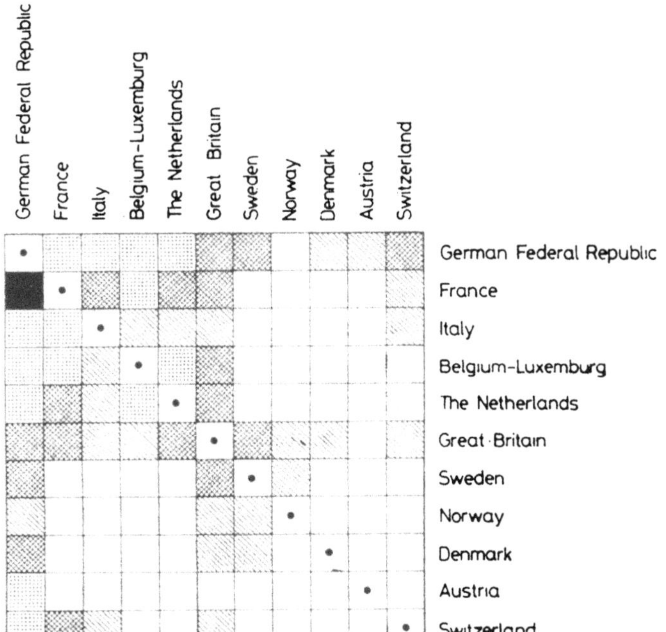

Fig. 10. **Distribution of the West-European commodity trade by bilateral relations in 1968, total trade among each other = 100**

Source: The author's computations

Thus, the "map" of the lines of force of commodity flows shows above all the existence of a GFR centre in overall West-European dimensions, which is, at the same time, the centre of a much denser than average medium, of the Common Market of the Six. Also the outlines of a Great Britain centre may be discerned, though much dimmer, which has attractive power mainly for the North-European countries.

France is similarly an important exporter and importer within the Common Market, but outside the scope of the Six it has intensive relations with the British and the Swiss economies. From the point of view of the total West-European trade, her relations with the other West-European countries are peripheric.

Finally, the distributions also point to the existence of characteristic local nodes. Such is, e.g., the commodity flow of increased intensity within the Benelux states. A more exact picture of the intertwinings will be obtained if we set up the balance of regional trade relations also by main groups of commodities (see Fig. 11).

The first main group of commodities comprises the products of the basic-material type, including electric and primary energy (coal, crude oil, oil products, natural gas, waste gas, turf, firewood, etc.), ores, ore-concentrates, metals and rolled products, chemical intermediaries, building materials, minerals and industrial materials of agricultural origin. The second one is that of raw and finished foodstuffs. The third is the group of investment machinery, vehicles, equipments, instruments, inclusive of the intermediary products of the metal-working industries. The fourth is that of industrial consumer articles, including the consumer goods turned out by the metal-working and the chemical industries. The matrices of trade of the main groups of products do not show basic differences from total trade, perhaps only in the fact that the existence of the British "centre" is less perceptible in some main-group matrices than in the one relating to total trade.

Nevertheless, their closer examination reveals much about the pattern of the West-European power lines. Without aiming at completeness, only the most characteristic ones will be listed:

a) The commodity flows seem to be most concentrated in the food sector. Out of the 110 measured, about 15 per cent are intensive relations, transacting almost two thirds (62 per cent) of the food traded within Western Europe. Next comes the market of machinery, where the ratio of intensive flows to the total is 12 per cent, transacting almost half of the trade (47 per cent). Then follows the market of industrial consumer goods, where 15 per cent of the relations comprises 56 per cent of the trade, and then that of raw materials, where, similarly, half of the volume transacted appears in 15 per cent of the relations.

Outside the internal turnover of the Common Market, the exports of the German Federal Republic are significant, and, in some cases, the British exports (e.g. of machinery) to the Six.

b) The basic component of what I have just called "the GFR centre of West-European importance" is the export of the metal-working industry. In the second place partly consumer goods, partly food may be mentioned. In addition, also

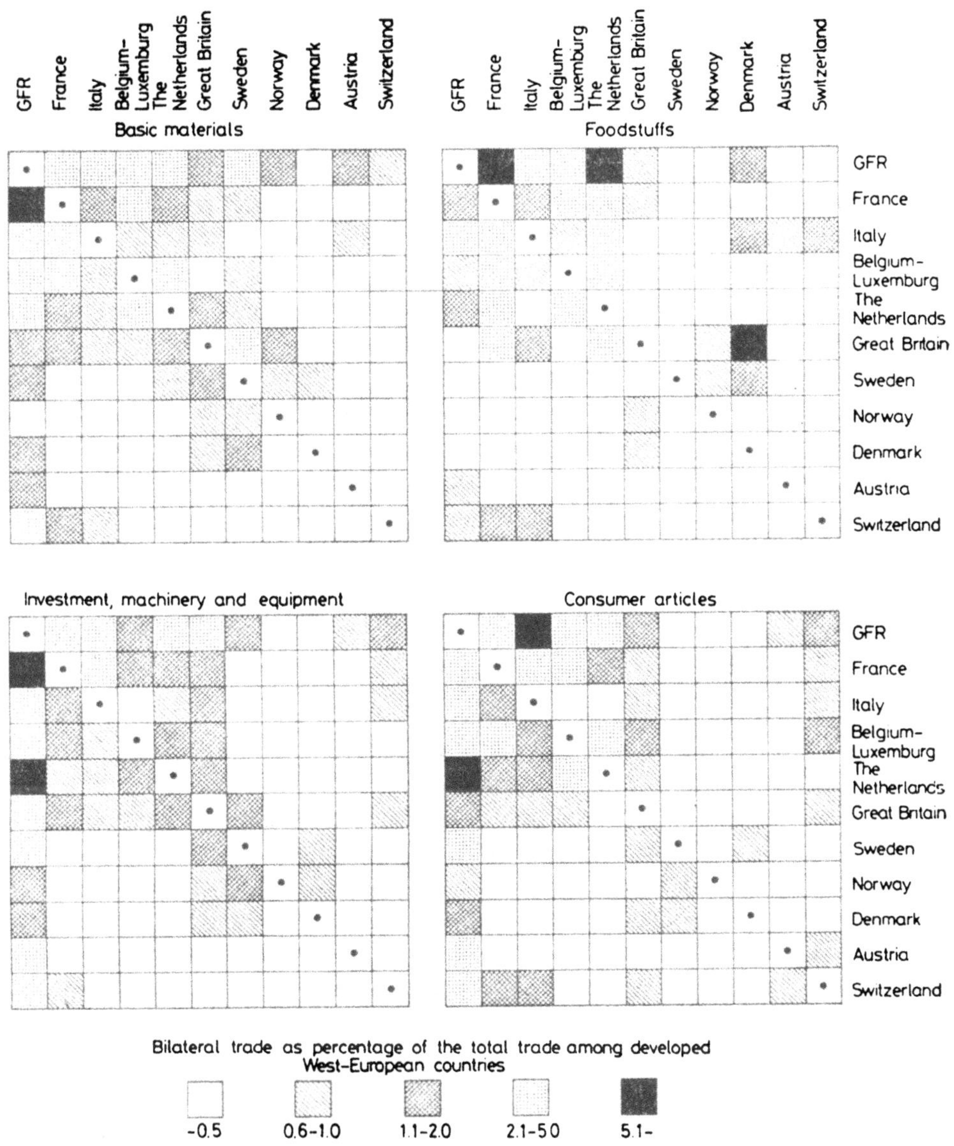

Fig. 11. Distribution of the West-European commodity trade by bilateral relations in 1968. (Total trade in the corresponding commodity groups among each other = 100)

Source: The author's computations

the imports of machinery and basic materials are significant. *West-German imports of food and consumer articles concentrate on the Six, while her total exports and the imports of basic materials spread over the whole of Western Europe.* Her export items to the smaller countries also belong here. The above statement, that in Western Europe there exists a GFR centre, may now be rendered more exact. This centre concentrates almost four-tenths of the machine exports (one-fourth of the net trade in machinery), three-tenths of the export of industrial consumer articles (one-tenth of net exports), one-fourth of both the exports and the imports of basic materials, and about one-fourth or one-fifth of the net trade in food. Considering that the trade of eleven countries is affected, a quarter of whose national income is produced by the German Federal Republic, this degree of concentration seems to be rather high.

c) As regards the Common Market of the Six (this group of countries contributed two-thirds of the national income of the developed Western Europe), almost half of the total trade in machinery, more than half of the trade in basic materials and industrial articles, six-tenths of the trade in food are transacted among each other. One-fourth of the total trade in machines of Western Europe was exported to non-Common-Market countries (exclusively by the German Federal Republic). The whole of the Common Market is a net exporter of industrial consumer goods, but also of basic materials and, slightly, of food. (The latter is divided between France and the Netherlands.)

d) Looking at the problem by main groups of commodities, the British "centre" seems to be much less concentrated. Her exports to the Six attained the level of a "medium" flow, the imports from Sweden and Norway attained the same level in some places. The sole exception is her food import from Denmark which is one of the most intensive flows in Europe.

Finally, it is worthwhile to dissect the bilateral flows of trade in Western Europe, related to the national income of the exporters.

I consider the relations between two economies to be organic if a country exports to another or imports therefrom a volume of commodities that exceeds 2 per cent of its national income. Insofar as units of different size transact trade with each other and, as a consequence, the volume of mutual trade related to national income is half of that in the other country, the relations are asymmetrical. Mutual relationship is much more important for the smaller party than for the bigger one. Let us examine when the "width" of trade exceeds the critical value of 2 per cent, and where we can speak about "intergrowth", that is, an organic relationship which is of more or less the same specific extent for both parties, and where we may call it "clinging", that is, a relationship where the volume sold or bought is particularly important for one of the parties.

Intergrowth can be found above all between the *GFR and France*, as well as between the *GFR and Italy*. As we have seen, the main element in the former is

Table 5

Exports as percentage of the national income of the exporting country in 1968

Importing country \ Exporting country	German Federal Republic	France	Italy	Belgium–Luxemburg	The Netherlands	United Kingdom	Sweden	Norway	Denmark	Austria	Switzerland
German Federal Republic	—	3.84	4.80	15.31	20.41	1.25	4.49	5.15	6.34	6.69	6.33
France	3.87	—	3.23	13.57	7.72	0.90	1.79	0.97	1.39	0.64	3.84
Italy	2.39	1.90	—	2.76	3.52	0.62	1.21	1.29	1.96	2.95	3.92
Belgium–Luxemburg	2.35	2.09	1.06	—	10.50	0.91	1.77	0.66	0.89	0.35	1.09
The Netherlands	3.20	1.03	1.19	15.38	—	0.94	1.77	1.11	1.35	0.89	1.18
United Kingdom	1.27	0.98	1.13	3.19	6.27	—	5.67	7.56	10.82	1.81	3.43
Sweden	1.21	0.33	0.40	1.26	2.03	0.99	—	5.96	7.85	1.05	1.59
Norway	0.45	0.12	0.12	0.60	0.73	0.48	4.01	—	3.77	0.30	0.50
Denmark	0.76	0.19	0.26	0.70	1.02	0.63	3.65	2.78	—	0.53	0.96
Austria	1.39	0.14	0.43	0.42	0.74	0.19	0.42	0.20	0.73	—	2.22
Switzerland	1.79	0.98	1.15	1.46	1.50	0.48	0.92	0.44	1.23	2.63	—
Developed Western Europe, total	18.73	11.66	13.82	54.71	54.49	7.45	25.14	26.17	36.38	17.88	25.12
World total	31.46	20.65	25.70	73.13	73.42	24.08	38.56	39.29	51.36	28.63	45.56

Source: The author's computations

the exchange of West-German machines and basic materials for French food. In its dynamics this intergrowth is somewhat asymmetrical, and this appears in the growing deficit of the French balance of trade. (The surplus of the GFR imports was in 1961, 8.4 per cent of the French exports to the GFR but in 1968 this was already 29.8 per cent.) There are no exact efficiency computations available for the particular West-European industries, but from the results of other computations it is likely that the export of agricultural articles against machines and industrial basic materials involves comparative losses, particularly for an industrialized country. The French–German intergrowth is laden with tensions also in this respect. The basis of the other—the West-German and Italian—intergrowth is the export of West-German machinery and basic materials against Italian agricultural goods and some exchange of industrial consumer articles between the two countries, with a surplus for Italy. In this respect the Italian–West-German intergrowth comprises more dynamic elements than the one between France and West Germany.

There is also a third intergrowth process emerging: that of the *French and Italian economies.* The French sell on the Italian market, too, mainly basic materials and food, while the balance of machines and industrial consumer goods is in the red. In spite of this, the net exports to Italy attained one-third of the export volume in 1968, while in 1961 France had an import surplus in this relation.

The three minor countries of the Six are similarly in a state of mutual intergrowth, about 10–15 per cent of their national income is realized in mutual trade. The pattern of this trade is not particularly characteristic, perhaps the mutual trade in machinery is a shade weaker than in other sectors, which is common in the case of mutual trade between developed small market economies. Each cling to the GFR economy, and this contains certain germs of mutual intergrowth, too. The French economy exchanges particularly with the Belgian–Luxemburg complex, but also with the GFR and the Netherlands, more than the critical 2 per cent of her national income.

Signs of intergrowth may be observed in the *Danish, Swedish and Norwegian economies.* But as regards their weight, these do not cover particularly important commodity flows, except for the exchange of machines for food between Sweden and Denmark, which belongs to the "medium" flows.

The "clinging" of smaller countries to the bigger ones is a general phenomenon. Switzerland established such relations with four, Belgium and the Netherlands with three major countries, Austria, Denmark, Sweden and Norway with two. The partners to which the countries are "clinging" are in most cases Great Britain and the German Federal Republic, in some cases France and Italy. This "clinging" is highly important for some smaller countries: Belgium realizes 15.3 per cent of its national income in West Germany, 13.6 per cent in France and 15.4 per cent in Great Britain; that is, half (!) of its national income is realized in these three markets. The Netherlands realizes on these same markets one-third of her national income. 17 per cent of the Swiss national income is exchanged on the markets of the GFR, France, Great Britain and Italy. The situation is similar with the Scandinavian countries.

As shown by the data, the developed West-European countries are situated in a power field with three poles. These three poles, whose movements are essentially independent of the others, are the German Federal Republic, France and Great Britain. These are moving mainly in each other's power field (as well as in the power fields of centres of attraction outside Europe, but the effect of the latter has now been left out of account). The GFR and France are near to each other, Great Britain was rather far in 1968, but the interaction was already palpable (2 per cent of her national income was exchanged with these two countries, and both her exports and imports to and from West Germany and France belonged to the "wide" and "middling" flows!).

At any rate, at the end of the sixties Great Britain was still far from exchanging 3–4 per cent of her national income of 60 billion dollars with any European country, and the volume of goods exchanged in any bilateral relation, from

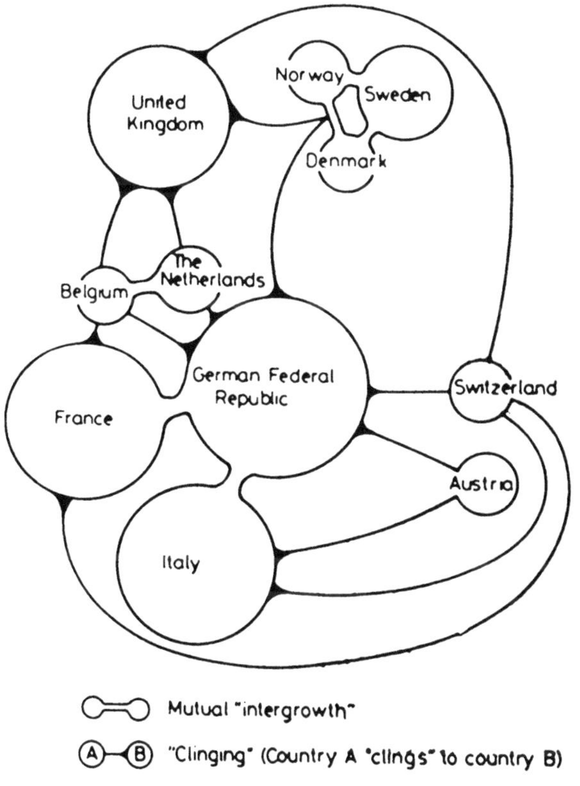

Fig. 12. "Intergrowth" and "clinging" in Western Europe

reaching one-twentieth of the West-European trade. Thus, the triangle we may draw at the poles of the West-European power field will not be an isosceles one.

At the same time, the pattern of trade between Great Britain and Western Europe does not make the approach hopeless. On the one hand, among the bilateral items of her trade in machinery there are several "broad" and "middling" flows, as e.g. in the case of France. On the other hand, even today, the Scandinavian countries are clinging to her more closely than either to the GFR or France. Finally, the three minor economies in the Common Market of the Six, Belgium, Luxemburg and the Netherlands, while being intertwined with their partners in the Market, lean with their back to the British market. Therefore, *the British economy may be conceived of as the biggest centre of attraction after West Germany*. This strongly modifies also the position of the minor countries which are basically situated in the British power field. The same does not hold conversely, that is, the fact of being linked to the British economy only slightly modified the path of those situated in the power field of the GFR.

The French economy has a special role in this three-pole power field. It does not hold any smaller country in its own power field, not even Switzerland or Belgium with whom its relations are the closest. But it is the "second partner" for many smaller countries and thus secures for them the possibility of a healthy

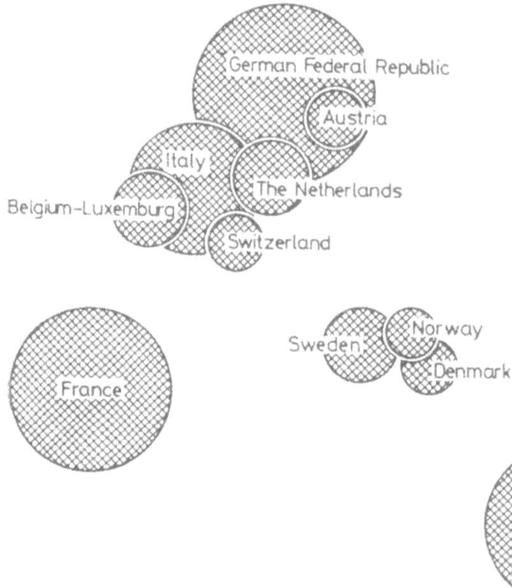

Fig. 13. Position of the developed West-European capitalist countries in the three-pole field

(Note: The area of the circles indicating the countries is proportionate to the national incomes, their relative positions indicate the intertwining with the economies of the three big economies.)

market division among the big European countries. Its attractive power is thus of a path-modifying nature.

The expansion of the EEC seems to support in itself the fact that the true framework of the West-European region is constituted by the mutual "gravitational balance" of the three West-European economies with a somewhat bigger than medium potential: the GFR, Great Britain and France, and to these there are attached, with smaller or greater intensity, other minor economies, almost independently of the quality of their relations to the institutional cooperation.

b) The "single-core" East-European region

From among the three established regions it is only the West-European one which has no single core constituted by one big economy. The North-American region with a "single core" is, however, the ensemble of a big and a smaller economy and is thus a highly specific international economic phenomenon, which cannot be considered a model. I will examine, therefore, the region whose centre is a big economy through the example of the East-European socialist community. Of course, Eastern Europe also has its characteristic features. This follows partly from the specific development relations of Eastern Europe and partly because the region develops according to the laws of socialism.

The East-European socialist countries are strongly attached to the division of labour established with the Soviet economy in the second half of the forties which have become organic since. A little more than one-third of the exports and imports within the region are transacted with the Soviet economy. This is a much higher ratio than the one measured in Western Europe in the case of any economy constituting the "core". It is about the same size as the importance of the trade between the West-European core and the surrounding minor economies. (34 per cent of West-European exports and 30 per cent of imports. The trade between the three medium-sized or major economies constituting the "core", amounts to 15 per cent of the West-European regional trade.) A further one-sixth of the trade is transacted with the GDR, one-seventh with Czechoslovakia, one-tenth with Poland, one-twelfth with Hungary and Bulgaria, one-twentieth with Romania. True, half of all these ratios falls to the Soviet Union. Thus two-thirds of the trade transacted within the East-European region come from the USSR or go thereto. This is a very high degree of concentration.

The degree of concentration is even higher if we consider that the exchange between the USSR and the GDR constitutes one-tenth of the total regional trade, and the trade between the USSR and Czechoslovakia, and between the USSR and Poland, about 7 per cent each. In the trade among the smaller socialist countries there is no bilateral relation whose extent within the total regional trade would reach 3 per cent. This pattern became established in the fifties and no major change has occurred since 1960.

From the diagrams showing the density of commodity flows it may also be read that the "middling" flows developed rather among the earlier industrialized countries as well as among the latter and Poland, which has a fairly big area and population. The major trade relations of Hungary—which may be said to be moderately developed by East-European standards, with a small absolute potential, but fairly strongly participating in the division of labour—with countries other than the USSR belong to the "narrower" flows, while her relations with Bulgaria and Romania are among the most insignificant. With the exception of the Soviet relation, none of the flows attained one-third of the regional trade in 1971.

The more significant changes, too, affect the "broad" commodity flows with the USSR. It may be observed that the importance of the later industrialized

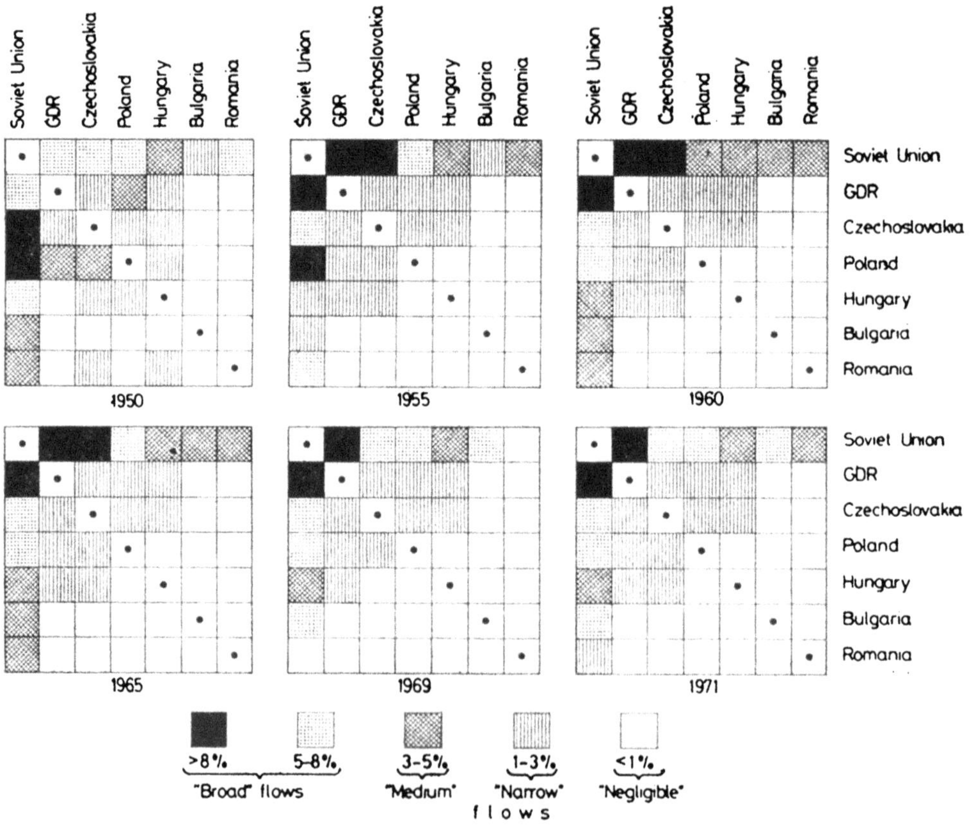

Fig. 14. Distribution of mutual trade among the countries of the East-European region

countries is growing in the trade with the Soviet Union. In 1960, Poland and Bulgaria exchanged with the USSR about 8.7 per cent of the regional imports and 10.2 per cent of the regional exports, by 1971 this increased to 12.9 per cent, while their trade with the German Democratic Republic and Czechoslovakia does not show any characteristic change. The mutual trade of the later industrialized countries also developed faster than average. (The Polish–Bulgarian and Polish–Romanian trade, even when combined did not reach 2.5 per cent of the regional trade in 1971.)

Thus, in the East-European socialist region a double process may be observed. On the one hand, *the Soviet economy strongly attracts the smaller ones* and this attraction increases in direct proportion with the industrialization of the latter. On the other hand, *the smaller, earlier industrialized countries attract much less those industrializing later*, than either the Soviet economy or the latter each other. Even the Romanian economy, whose Soviet trade relations do not belong to the "broad" flows, shows a higher growth rate of exports and imports with Poland and Bulgaria than with Czechoslovakia or the GDR.

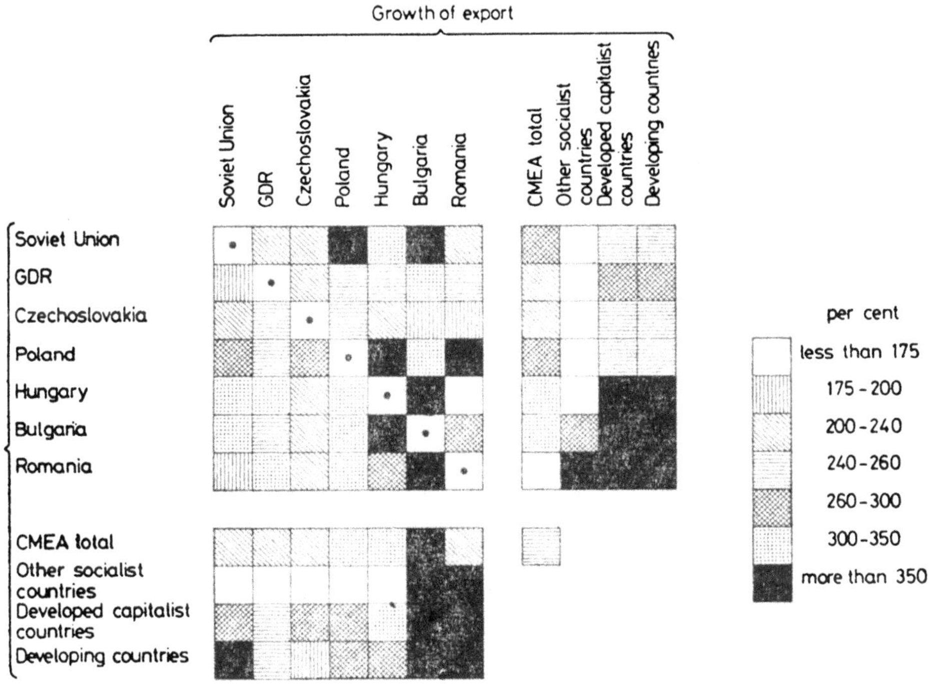

Fig. 15. Dynamics of the foreign trade of the East-European CMEA region, exports in 1971 as percentage of 1960

Source: The author's computations

In the preceding chapter, studying the regional flows in Western Europe, I also mentioned certain "ebbing flows". There are no such flows in Eastern Europe, in spite of the fact that the exports and imports of Czechoslovakia developed generally more slowly than the average, and also in the Soviet–GDR–Czechoslovakia relations an average or slower development can be measured. The former may be explained by the temporary halt in the Czechoslovak economy in the mid-sixties—which has since been overcome—while the latter by the exceptionally high rate of growth of the Polish, Hungarian and Bulgarian exports and imports, that is, by the accompanying phenomena of industrialization. *In the relations between the Soviet "core" and other economies of the region, a new equilibrium is being created.* I will later return to this idea in greater detail, now I would stress only the most general tendency, namely that the importance of the trade of the later industrializing countries within the region is growing mainly through their trade with the USSR. The regional "core" acts here as a catalyst linking the developing countries more intensively to the division of labour.

From Figure 15 it may be also read that the development of relations with regions outside Eastern Europe shows a similar tendency, since the fastest growth is to be found in the case of the later industrializing countries.

Thus, a certain unequal development trend may be discerned in the development of the foreign-trade relations of the East-European region, as well as in the structure of these relations. As distinct from the West-European development, where the basic factor of the unequal development is the effect of the constantly changing "power field" of three major economies on the smaller ones, *in the East-European region it is the gradual approximation of the structures and development levels which somewhat modifies the "power field" otherwise firmly determined by the attraction of the Soviet economy.*

The intertwining is exceptionally strong, but its unequal state is verified by the export ratios of national income (see Table 6).

The indicators of the East-European countries showing the relationship between exports and national income on the whole correspond to world tendencies. Their participation in the world division of labour is neither more intensive nor slacker than that of the industrialized countries. At the same time, relative to their population they are less export-oriented than the following six of the Common Market: Belgium, Luxemburg, the Netherlands, the German Federal Republic, Italy or Great Britain. These are all traditional trading countries, while no such countries developed in the East of Europe in the past. Their participation rate is much higher than that of the peripheric countries of the Mediterranean, i.e. Greece, Spain or Portugal, which is an indication of the fact that socialist Eastern Europe is no longer a part of this sector of the world economy.

The countries most linked to the region are Bulgaria and Hungary, the first exports to the other countries of the region a volume of commodities correspond-

Table 6

Exports and imports as percentage of national income in 1971

Importers \ Exporters	Soviet Union	GDR	Czecho-slovakia	Poland	Hungary	Bulgaria	Romania
Soviet Union	—	14.43	12.94	9.12	15.89	27.61	5.82
GDR	1.10	—	4.25	2.04	4.43	4.28	1.34
Czechoslovakia	0.78	3.60	—	1.80	3.62	2.29	1.26
Poland	0.83	3.40	3.21	—	3.40	1.58	0.85
Hungary	0.56	2.28	2.29	1.02	—	1.00	0.73
Bulgaria	0.63	1.32	1.17	0.58	0.83	—	0.29
Romania	0.27	1.14	1.38	0.51	1.21	0.87	—
East-European region, total	4.17	26.07	24.54	15.07	29.38	37.63	10.29
Total exports	8.05	37.70	38.37	25.47	45.68	50.09	21.41

ing to almost 40 per cent of her national income, the latter, a volume amounting to 30 per cent. From the two, the links of Bulgaria are more concentrated, about two-thirds of her exports to Eastern Europe go to the Soviet Union. Half of Hungary's exports go to the Soviet Union and the other half to the rest of the CMEA countries. The GDR and Czechoslovakia belong to the region to the extent of one quarter of their national income. From the two, the GDR is somewhat more closely linked to the Soviet market than Czechoslovakia. The ratio of exports to national income is 15 per cent for Poland and 10 per cent for Romania. The Polish economy is more intensively linked to the Soviet "core" than Romania. In Western Europe we meet similar data, with the difference that there the link with the triple "core" can be compared with the links of the smaller East-European countries with the Soviet market. The relative instability of the triple "core" is indicated by their weak links with each other (2–5 per cent), as against the fully integrated monolithic appearance in the world economy of the Soviet Union. Considering also the export ratio of the national income, the relative underdevelopment of the non-Soviet relations is remarkable. The specific flow of commodities between the two industrially developed neighbour countries, the GDR and Czechoslovakia, is identical with the relations between Sweden and Holland. And the relations of Bulgaria and Romania, which are also neighbours, is identical with those between Switzerland and Norway. Considerable intertwining (exceeding 2 per cent of the national income) can be found in the following cases:

Mutual intertwining between the GDR and Czechoslovakia, between the GDR and Poland, and between the GDR and Hungary.

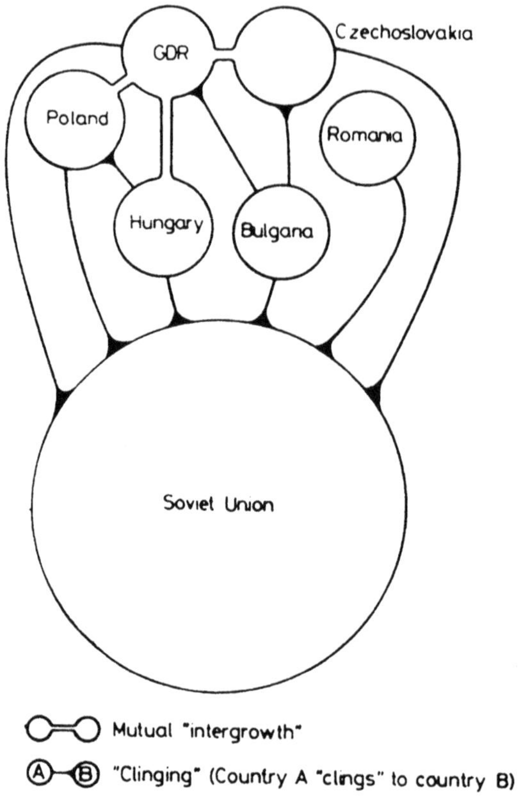

Fig. 16. "Intergrowth" and "clinging" in Eastern Europe

One-sided relations ("clinging"), besides all Soviet relations, between Bulgaria and the GDR, between Bulgaria and Czechoslovakia, and between Hungary and Poland (see Figure 16).

The other bilateral relations do not attain the 2 per cent rate. That is, beside the Soviet "core" a secondary GDR–Czechoslovak–Polish circle has also emerged, which affects 3.1 per cent of the export/national income ratio of the participants, against the 7 per cent of the Soviet relations. Thus, today we cannot yet speak of a subregion, all the less since the rate of development of trade within this circle is average or somewhat lower—as it was shown above. In Western Europe there does exist such a subregion: we have seen that the Benelux countries and the Scandinavian ones may be considered as such. The average export/national income ratio of the former is 13 per cent, against the average 5.2 per cent link to the "triple core". The average link between the Scandinavian countries may be characterized by an export/national income ratio of 4.5 per cent. The Benelux countries are a strong tripartite integration. The "intertwining" of the Scandinavian countries hardly justifies this term, but the "force of field" of the cooperation approaches the value of the cores.

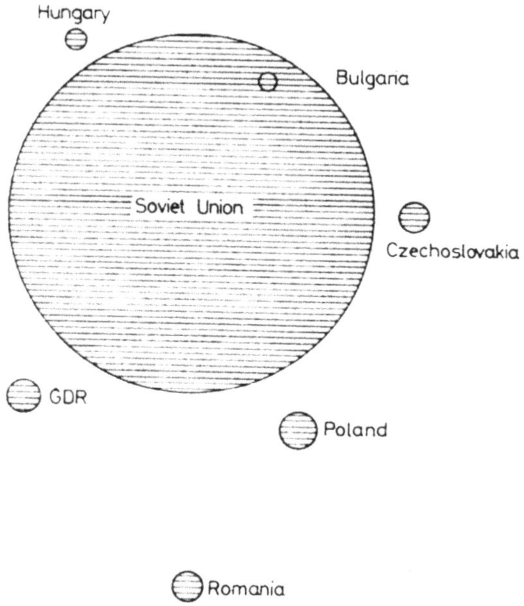

Fig. 17. Position of the East-European socialist countries in the "single-core" power field of the CMEA

(Note: The area of the circles is proportionate to the volumes of national income in 1971, while the distance between the centres of the circles is proportionate to the quotient of the volume of bilateral trade and the national income)

If one attempts to construct the East-European field of gravitation, analogously to Figure 13, the "single-core" nature of the region will become quite conspicuous.

Compared with Figure 13, Figure 17 shows firstly that the production potential of the smaller countries in the East-European region is negligibly small relative to the "core"—its totality does not attain one-third of that of the Soviet economy. Such a difference in size is not found in the West-European region, even if we add the national incomes of the three "core" economies and compress it into a single circle. It secondly shows that the position of the smaller East-European countries relative to the Soviet "core" is very similar to the five West-European countries situated round the West-German centre with the single exception of the Romanian economy. Later it will be shown—now we only mention it—that the factors of attraction highly differ in the case of the Soviet economy from those of any economy in the West-European "core".

The socialist division of labour is rather strongly restricted to an exchange of *basic commodities* important for the functioning of the national economies. Lines of the division of labour became established through which manufactured goods are exchanged for raw and basic materials as well as for primary energy, and others through which investment goods, or basic materials and primary energy are exchanged for basic foodstuffs. A few countries are willing to cover also their need for industrial consumer goods against basic materials, primary energy and food. A considerable portion of the commodity flows between the CMEA countries is composed of these goods.

It would be a poor argument to pass a summary judgement on the CMEA division of labour because of this pattern of trade. It should be taken into account that—as distinct from the conditions of the West-European integration—the CMEA has solved, and will continue to solve its material, primary energy and food-supply problems by relying on its own natural resources. The share of these commodities in the internal trade of the CMEA is expected to remain much higher than in other integrations also in the future. In fact, in view of the unequal distribution of natural resources, it may be expected that a *very considerable part of the commodity flows between the CMEA countries will continue to consist of the exchange of products processed to highly different degrees.*

This being so, serious work is needed to figure out the practical implementation of the principle of mutual advantages for the case when products processed to different degrees are exchanged. For the time being, the share of these commodity flows is overwhelming in the international trade within the CMEA and *thus their unsolved problems overshadow the whole of the international division of labour* and hinder the development of the mutual exchange of manufactured products.

In the mutual exchange of the results of *extracting industries* the remnants of preferences of the first industrialization period are perceivable. The products whose acquisition was of primary importance in the period of accelerated industrialization (laden also with the burden of the development preferences forced upon us by the political environment of cold war), were highly overvalued against other raw products. Only on the basis of such considerations can it be understood how, in a community situated mostly to the North, in whose greater part the supply of the population with vitamin-holding vegetables and fruits meets with difficulties, these products could become "soft" against other raw materials in which the community as a whole is self-sufficient and even transacts large exports (e.g. in wood). These no longer rational preferences considerably hinder the development of a rational division of labour in the extracting industries and in agriculture, and impair the development possibilities of countries possessing optimal productive possibilities in respect of the "non-preferred" products in general, and in respect of the development and modernization of the affected productive activities in particular.

Remnants of the above-mentioned preferences may also be encountered in the valuation of *manufacturing activities*, though to a much smaller extent than in extraction. The basic problem here is of a quite different nature.

Accelerated development carried on with concentrated means in different countries and to different extents resulted in the development of *definite finished-product capacities*, in an order dictated by necessity and to an extent allowed by the material means available to the economies. These end-product capacities were developed to a full vertical scale, inclusive of all work phases and the production of parts, irrespective of the optimal scale of production of the particular phases or parts, since the structure, being still in the gestation process, could not yet "accommodate" specialized plants for the production of parts.

As a consequence, considering the industrial pattern of the manufacturing industries, they radically differ from their counterparts in the West particularly in engineering. In Western Europe the network of enterprises within an industry is composed of a relatively small number of huge enterprises releasing end products, endowed with massive capital and possessing a research and development basis, and of a legion of modern, specialized medium-sized plants producing units, parts and auxiliary materials. In the CMEA countries, however, we find combines where the whole of the technology, or at least its bulk, is present. Although as regards the size of employment, the value of output or the amount of products released, these enterprises frequently belong to the major ones in Europe, their efficiency is much impaired because the majority of the intermediary products is produced on suboptimal scales.

When decision was taken on the size of these productive units, the possibility of exports was also reckoned with, particularly in the smaller socialist countries. The overwhelming part of the trade in machines within the CMEA is borne by such enterprises, of which two undesirable conclusions follow:

One is that, *in spite of large-scale production, the machines sold are not sufficiently cheap*, and the other, that *the exchange of commodities suited for final use is predominant in the division of labour*. The industrial structures firmly withstand deeper specialization, since breaking up of the combines into independent plants, as a function of the optimum scale of production would imply a complete reorganization of the industrial capacities just established and this would involve huge sums. I would add that the valuation of the work performed in the individual technological phases also developed—more or less consciously—according to necessity and this makes the enterprise interests neutral, or even resistant, to specialization, not only on an international, but even on a national scale.

It has also become characteristic of the forms and modes of the division of labour that the industrializing national economies created, for the control of the production process, essentially *technologically centred centralized organizations*. The division of labour among the national organs for the control of productive processes developed in such a manner that the decision centres became delimited according to the technology used. The various "user industries" availing themselves of the different products in a complex manner either have no organization or are authorities far from the productive investments, technological development, etc., and frequently alimented from the state budget. (For example, the production of railway machinery is generally controlled, because of the similarity in technology, by the Ministry of Engineering and not by the Ministry of Transport. Decisions on the production of pharmaceuticals are taken by the same organ which is responsible for the production of phosphoric acid and fertilizers, and not by the authority responsible for health care, in general.) As a consequence for the international division of labour, for the time being, *the complex forms of cooperation would be suited for the common development of comprehensive technical cultures and for implanting these, could not yet sufficiently develop.*

The efficiency of the division of labour is *evaluated* in a particular manner by the participating countries. As the CMEA is a community whose cooperation looks back upon a tradition merely of a quarter of a century, and in view of the fact that in the course of development cooperation was shaped in a manner enabling it to link firmly controlled and planned national economic units on a macro-economic level, its members evaluate the efficiency of the division of labour from two viewpoints:

— Each act of division of labour is evaluated from the viewpoint of its *total national economic utility*. It is not "business" confronting another "business", but the *entirety* of specialization and commercial relations on the side of one macro-economic unit facing the same on the side of the other unit. In this respect, the efficiency of some specialization, sale or purchase of commodities, or cooperation is taken into account above all as a part of the complex bilateral (or multilateral) cooperation. In this case, the social valuation of efficiency moves between *national* limits.

— Since the embargo has been essentially lifted, the CMEA countries can openly step forward as sellers and buyers on the capitalist world market. It follows that they increasingly tend to *compare* the efficiency of their transactions among each other *with the efficiency of purchase and sale on the capitalist world market*. This is the basis of comparison, even if the comparison is, in the majority of cases, favourable for the socialist exchange.

In fields where the CMEA countries have real possibilities to sell or purchase in the West, they judge and satisfy the identical CMEA demand and supply with a view to the Western possibilities. Thus, *criteria borrowed outside the community* strongly affect the judgement of the efficiency of relations. A *regional, CMEA element* of judging and evaluating the efficiency of cooperation could not yet sufficiently develop. The above-mentioned two criteria are necessary and realistic elements of the domestic decisions about fitting into the international division of labour. But, without a development of regional criteria and incentive systems based on them, it is difficult to imagine a cooperation which would bring to the surface the reserves inherent in regional integration.

CHAPTER FIVE

The requirement of equalizing the development levels

Up to now I have tried to expound the historical and structural characteristics which make the integration of the CMEA countries characteristically *"East-European"*. In reality however, it is very difficult to separate what is characteristically *"East-European"* from what is characteristically *socialist*, since the CMEA countries solve the actual tasks deriving from their East-European situation by using the advantages deriving from socialism, and are building socialism under the actual East-European circumstances. At any rate, it is clearly visible that an effort to make up for the lag on a regional scale is not necessarily a socialist feature in itself. Up to now this has been a *basic* feature of *every* integration, thus also of the West-European one. Nor does it follow from the socialist nature of the integration that the division of labour developed in lack of capital relationships: this is a historical heritage of the East-European region which long preceded the socialist transformation. Even such features in the pattern of the division of labour as the preponderance of the manufactured finished-product–raw-material flows cannot be ascribed to socialism. The industrializing countries which are short of raw materials have always based their industrial development on massive imports of raw materials and exports of finished goods.

A feature which does not directly follow from the East-European nature of the division of labour is the *stubborn collective struggle against the differentiated development of national economies within the region, and for balancing the historically developed differences in the development levels.* This is quite a new phenomenon, since it would be quite impossible to solve it with the natural system of targets and instruments of the capitalist integration. The task is particularly difficult if we consider that, on the one hand, the resources of the less developed countries are smaller by orders of magnitude than those of the more developed ones and, on the other hand, that the process of levelling takes place in the framework of an exceptionally fast development of the whole region. *We are thus witness to an experiment with a group development model in which the considerable development-accelerating effect is attained through the favourable conditions of the international division of labour, above all by releasing the internal resources.*

External help above all serves the purposes of securing markets and the material and technical conditions of development. The international regrouping of actual values takes place first of all in the form of handing over patents, designs, production procedures and know-how. In addition, of course, an important role is played by the international regrouping of material assets, as e.g., credit or aid, but this is always related to an actual development project of the country in need of it. The technical and material supply to aid the less developed CMEA countries enjoys a preference also in the industrial development of the more advanced countries as an international development target.

In vain would we look for this feature in the system of goals of the West-European integration. Not only because the possible tasks of levelling are smaller there, but also because of the basic conditions of the integration relying on "natural selection". The instruments which are available for the development of backward areas through the European Investment Bank serve rather political than basic economic purposes. The agricultural provisions, though helping to maintain uneconomical activities, do not provide satisfactory possibilities for raising them to the level where they could be viable even without subsidies. This is the reason for the phenomenon that those countries of the European Economic Community which have most to fear within it, grasp hurriedly at the American capital flowing into the countries or strengthen the hidden protectionism, actually hindering the integration of the region in both ways. *The system of goals of the West-European integration is aimed above all at increasing the efficiency of those at the top, and maintaining and protecting the cooperation "pyramid" serving the top.* (Inclusive of the conditions of the free flow of labour.)

If it produces something different from that, it is foreign to the basic model, contradicts it, and is usually done to forestall the sharpening of internal political tensions. As an organic part of the capitalist world system developing in an increasingly polarized manner, the West-European integration, even if it wanted to, could not but work towards the polarized development model. Otherwise even the peak sectors of the member countries would quickly drop behind in the economic–technical competition dictated by the giants of the United States, and this would produce unsurmountable political and economic tensions in Western Europe.

As a matter of fact, the CMEA cooperation is also tempted from time to time by the expediency of implementing such a West-European model which clearly favours the acceleration of the development of the most advanced countries. It is just the requirements of competition with the developed environment that work towards the one-sided preference of developing the peaks. In reality, however, the CMEA can implement *only a hybrid of the two models which does not basically hinder the process of levelling.* In the opposite case, it would get into conflict with the socialist base on which it has evolved and would help to foster such political tensions which would weaken the basic cohesive force of the socialist integration mentioned above.

Thus, both integration processes are forced to make a certain compromise between the levelling and the polarizing development models. The radical qualitative difference is to be found in the starting points. Though, deriving from its essence, the West-European integration is based on the polarizing model, it is forced to make concessions to the demands of the less developed and weaker areas or industries. The East-European socialist integration must, by its nature, lead the participating economies towards levelling, and tries to reconcile this goal with the higher development needs of the more developed economies. Both models have their advantages and special difficulties.

No doubt, the West-European model could demonstrate spectacular results in the short run, since it selects the development solutions that are most handy. It concentrates resources to where they are capable of attaining the greatest efficiency within the shortest time with the least effort. For a highly developed region which is free from greater differences in development level this model is practically feasible. Namely, the bridging of existing tensions does not, for the time being, introduce so many elements "alien from the model" into the cooperation as to paralyse it. But we do not yet know its effect on the whole of the capitalist world economy. Nor do we know whether in a few decades this will end in a fast development carrying with it the whole region or will necessarily polarize the forces of production of the region.

The road chosen by Eastern Europe, centred on levelling, is not free of contradictions either. Levelling as a basic tendency has to be reconciled with the demand that the earlier industrialized countries should keep pace with world development which is a no less important basic tendency. This is required for the continuous reproduction of the unity of economic and political interests. Braking the development of the forces of production of the most advanced countries relative to the Western peaks may, within a given limit of tolerance, reduce the size of advantages to be derived from the division of labour as against the trade transacted with the Western centre. Thereby, the centripetal force of the integration would diminish and centrifugal tendencies may transitorily become preponderant. At the same time, in the long run the East-European socialist integration tries to bring about through levelling the very economic homogeneous medium whose lack hinders most the development of the forces of production in regional dimensions. In this respect, therefore, the model chosen by the CMEA fully suits the prevailing conditions of the region, and in the long perspective, considering both its political and economic effects, it is more advantageous than the West-European alternative carrying with it the possibilities of polarization.

a) The socialist nature of levelling

The classical bourgeois concept holds that public welfare is an automatic result of the free competition of individuals in legally identical positions. The centuries-long experience of capitalist world economy proved that formal equality in the competition of national economies competing and cooperating under unequal material conditions bears in reality inequality, one-sided dependence. The difference in the development levels increased instead of being reduced. If we consider only the sixties, the differences in development level between the industrialized and the developing countries grew immensely. In 1960, per capita GDP of the developing countries amounted to 9.4 per cent of that in the advanced capitalist countries, while the same figure fell to 7.7 per cent by 1969. It indicates the failure of the idea of bourgeois equality that by the second half of the 20th century about 20–30-fold differences could develop between advanced and backward countries in per capita income. In the USA per capita national income (NNP) stood about $ 2,700, in the early seventies at the same time more than one billion human beings existed in the world under circumstances where the per capita income is below $ 100–150.

The socialist world has not adopted the bourgeois concept of formal equality. When socialism overstepped the limits of the framework of a single country and became an international system in Eastern Europe, it had to clarify the guiding principle of further development.

The deeper we penetrate into the theoretical and empirical knowledge of the international relationships of our own society, the clearer it becomes that *socialism, in all its economic, political and cultural aspects, means a deliberate and massive struggle against the polarization of society*. Every kind of egotism is alien from this society, be it the egotism of the individual, of a social group or class or even of a nation organized in the framework of a given state. The structure of socialism does not tolerate the exclusivity even of welfare acquired through work. The welfare, riches, and material safety which the more talented, clever, better educated or privileged people acquire and develop simultaneously obliges them to help others to create the conditions of welfare and culture. This basic social requirement is made compulsory not only by the socialist *morals*, but also by the well-conceived *interests*. The elevation of humanity from misery, ignorance and discords demands such huge efforts and such complicated productive and organizatory activities which exceed, and will continue to exceed, the ability of any kind of "élite". Socialist society is capable of faster development, both politically and economically, in a relatively homogeneous medium, since its pattern is devised for cooperation, not for competition. This follows from the global social control of the factors of production. Therefore, the basic objective and internal meaning of socialism would be jeopardized, or become illusory, if the individuals, productive collectives or nations who, for whatever reason, are capable of greater efforts today, did not do everything in their power to increase, as fast as possible, the productive capacity of those lagging behind.

I believe that the *active* influence of those starting from a higher development level on those starting with a handicap is a highly important factor. Socialism fundamentally differs in this respect from the societies preceding it. In principle, the capitalist social relations also secure the equality of development possibilities, but this is nothing else than the formal equality of participating in competitive activities. This is why the exclusion of competition in favour of the weak or backward party is alien from the logic of capitalism. The experience of the socialist countries in building up their economies as well as that gained in the almost 25-year experience of international economic cooperation within the CMEA testify that the great differences in the initial positions can be reduced or eliminated—in a historical perspective—only if the principle of competition relying on formal equality is replaced in economic strategy by *mutual aid.* In this case the development of the economies will tend, instead of polarization, towards the equalization of development levels.

b) The facts about and the contradictions of levelling within the CMEA

The conditions of building socialism are rendered complex in the countries of Eastern Europe, on the one hand, by the general *historical, inherited backwardness* of the forces of production of the region causing a lag behind the industrial countries of the world, and, on the other hand, by the *differentiation* of the extent of this lag among the national economies of the region. Besides many other things, this circumstance lends a special hue to the features of socialist economic cooperation between the CMEA countries. It is also one of the causes why catching up with the advanced capitalist countries and, simultaneously, matching the development levels within the CMEA have been in the focus of cooperation, as a double requirement, right from the start.

Examining the development within the CMEA, we see a picture of a diversified process. If we set out, for the time being, from the indicator of per capita national income, we find that the countries which were at a disadvantage, that is Bulgaria and Romania, have caught up with the development of the countries which, until the sixties, were said to be moderately developed (Poland and Hungary). Furthermore, the Soviet Union, which was moderately developed in the early fifties, has caught up with the most developed ones. Thus, the relatively evenly scattered field became divided by the early seventies—while there was a generally fast development in two distinct groups. The difference between the two (1.5:1)

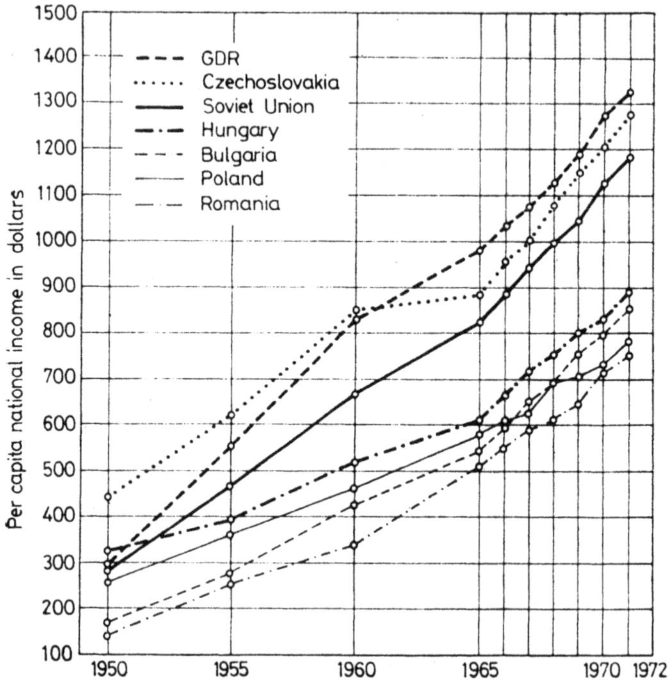

Fig. 18. Per capita national incomes in the East-European socialist countries, 1950–1972

Source: The author's own computations

corresponds on the whole to the difference in 1950 between the moderate group and Czechoslovakia, but is much smaller than the one prevailing between Czechoslovakia and the lower stratum in 1950 (2.9:1). In other words, we may speak about a matching between Romania and Bulgaria on the one hand and Poland and Hungary on the other; about an approach between the former two and the Soviet Union as well as the most developed Czechoslovakia and the GDR; and about a roughly parallel development as regards the Hungarian and the Polish economies on the one hand and the GDR and Czechoslovakia on the other.

Thus, the development of the CMEA reduced the inherited differences in development levels in most respects, but this effect was not quite unambiguous nor of equal extent. It may also be observed (see Figure 18) that the contradictory nature of this tendency emerged already in the second half of the fifties. It was then that the Soviet development broke away from the "moderates" and the distance between the less developed states and the moderates began to diminish. In the early sixties development again became more or less parallel (except for the grave lag of Czechoslovakia behind other CMEA countries), and in the second half of the sixties the two groups were already clearly perceivable.

Thus, the dialectics of the levelling process may be most expediently examined if divided into two historical stages. The first coincides on the whole with the fifties and may be called the stage of evolving industrialization, while the latter, in the sixties, is the stage when the contradictions of industrialization began to unfold.

c) Industrialization, cooperation and the approaching of development levels in the fifties

As has been mentioned, the CMEA cooperation was built out among countries with different "initial conditions". Bulgaria and Romania were only at the beginning of industrialization, Hungary and Poland were in a rather advanced stage, while Czechoslovakia and the German Democratic Republic could be considered as industrialized countries. The USSR should be analysed separately. On the one hand, it necessarily belongs to a different "weight group" by its size and, on the other hand, because of the strongly selective, fast industrialization before and during World War II, it possessed highly developed forces of production capable of high performance, in certain fields, while in others its forces of production were similar to those of the less developed countries.

Owing to the discriminatory policy of the imperialist powers, the whole community was almost hermetically separated from world economy. It could rely essentially only on its own forces, as regards both the sources of accumulation and the technical conditions of developing the forces of production. Thus, the given historical form of economic cooperation among the socialist countries, the *community of interests in industrialization*, developed almost under "laboratory conditions".

Under such conditions the countries possessing more developed forces of production secured their needs for raw materials and food, the markets for their manufacturing industries and, in the last resort, their fast growth and economic equilibrium by contributing to the industrialization of the less developed countries. The latter could carry out the accelerated industrialization only because the necessary production experience and a considerable part of the equipment was imported from the more developed countries, and a considerable part of the products of their newly-created industries was exported to these countries. The Soviet economy played, as a matter of fact, the roles of both "parties" relying on her huge natural resources, absorptive market and her capacity to provide technical help in the most developed industries on the one hand, and also because of the historical situation hampering the simultaneous development of every branch of production to a satisfactory extent. Thus the Soviet economy was partly providing help with industrialization, and partly imported the assets necessary for industrialization too. Her huge and diversified market was suited for absorbing both the higher-level products of the more developed countries and the simpler ones of the less developed nations. At the same time, she could supply the other socialist countries with the greatest part of the raw materials they needed.

The basic task of cooperation was to accelerate the creation of a strong and diversified industry in all CMEA countries, and to secure simultaneously the operational conditions for industry through the supply of raw materials, technical cooperation and by providing markets. In this respect the structures of the countries of different type could complement each other. Considering also the "Janus-faced" nature of Soviet economy, we may claim this complementarity as almost perfect. The commodity flows developing between the CMEA countries were the same as generally among the advanced industrialized and the less industrialized countries anywhere. From the more developed countries manufactured articles, mainly means of production, were flowing into the less developed ones. The latter balanced the trade initially with less processed industrial and agricultural materials and food.

Thus, the division of labour apparently developed according to the classical Ricardian principles. In fact, the composition of the imports of the less developed countries foreshadowed the upsetting of the Ricardian division of labour. Namely, according to the classical principle of comparative costs, the less developed countries should have imported, above all, means of production which intensify their existing comparative advantages, i.e., mining, agricultural, food-industrial and—perhaps—metallurgical equipment. As a matter of fact, a considerable part of the means of production imported were not suited for the development of those branches of production in which these countries had "original" comparative advantages, but for developing such new industries in which they could not even hope to attain the lowest limit of competitivity, at least in the short and medium run, let alone comparative advantages in a world economy based on competition. In the CMEA countries which started with a handicap machine building, electrical engineering manufacturing, transport equipment, instrumentation and chemical industries developed. It should not be forgotten that this took place in the second half of the 20th century, at a time when these branches had been raised to a high level already several decades before in about two dozen countries of the world which could supply the world market competitively with their mass products.

It should be clearer that, under such conditions, in the less developed countries it was necessary to secure very strong protection for the maintenance and development of the emerging new industries. And this not only on the internal markets, but on the market of the whole community as well. Protection could not have been provided through any kind of traditional instrument—customs duties, subsidies, etc.—nor through the quota systems known in capitalist world economy. Much more drastic measures were needed: the undertaking of mutual selling and purchasing *obligations*. The less developed countries undertook obligatorily to satisfy the needs of the more developed ones for basic materials and food and, in exchange, the more developed ones undertook to purchase the manufactured products of the less developed ones, at highly favourable prices.

In order to realize all this, the demand and supply effects induced by the microsphere, and less conspicuous from the viewpoint of economic strategy, had to be eliminated from mutual economic cooperation. If, namely, the economic exchange between the CMEA countries had been regulated in those times by demand and supply relations, the products of the new industries of the less developed countries could have been sold—even with the maximum of national protection—only in the narrow domestic markets. And, with the exception of the Soviet Union, these domestic markets are not of a size in any of these countries that would allow to implement industrialization on an economic scale from the beginning. However, the latter was a basic condition for such a rapid development in the CMEA countries that were lagging behind in industrialization which promised doing away with backwardness in the longer perspective.

Socialist cooperation brought about such a peculiar system of economic protection which is unique in world history. The maximum performance of the classical bourgeois national systems of economic protection was to protect the *internal* market against foreign competition. The maximum performance of collective economic protective systems of an integrational character, e.g. the Common Market, is to defend the market of the region against competitive effects from outside the region. But it is not their task to protect the less developed countries or less developed areas of the region against the competition of the more advanced countries or industrialized areas of the region. Thus, bourgeois protectionism means either the fight of an abandoned weaker economy against the outer world, or the collective attack of strong sectors of several countries on the weaker ones within and outside the region in order to gain economic power. The basic feature of the CMEA was to make the *national industrial development* of the small industrializing countries, with relatively weak production potentials, the *common cause of the whole community*. This is why it created markets for the emerging new industries and secured safe supply for economies poor in raw materials, and increased development possibilities deriving from the size of the community available to all. This is the secret which made it possible that very strong cooperation links should develop between countries with relatively big differences in development levels and between big and small economies which not only did not disturb, but even promoted the development of the weaker ones.

This mechanism and the regional development model emerging with its aid was satisfactory for all three types of countries and secured mutual advantages as long as the strategic changes aimed at did not take place in the economic structure of the community. The less developed countries obtained the necessary technical equipment, production experience and markets needed for their realization as well as increasing amounts of raw materials. The development of their industries did not start with a small-scale framework and did not grow into large-scale structures in the process of concentration and centralization sharpened by competition—this could not have been successfully accomplished any longer in the second half of the 20th century—but in a medium which undertook to create markets for the products of their newly established industrial plants even in the case when these, initially, did not fully come up to the requirements of the world market.

Market opened for the manufacturing industries of the more developed countries and, in exchange, their raw-material and food supply was secured. It is true that while the earlier industrialized CMEA countries spread their forces of production, their technological "monopoly" ceased gradually in the other countries. But their growth, faster than the world average, relied precisely on that; the less developed countries had to be provided with the knowledge and technology they had possessed themselves until then.

There is no such bourgeois world-economic model which would not qualify this activity as insane in the long run. In capitalist world economy everyone who transplants his own technical knowledge to other countries on the same level, creates competitors for himself and risks his inherited and acquired advantages. But the experience of cooperation within the CMEA proves that the flow of higher development standards into other countries *does not necessarily create competitors under socialist relations, but rather cooperating partners.* It may raise whole countries to a level where the division of labour brings essentially more fruitful results also for the earlier industrialized countries. The socialist social order, which denies competition *against* each other and whose vital medium is cooperation, could produce such transfer of technology where the *loss of development monopoly turned not into a disadvantage but into a potential advantage of the partner who had brought itself to it.* The Bulgarian, Romanian, Polish or Hungarian economies which had hardly possessed manufacturing industries under the capitalist system, became production partners in machinery and chemical of such traditionally industrial countries as the GDR or Czechoslovakia and established many-sided and fruitful division of labour with such an industrial big power as the Soviet Union.

It became possible for the USSR to abandon the autarkic model of economic development forced upon it by its earlier history. It could establish division of labour with a significant group of countries. Furthermore, cooperation with the CMEA partners facilitated the quick introduction of several such industries, processes and technologies for whose development it had neither energy nor possibility in the former decades.

In the final analysis, this process worked towards levelling from two directions. On the one hand, the less developed countries quickly increased the share of those industries in which their labour productivity was acknowledged to be higher than in their traditional industries both on the international and the domestic markets. On the other hand, the efficiency of the newly introduced industries was high from the outset, because of the cheap material supply and the massive export possibilities guaranteed under long-term agreements. Thus, the mutual approach of levels manifested itself partly in the approximation of structures, and partly in that of the technological equipment levels. Agricultural employment rapidly fell in every industrializing socialist country, while the ratio of those employed in the manufacturing industries, which are the carriers of technical progress, quickly increased within the economically active population. In 1960 in Bulgaria, the ratio of those employed in the engineering and the chemical industries did not attain 20 per cent of the economically active population (the corresponding figures were 43.8 per cent in the GDR, and 36 per cent in Czechoslovakia); by 1970 it already exceeded 27 per cent. Electric energy used by a worker in Bulgaria was, in 1960, two-fifths of that in the GDR, and in Romania it was half of it; by 1970 the corresponding values increased to two-thirds and four-fifths, respectively. (The parallel development of the Polish and the Hungarian economies with the German one is proved by the fact that in the sixties they could not overtake the GDR level in respect of either the ratio of those employed in the industries which are carriers of modern technology, nor as regards energy consumption per industrial worker.)

Economic measurements make the assumption probable that the structural factor was more important in the approximation of levels than the second-mentioned factor. The increase in the volume of fixed assets preceded the growth of live labour productivity in many productive branches. In about half of the productive branches of the CMEA countries a diminishing efficiency of fixed assets could be established in the course of measurements, in one-third of the cases this attained 8 per cent. Improvement in efficiency could be found in 36 per cent of the industries surveyed, of which 26 per cent exceeded an 8 per cent improvement. (It should be noted that the fastest increase in productivity can be measured in the engineering industries of the newly industrializing countries. But we know from experience that this fast growth is partly only apparent to an unknown degree and derives from overpricing new products.) The productivity-increasing effect of technological equipment was strongly hampered because of the inexperience in using new technology, in planning development, in organizing work, and also because of fragmentation of micro-structures and investments, parallel development of capacities, and low indication in developing production, that is, by all the unfavourable phenomena which accompanied the industrialization of East-European socialist countries. This is the reason why the differences of per capita national income of the East-European socialist countries are somewhat greater than would be justified by the differences in economic and, particularly, in industrial structures.

Thus, industrialization secured a huge source for growth also for the country which created the new structure, since it could channel its factors of production into industries whose products were judged to be "more valuable" by both domestic and international markets than those of the traditional industries, and also for the country which provided the possibility for this structural transformation by exporting machinery and equipment. It acquired wide and quickly expanding markets for the products of its productive activities which were judged to be valuable also in the world exchange of commodities. This did secure firm motivation both for the earlier industrialized and the newly industrializing countries of the CMEA in the stage of evolving industrialization.

Of course, in spite of all this one should not believe that economic cooperation in the first decade of industrialization was a state of Paradise, free of contradictions and tensions. Quite a few of the latter existed. The contradictions were focussed on the manufactured products to be exported of the less developed countries, mainly on the products of the industries which were carriers of modern technology. The greater the claims of the less developed countries became to export machinery and equipment to the more developed ones, the sharper became the problems deriving from the poor technological parameters, the unsatisfactory quality of the products and the laggard servicing accompanying them. As formulated in classical terms, the products of the new industries in the less developed countries were not competitive on the markets of the more advanced countries, their use did not sufficiently raise efficiency in the latter countries on either national or enterprise levels. Not infrequently it seemed to be worthwhile to produce parallelly these products, originally "assigned" to the less developed countries, because domestic small-series production—uneconomical in itself—was still more favourable than purchase of poor-quality products, released by the young, inexperienced industries. At the same time, the need of the newly industrializing countries to export their manufactured products became so pressing that they began to render their raw-material and food-supply commitments increasingly dependent on the former. The phenomenon of "linking" needed to unrequired exports began to emerge on a mass scale, a sure sign that the harmony of mutual interests was upset.

d) Tensions caused by differences in development level between member countries in the present stage of development

The more the macro-structures approached each other, that is, the more competitive the originally complementary structure of the economies became, the more unstable the unity of interests of more and less advanced CMEA countries became. By the mid-sixties the industrial structures were *already* strongly matched, but the productivity levels and technical cultures of the manufacturing industries did *not yet* come near enough to trigger a closer industrial intertwining—and a rebirth of the unity of interests—on micro-levels.

In the sixties a certain approximation appeared among the similar industries of the member countries in respect of *efficiency*. The changes in the efficiency indicators of industries may somewhat contribute to understanding the trends in the aggregated indicators of the development levels (see Table 7).

It may be observed that, in about half of the industries examined, the level of per unit inputs approached that in the GDR. The engineering and the light industries, employing great amounts of labour, were catching up with the most developed GDR level in Poland, Bulgaria and Romania. In the case of Poland this was counterbalanced by the relative lag in agriculture. The Soviet advance to the GDR level is explained by the quick increase in efficiency partly in agriculture and partly in the basic-material producing industries. The detrimental factor in the stagnation of the Czechoslovak and the Hungarian economies relative to the growth rate of the GDR was the slack development of efficiency in the extracting and engineering industries, which was barely counterbalanced by the relatively fast increase of efficiency in agriculture. But the fact that in the sixties the lag in efficiency occurred in the industries producing means of production foreshadows—if this tendency continues—a lag based on the obsolescence of the technical culture—which is difficult to make up for.

Altogether, the development of *identical* industries within the CMEA shows rather more levelling than polarizing tendencies.

But the sometimes slack and uneven levelling tendency which can be read from the international comparison of the development of identical industries involves, at the same time, the spreading differences in efficiency within a country among different industries. This phenomenon, however, usually makes the conditions for cooperation difficult.

Tensions between industries are the strongest *precisely in those countries where the particular industries have approached the GDR level—which is considered to be the peak within the CMEA*—the most, that is, in Bulgaria, Romania and Poland; though the other economies are also characterized rather by growing differences in efficiency than by levelling. This, too, is a difficult problem.

Table 7

Social input in some productive branches of the CMEA countries, relative to the input in the same branches in the GDR.*
(Values smaller than 100 indicate higher, values bigger than 100, lower inputs than in the GDR.)

Productive branches	Soviet Union		Czechoslovakia		Poland		Hungary		Bulgaria		Romania	
	1960	1969	1960	1969	1960	1969	1960	1969	1960	1969	1960	1969
Engineering	80	79	103	116	186	167	176	193	245	205	191	149
Production of fuels	95	88	108	374	143	143	246	253	305	271	228	197
Ferrous metallurgy	60	55	98	107	162	147	195	192	416	417	174	240
Non-ferrous metallurgy	91	90	135	167	239	237	213	240	500	550	338	369
Chemical industry	122	128	118	100	266	222	270	238	279	243	251	162
Construction materials industry	121	119	120	118	239	231	188	226	213	182	231	202
Agriculture	212	192	124	92	211	244	164	143	220	184	360	295
Food industry	127	137	107	110	212	244	166	168	196	162	267	244
Textile industry	144	173	89	117	144	145	128	156	176	205	157	169
Other light industry	111	115	95	141	193	182	186	204	187	160	147	117

* Per unit social inputs are used as indicators of efficiency. They express the man-years necessary in the whole vertical chain of the production process necessary to produce end products for final use worth one million transferable roubles, inclusive of the labour demand of producing fixed assets returned in the year, as well as that of the export products necessary to balance the products imported for productive use.

Within the economy of any country, productive forces of the most diverse levels coexist and are interlinked and interdependent. The forces of production of different development levels establish inter-industry relationships asserting themselves in the commodity relationships. These productive forces pertaining to different development levels bring about a technical and economic interrelation burdened by tensions. The growth rate of such an economy with heterogeneous forces of production is finally determined by the character and size of the sectors carrying developed forces of production, and the rate at which these sectors can draw the others after themselves.

The relative backwardness of an economy (the presence of obsolete technology, scanty mechanization, insufficient know-how, relatively low degree of skills, and lack of organizing talent), however, will restrict the sphere in which higher forces of production can be introduced.

There exists a technical structure of the economy which expresses the weight of the forces of production which are in different stages of development in the whole economy. The technical structure of an economy might be considered completely optimal if the more developed sectors help the less developed ones in their progress. In reality, of course, perfection cannot be found, but the structure is near to the optimum if those forces of production are present which, as if by chain reaction, can draw after themselves the lagging ones, if there are no gaps between the forces of production on different development levels, if mutual smooth relationships are secured.

The technical structure is not independent of other factors in the development of the economy. It is influenced by the general development level of the economy, its industrial structure, the size of the country, as well as by the degree and mode of participation in the international division of labour.

The actual structure of the economies which are industrialized at an accelerated rate mostly differs from the ideal one. There may exist, for instance, such a modern economic sector which is above the average by two or three phases, as a result of the import of technology or of an exceptional centralization of the internal research and development apparatus and of accumulation. In this case there is grave danger that the modern sector becomes detached from the economic background, its maintenance either requiring continued external capital and technical resources or a continual systematic regrouping of the resources of the economy—at the expense of raising the general level. Such an economy may be said to have a "technically overstressed structure".[14]

Such an economy is characterized by a high rate of accumulation, a strong lag of personal consumption behind the growth rate of the national income,

[14] In extreme cases we may speak of "dual economy".

a gap between industry and agriculture, as well as an abyss between the bulk of the industry and the sector causing the tension. All that leads to a dynamic growth which is, however, unbalanced and periodically increases the tensions in the economy. The overstressed economy handles with difficulty the thresholds of qualitative stages of development, even if the pioneering forces of production develop in the most dynamic industries. Namely, the technical influence of the pioneering sector on the bulk of the economy is insufficient because of the large gap in the respective development levels. The pioneering sector, instead of helping the lagging average economy (with technology, tools of labour, expertise, organization methods, means of accumulation, etc.), rather hinders its development, since it relies on the less developed sectors in respect of accumulation, supply of materials and labour replacement.

The other distorted type is represented by economies where the development of the forces of production progresses in too small steps. Transition to a level slightly above average takes place at a moderate rate but on a wide terrain. This structure may be said to be "without tension". The advantage of such an economy is relative stability, the possibility of maintaining an equilibrium without major shocks. Its disadvantage is the lack of internal dynamism, which results in the fact that it can show a relatively fast growth rate only in the stages of quantitative growth while development is slowed down before qualitative leaps: the sector which would be able to raise the economy to the next stage of development is missing.

Thus, a too homogeneous technological level has a similar breaking effect on the economy as too heterogeneous sectors with widely different development levels.

No general recipe can be given as to what should be the percentage distribution of sectors representing different development levels in an economy, or what their industrial distribution should be. It is, however, a rather general experience that the implantation of a sector exceeding the general development level of the basic sectors of the economy (in the CMEA countries: of the industry) by two qualitative degrees will already cause overtensions. The complete lack of a level higher by two degrees causes development to be "without tensions", and a lagging of agriculture two degrees behind the level characteristic of industry may become a strong brake on the development of the forces of production.

Let us denote—to facilitate further discussion—the development level characteristic of the bulk of industry by n. The technical structure of industry will be accordingly

$$a_{n+2}+b_{n+1} = c_n+d_{n-1} = 100.$$

This means that a per cent of industry is on a level two degrees higher than the bulk of industry, b per cent is on a level higher by one degree etc. The a, b, c

and d weights are empirical figures to be derived from the input—output tables, the established ratios of the labour structure and of accumulation and consumption.

The lower the general level of technology n, the smaller the ratio of pioneering sectors a can be. If, e.g. in some country a low level of industrial development is characteristic, if basic mechanization is just starting and the dynamic sectors are missing, there are only slight possibilities for the creation of automated productive units organically linked to the whole of the economy. If the economy does not make use even of this slight possibility, it will become lazy, lacking tension; if it exceeds it, it will become over-tense, with all the consequences involved.

It is an important condition of the dynamic pulling effect that in the sectors of the development level $n+2$ and $n+1$ the share of the industries carrying technological progress, that is, of energetics, metallurgy, engineering, chemical industry and construction, should be adequate. If this condition is not met, technical progress will spread slowly to the less developed sectors. The economy which satisfies this requirement may be said to have a "proportionately tense structure".

It is well known that the equilibrium of an economy is the less stable the greater the differences in efficiency between its industries, e.g. the more backward the agriculture on which a newly established industry relies. In such national economies a high rate of growth can be secured through the maximum increase of non-agricultural employment. A worker in industry or construction, etc., can increase productivity quickly and simultaneously expand the market, both as a producer and as a consumer. Structural transformation thus "gears up" growth from both the productivity and the market aspects. This is the basic principle of socialist industrialization. But if this structural transformation puts excessive pressure on the resources for accumulation, it will unavoidably lead to overtension in the markets of food and industrial consumer goods, because the technological equipment of agriculture and light industry does not keep pace.

If the 1969 columns of Table 8 are examined, it will be found that the efficiency differential between particular industries is different in the various CMEA countries. The dispersion is greatest in the Soviet economy, where the individual industries show values between 0.4 and 2.5-fold of the national economic average. The standard deviation is 4.11. The Romanian and the Bulgarian economies with a standard deviation of 2.85 and 2.38 show a more levelled picture, while the values of 2.13 and 1.91 of the Polish and the Czechoslovak economies reveal a moderate tension. It seems that the GDR economy is best balanced with a coefficient of 1.03, and here we find a more or less healthy relationship between the industries which are less and those which are more efficient than the average.

Table 8

Deviation of the efficiency indicators of some productive branches from the industrial-agricultural average in 1960 and 1969

Productive branches	USSR		GDR		Czechoslovakia		Poland		Hungary		Bulgaria		Romania	
	1960	1969	1960	1969	1960	1969	1960	1969	1960	1969	1960	1969	1960	1969
Engineering	46	37	70	60	66	51	66	50	66	60	66	49	55	40
Fuel industry	57	60	75	86	75	207	55	62	101	113	88	93	71	75
Non-ferrous metallurgy	62	64	85	90	106	111	104	106	99	111	163	195	120	146
Ferrous metallurgy	41	46	87	107	78	86	71	79	92	107	139	178	63	114
Chemical industry	68	63	70	62	76	46	96	68	103	77	75	59	73	45
Construction material industry	84	76	87	80	95	138	106	93	89	94	71	57	84	72
Textile industry	160	176	140	128	114	112	96	99	94	104	96	105	92	97
Other light industry	82	77	93	84	81	88	91	76	93	88	66	53	57	44
Food industry	141	159	138	147	136	120	151	179	125	128	103	95	142	160
Agriculture	256	240	154	157	176	109	166	192	137	117	132	115	231	207
Approximation to the average	24 points		31 points		130 points		25 points		43 points		31 points		70 points	
Departure from the average	61 points		51 points		195 points		121 points		71 points		139 points		126 points	
Increase (+) or decrease (−) in the structural tension of efficiency	+37 points		+20 points		+65 points		+96 points		+28 points		+108 points		+56 points	

The 0.37 indicator of the Hungarian economy seems again to be exaggerated—this time in the opposite direction (see Figure 19).

Another danger of an "over-tense" industrial structure is that the fast development of the dynamically increased industries is not accompanied by the needed quality and technological features, and thus the export capacity of manufacturing diminishes all the more because production traditions are missing while the qualification of labour and the organizing ability of cadres is not sufficiently high. The technological equipment of agriculture, the development of the light industry, the supply of materials, and the modernization of the heavy industry all assert themselves in a cumulative manner towards the end of the first period of fast industrialization. However, the national economies are not yet in a position to satisfy simultaneously all these pressing requirements. Thus, the end of the first industrialization period sharpens the internal growth and equilibrium problems in each country. The faster a country was industrialized, and the more blank spots there remained in the quickly developed industrial structure, and the more industrialization aimed at quickly increasing the non-agricultural workplaces, the sharper and more pressing these problems will become. Curiously, in the fast industrialized countries, the faster their development had been, the sharper the problems of further development are. The rapidity of growth does not reduce their economic troubles, the feeling of a "low development level" does not disappear in either the population or the economic leadership.

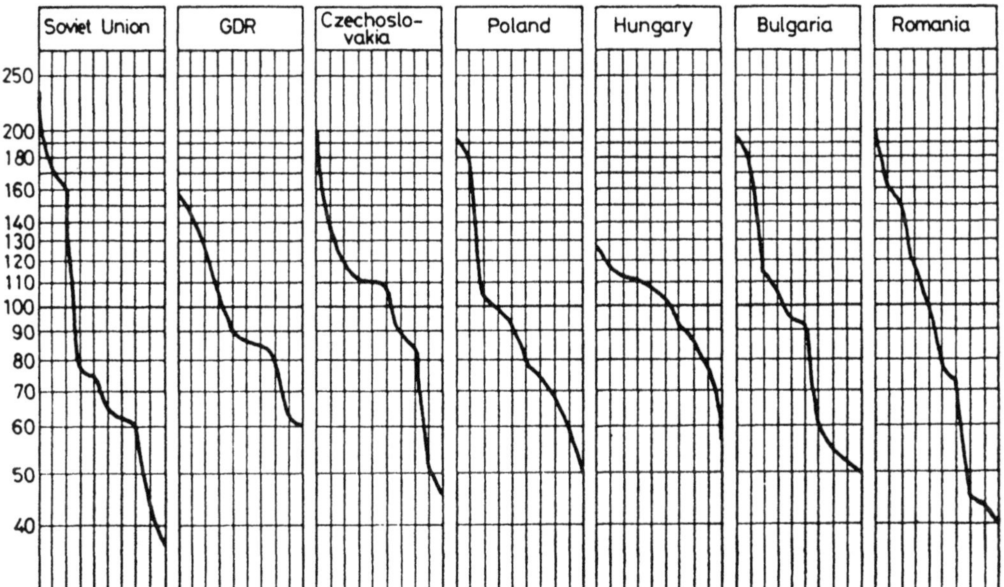

Fig. 19. Distribution of efficiency by industries, national average = 100

Source: The author's computations

An interesting conclusion will be arrived at, if the *territorial* dispersion of development levels within countries is analysed (see Figure 20). Of course, one cannot find a country made up of equally developed areas, regions, thus we would, in vain, look for such an international region either. Both Western Europe and the socialist Eastern Europe are diversified conglomerates of more and less developed areas. But a survey of the UN relating to 1968 shows that in Western Europe—not counting the countries of the Mediterranean periphery—there are only two regions where the productivity of social labour does not attain seven-tenths of the average European level (Southern Italy with the islands, as well as Northwestern Ireland), while in big interrelated areas it is higher by 30 per cent. In the socialist Eastern Europe we find four major regions (Eastern Poland, the Southern and Eastern parts of Romania, Southern Bulgaria, and four Middle-Asian republics of the USSR), where the productivity of social labour is below 70 per cent of the European average. On the other hand, a considerable part of the GDR, the Bohemian Basin, as well as two Baltic republics of the USSR and the Middle-Russian industrial region show productivities above the European average, i.e. 110 per cent. (See Figure 21)

If we consider not only the area, but also the number of population living there, we arrive at Table 9.

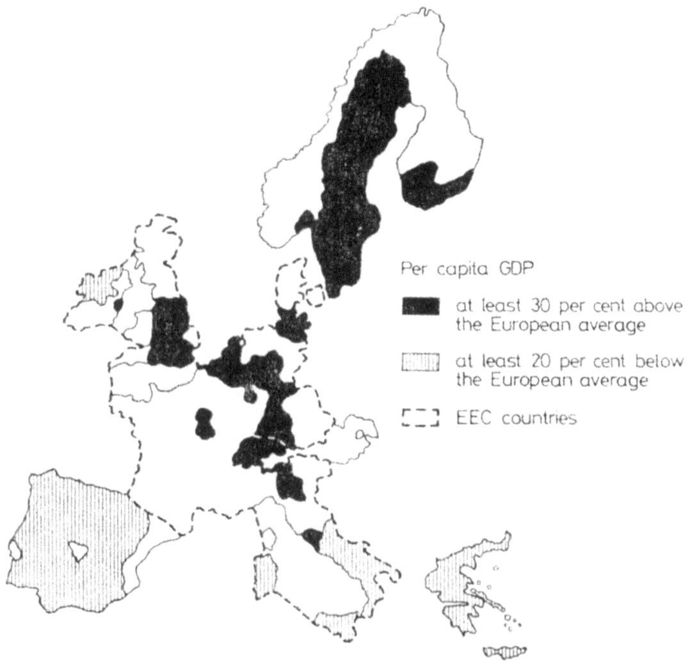

Fig. 20. Backward and developed areas in Western Europe, 1968

Source: The EEC Region in figures, UN New York, 1972

In the majority of CMEA member countries the population is dispersed along a wide scale between relatively higher and lower developed areas. These areas differ not only as regards the working conditions, but also as regards the general living circumstances. Similar phenomena may be found in only a few of the

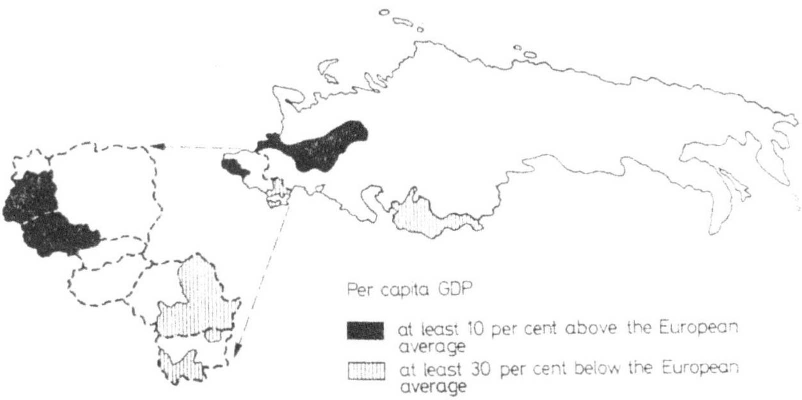

Fig. 21. Backward and developed areas in Eastern Europe, 1968

Source: The EEC Region in figures, UN New York, 1972

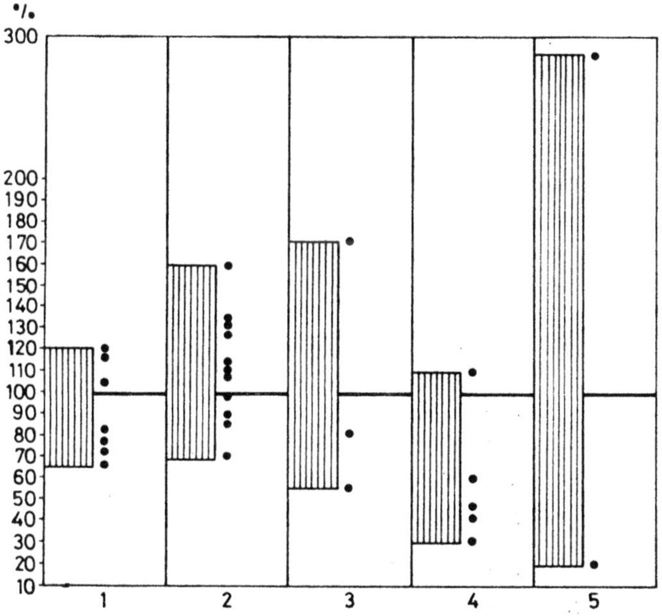

Fig. 22. Dispersion of per capita national income in various regions of the world economy, 1969, weighted average of the given group of countries = 100

Table 9

Position of the population of European socialist and capitalist countries in areas with different development levels, 1968, per cent

Regions where per capita national income produced is	European periphery					Socialist countries						Developed European capitalist countries											
	Turkey	Portugal	Spain	Greece	Ireland	Romania	Bulgaria	Poland	Hungary	Soviet Union	Czechoslovakia	GDR	Italy	Austria	Finland	Norway	France	Denmark	GFR	Belgium–Luxemburg	The Netherlands	United Kingdom	Switzerland	Sweden
— much below the European average	93	45	52	12	—	32	—	—	—	1	—	—	—	—	—	—	—	—	—	—	—	—	—	—
— below the European average	7	32	48	59	21	68	82	45	41	33	—	—	36	—	—	—	—	—	—	—	—	—	—	—
— around the European average	—	—	—	29	51	—	18	45	59	54	31	12	31	69	43	21	20	—	—	—	—	3	—	21
— above the European average	—	23	—	—	28	—	—	—	—	22	69	88	33	10	57	66	62	100	82	81	53	57	82	66
— high above the European average	—	—	—	—	—	—	—	—	—	—	—	—	—	21	—	13	18	—	18	19	47	40	18	13

European countries with capitalist social systems, and not accidentally in those where development conditions show features similar to those in CMEA countries prior to socialism.

It might be said with some simplification that the fields between the fast developing industrial regions of Eastern Europe are filled with "mezzogiorni". The process of levelling has not ended even within the particular countries, it has not even reached its middle phase. This, too, endangers the internal equilibrium of the countries.

Knowing all this, one can find an explanation for an extremely curious phenomenon. If the per capita national incomes of CMEA countries are compared, it may be found that the difference in development level between the most advanced and the least developed European CMEA countries is *much less than in other parts of the world economy.* This difference is, e.g., much smaller than the one between the USA and the West-European developed capitalist economies, or between the latter and the medium-developed countries of the Mediterranean area, or between the USA and Japan, not to mention the differences between the developed and the developing countries.

As regards per capita national incomes, in the early seventies the CMEA seems to be one of the most homogeneous regions of the world economy. If only these data are considered, it does not seem self-evident why the elimination of differences in development level stands in the forefront of the whole economic policy conception of the CMEA. If, however, we also consider *the differences between sectoral efficiencies and in development levels between areas* due to historically inherited *sectoral and regional structural tensions*, as well as those that emerged in consequence of the fast rate of socialist industrialization, it will become understandable why, in spite of the relatively homogeneous regional levels and the measurable tendency of levelling, the matching of development levels will remain one of the basic elements in CMEA cooperation also in the future. Namely, these tensions of internal equilibrium and growth can be overcome only with difficulty by relying merely on internal material and intellectual resources. It is a vital interest of the member countries to include, by joining the international division of labour, also *actual external sources* into development, that is, to raise credits and to attain price gains. Furthermore, it is important for them to find such methods in the course of specialization *which save above all investments*, since the existing internal sources of accumulation have to be used first of all for eliminating the cumulated sectoral and regional disproportions, while securing fast growth and full employment, and helping the modernization of the productive machinery.

CHAPTER SIX

Rearrangement of the advantages derived from the division of labour in the course of industrialization

In the preceding chapters we have already mentioned that the motivation of the more developed CMEA countries to cooperate with the less developed ones decreases the more they are compelled to buy the manufactured articles of the latter in exchange for their own manufactured goods, particularly machinery and equipment. I may also add that the whole industrial development program of the more developed socialist countries was partially adapted in the last decades to the industrialization needs of the less developed countries and regions. This, too, contributed to the fact that the world-market competitivity of their manufacturing industries did not keep pace with the extension of their industries. Thus, the earlier developed countries found themselves in a situation where the marketing possibilities of their manufactured products became concentrated to the CMEA area, similarly to those of the later developing ones.

At the same time, parallel to this tendency, both the earlier developed countries and *those industrializing in the last decades* have attained the critical development level where the problems of economic policy can be solved not so much by regrouping the agricultural population with low skills to industrial workplaces, but through a continuous technological development of the whole national economy. The later developed countries are not yet able to meet these new demands. And the earlier developed countries have become too specialized in supplying industrialization with the means of production and, therefore, they, too, cannot satisfactorily meet the increased qualitative demands for either themselves or for their CMEA partners.

Viewed from the side of the more developed economies, the common interests based on the complementary structures of the fifties *were embodied in the classical comparative advantages*. By becoming the main suppliers of machinery and equipment to the CMEA countries starting to industrialize, they boosted the least fixed capital-intensive industries and those which seemed to be the "most productive" because of fetching high prices, so that these became preponderant. The big and ever increasing export of manufactured articles, mainly of machinery and equipment, replaced in these economies the extractive activities, hence they could avoid considerable advances of capital. All that entailed great comparative advantages for the earlier developed CMEA countries. They used an important part of this advantage for expanding the manufacturing industries. The result was an *even greater number* of "accessories of industrialization", demanding and making possible even greater imports of raw and basic materials.

As regards the economies starting with a bigger handicap in development, their interests became realized mainly through putting to work the imported industrial means of production, that is, as advantages of adaptation. The equipments received in exchange for the raw materials and food, produced with relatively low efficiency in international comparison, allowed the fast expansion of a manufacturing industry of relatively high efficiency, as a consequence of which they had a greater gain in national economic efficiency than the possible comparative disadvantage in the actual commodity exchange. At the same time, following from the *socialist* nature of cooperation, the countries with less developed forces of production were not compelled to squeeze the scope of imported technology into the development of the sectors which were momentarily the most efficient. The Hungarian imports of technology were not restricted to the mechanization of the production of bauxite or wheat, nor the Romanian ones to that of oil and natural gas. The newly developed industries *copied* the technological level—and partly also the production pattern—of the industries of the earlier developed countries, they multiplied them in CMEA dimensions. This development made its way also in the efforts to level *export structures*, particularly in the sixties.

The accounting of comparative advantages was based first of all on the total domestic input necessary for producing a unit of foreign currency for export, as against the domestic input of import-substitution. While in the fifties Bulgaria and Romania had hardly any basis for comparing the extracting and manufacturing activities, in the sixties almost every country possessed a manufacturing industry which provided realistic bases for computing and comparing the domestic inputs of export activities and import savings necessary for earning or saving a unit of foreign currency. The *G* indicators already showed that for earning a unit of foreign currency more social labour had to be expended in the extracting industries than in manufacturing and that a considerable part of the surplus derives from higher investment demands. Therefore, the countries exporting mainly raw or partially processed products and importing mainly highly processed manufactured ones had to book comparative losses. The computations of Table 11 show this tendency already for 1960.

The method of the computations agrees with what was described in Part Two. Figures higher than unity indicate comparative losses, that is, the country in question expended more social labour on the aggregate of exported products

Table 10

Changes in the commodity pattern of exports in the sixties

I. Countries interested in a 1:1 tendency

Bulgaria

Commodity groups	1960					
	Hungary	GDR	Poland	Romania	USSR	Czechoslovakia
A	30.5	3.0	1.6	3.2	16.4	24.0
B	20.7	4.4	18.5	17.1	8.9	12.2
C	11.8	—	0.1	5.5	2.0	0.8
D	0.5	0.4	—	1.4	0.4	1.2
E	9.1	38.3	43.4	14.3	17.1	23.8
F	23.2	48.7	32.6	49.3	27.3	36.4
G	4.2	5.2	3.8	9.2	27.6	1.6

Romania

Commodity groups	1960					
	Bulgaria	Hungary	GDR	Poland	USSR	Czechoslovakia
A	9.0	20.2	44.6	20.7	8.7	20.4
B	41.7	29.2	10.3	46.8	52.0	23.6
C	0.7	6.0	—	2.1	1.9	4.1
D	0.7	2.0	0.9	5.7	3.7	2.9
E	0.6	21.6	16.8	11.1	19.2	19.3
F	37.2	15.8	22.6	11.5	4.9	27.1
G	10.1	5.2	4.8	2.0	9.6	2.6

Poland

Commodity groups	1960					
	Bulgaria	Hungary	GDR	Romania	USSR	Czechoslovakia
A	54.8	35.4	25.9	32.5	40.2	38.6
B	31.5	44.3	63.9	42.6	33.6	50.3
C	3.3	7.4	0.6	4.8	1.7	2.3
D	0.4	1.0	—	0.5	0.4	1.1
E	1.2	5.0	2.2	7.2	1.3	1.5
F	—	0.7	5.9	5.7	5.3	3.4
G	6.8	6.2	1.5	6.7	17.5	2.8

USSR

Commodity groups	1960					
	Bulgaria	Hungary	GDR	Poland	Romania	Czechoslovakia
A	33.0	22.7	3.5	11.2	22.0	9.6
B	24.3	33.7	48.2	38.6	51.2	34.8
C	6.0	3.5	3.0	1.9	5.3	3.3
D	0.6	—	—	0.1	0.5	0.1
E	13.4	26.3	28.1	25.7	13.3	31.3
F	2.0	2.2	7.9	4.1	0.5	6.1
G	7.4	2.6	0.9	6.7	3.7	2.1

Bulgaria

Commodity groups	1969					
	Hungary	GDR	Poland	Romania	USSR	Czechoslovakia
A	47.4	34.8	49.3	45.4	29.3	31.6
B	9.3	1.0	5.2	16.8	3.8	6.7
C	9.7	3.7	0.6	5.0	1.3	1.9
D	2.1	1.0	0.1	0.7	1.1	1.3
E	9.0	5.5	2.9	2.7	9.3	14.3
F	12.8	49.1	30.7	22.2	32.9	36.3
G	9.7	4.6	11.2	7.2	22.3	7.9

Romania

Commodity groups	1969					
	Bulgaria	Hungary	GDR	Poland	USSR	Czechoslovakia
A	63.9	31.6	37.2	40.0	20.7	22.6
B	17.6	11.6	9.3	43.8	20.0	25.9
C	1.2	12.9	6.8	1.2	6.0	5.9
D	3.3	13.1	3.2	2.0	1.2	10.4
E	1.2	11.1	7.8	1.1	11.3	8.1
F	5.4	6.7	27.3	6.4	8.0	19.4
G	7.4	13.0	8.4	5.5	32.8	7.7

Poland

Commodity groups	1969					
	Bulgaria	Hungary	GDR	Romania	USSR	Czechoslovakia
A	64.8	42.8	52.5	47.8	52.5	56.7
B	13.6	35.0	27.3	38.5	16.5	22.1
C	3.7	3.6	2.5	0.9	4.1	1.4
D	0.9	0.8	0.7	0.2	—	2.7
E	2.4	2.8	5.1	1.5	0.8	1.9
F	2.0	5.1	4.2	2.0	1.6	2.8
G	13.4	9.9	7.1	9.1	24.5	12.4

USSR

Commodity groups	1969					
	Bulgaria	Hungary	GDR	Poland	Romania	Czechoslovakia
A	36,5	18.3	18.1	19.0	31.1	14.8
B	36.6	39.9	40.3	40.4	40.0	47.1
C	4.7	8.1	3.9	2.5	4.0	5.0
D	0.6	2.0	0.5	0.9	0.5	0.7
E	11.3	21.5	17.9	15.6	5.4	17.4
F	2.9	2.5	6.1	2.8	1.0	4.3
G	4.4	2.8	0.8	2.6	2.0	1.5

GDR

Commodity groups	1960					
	Bulgaria	Hungary	Poland	Romania	USSR	Czechoslovakia
A	67.3	51.5	45.2	69.8	59.1	49.5
B	1.4	8.6	11.9	6.0	20.1	10.0
C	12.1	15.9	23.5	9.7	6.8	22.0
D	1.4	2.9	0.7	0.5	0.3	2.0
E	3.3	6.0	3.5	3.2	1.0	2.6
F	1.6	0.9	2.7	0.2	0.2	0.5
G	12.9	14.2	12.5	10.6	12.5	13.4

Czechoslovakia

Commodity groups	1960					
	Bulgaria	Hungary	GDR	Poland	Romania	USSR
A	52.6	38.8	37.9	56.6	46.6	49.2
B	24.9	37.7	25.9	26.5	38.0	18.0
C	2.9	3.3	4.6	1.7	1.4	1.3
D	2.0	2.7	1.1	2.0	2.6	0.3
E	0.1	5.4	4.0	2.4	3.7	0.9
F	0.2	0.4	3.6	0.3	0.2	3.4
G	8.3	10.7	22.7	10.5	7.5	26.9

Hungary

Commodity groups	1960					
	Bulgaria	GDR	Poland	Romania	USSR	Czechoslovakia
A	52.4	32.6	35.1	32.1	58.2	37.0
B	26.9	10.6	29.0	38.5	6.4	20.7
C	3.3	0.2	1.2	2.5	3.3	1.3
D	1.3	0.4	1.3	3.6	—	1.0
E	3.0	8.0	7.2	6.8	3.1	7.8
F	0.3	31.9	5.8	1.7	5.8	27.9
G	12.8	16.3	20.4	15.0	23.2	4.3

A = Engineering products
B = Minerals and primary energy
C = Chemical products
D = Construction materials

GDR

Commodity groups	1969					
	Bulgaria	Hungary	Poland	Romania	USSR	Czechoslovakia
A	64.2	64.9	49.9	64.1	59.5	60.7
B	3.1	7.1	10.7	12.3	11.6	5.9
C	16.4	10.9	14.7	11.5	5.3	13.9
D	0.6	2.0	0.5	0.5	0.4	0.9
E	2.8	2.0	6.7	1.6	1.1	1.6
F	1.3	0.6	0.2	1.8	—	1.2
G	11.6	12.5	17.3	8.2	22.1	15.8

Czechoslovakia

Commodity groups	1969					
	Bulgaria	Hungary	GDR	Poland	Romania	USSR
A	70.2	46.1	59.2	67.3	57.5	61.3
B	11.5	24.5	19.1	17.4	27.0	12.1
C	4.7	5.1	3.6	4.0	2.8	4.3
D	1.8	5.0	1.8	2.1	4.7	0.4
E	2.3	6.2	2.6	3.2	1.5	1.4
F	0.7	2.6	1.0	0.5	0.8	0.9
G	8.8	10.5	12.7	5.5	5.9	19.6

Hungary

Commodity groups	1969					
	Bulgaria	GDR	Poland	Romania	USSR	Czechoslovakia
A	57.3	45.9	39.6	38.0	45.2	34.1
B	14.7	6.6	26.7	21.1	8.1	9.0
C	3.6	0.9	1.3	6.5	2.4	2.1
D	0.7	1.1	0.6	2.4	0.3	5.9
E	5.8	3.8	4.1	1.5	2.2	7.7
F	0.7	26.0	10.8	1.5	14.4	20.0
G	17.2	15.7	17.9	29.0	27.4	21.2

E = Industrial materials of agricultural origin
F = Foodstuffs and materials for the food industry
G = Industrial consumer articles

Table 11
Comparative advantages and disadvantages in 1960

Countries	USSR	GDR	Czechoslovakia	Poland	Hungary	Bulgaria	Romania
USSR	—	0.68	0.64	0.75	0.80	1.15	1.20
GDR	1.71	—	1.05	0.92	1.15	1.63	1.78
Czechoslovakia	1.90	0.92	—	1.06	1.09	1.38	1.94
Poland	1.39	1.01	0.91	—	0.99	1.38	1.19
Hungary	1.42	0.77	0.77	0.88	—	1.07	1.33
Bulgaria	0.71	0.55	0.65	0.50	0.83	—	0.70
Romania	1.29	0.72	0.64	0.94	0.87	1.22	—

than it would have expended on the domestic production of the products imported from the country indicated. By the same token, the figures smaller than unity indicate comparative advantages (savings). The computation is of a highly approximative nature and shows more the *tendency* than the *extent* of gains and losses. Where can we find the major comparative advantages (savings)?

— In the trade of the more developed small CMEA countries (the GDR, Czechoslovakia, Poland, Hungary) with the Soviet Union—to the advantage of the former;

— in the trade of the more developed small CMEA countries with the less developed ones (Bulgaria, Romania), similarly to the advantage of the former;

— in the trade between the USSR and Bulgaria (because of the high agricultural imports from the latter).

On the other side of the given relations we find *comparative losses*.

The mutual trade between the developed small countries was on the whole *indifferent*, in the sense that no major comparative advantage or loss appeared on the part of either party. *The computations have shown no relations where the partners gained mutual advantages from the exchange.*

The explanation for the result of the computations—or rather estimations—is simple. As it has been mentioned earlier (and as it can be read from Table 7), it is the engineering products which are the most efficient in every CMEA country, while the agricultural end products are the least efficient. The industries producing basic materials seem to be efficient in the USSR (though not relative to the engineering products), but less so in the other countries. Thus, the computations relating to the comparative advantages and disadvantages reflect the price problem which asserted itself strongly in the sixties, namely, the disproportionately high price level of manufactured articles, above all of machinery, relative to that of the less processed products. Every country enjoyed comparative advantages in whose exports manufactured articles, mainly machines, were dominating and in whose imports agricultural products and food were preponderant, and, conversely, every country showed comparative disadvantages which bought processed articles, mainly machines, in exchange for raw materials and agricultural products.

This situation regarding comparative advantages and disadvantages notwithstanding, *the turnover between the CMEA countries steadily increased*—in ten years to 2.3-fold—while in the meantime the national income of the CMEA countries approximately doubled. Of course, as regards bilateral relations, the dispersion is strong, as can be seen from Table 12, particularly in respect of export elasticity.

Table 12

Increase of exports relative to the growth of national income
(Growth of national income between 1960–1970 = 1)

To \ From	USSR	GDR	Czechoslovakia	Poland	Hungary	Bulgaria	Romania
USSR	—	1.29	1.22	1.71	1.71	1.51	0.84
GDR	0.93	—	1.49	1.31	1.41	1.24	0.94
Czechoslovakia	0.96	1.06	—	1.34	1.11	0.75	1.03
Poland	1.50	1.55	1.56	—	1.76	1.65	1.49
Hungary	1.48	1.70	1.21	1.74	—	1.54	0.74
Bulgaria	1.53	1.74	1.03	1.71	1.88	—	1.68
Romania	0.95	1.48	1.47	1.96	0.96	2.02	—

Table 13

Interrelation between comparative advantages and disadvantages and export elasticity

To \ From	USSR	GDR	Czechoslovakia	Poland	Hungary	Bulgaria	Romania	Agreement of percentage of total
USSR	•	+	+	+	+	+	+	100
GDR	+	•	—	—	—	—	+	33
Czechoslovakia	+	+	•	—	+	+	+	84
Poland	—	—	+	•	—	—	—	17
Hungary	—	+	+	+	•	—	+	66
Bulgaria	+	+	—	+	+	•	+	84
Romania	+	+	+	—	—	—	•	50
Agreement as percentage of total:	66	84	66	50	50	33	84	

Explanation of symbols

+ = direct relationship, i.e. comparative advantage—great elasticity, or comparative loss—export elasticity around or less than unity

− = inverse proportion, i.e. the degree of export elasticity is not justified by the comparative advantages and disadvantages

Let us compare the export elasticities with the table of bilateral comparative advantages (Table 11), and see whether the actual increases in turnover coincide with the realized comparative advantages and disadvantages, as motives of increasing or restricting trade?

From among the total of 42 cases 15 (or 36 per cent) show reversed proportions. The final result is not very characteristic. The individual explanations illuminate much more than the general tendencies do. At least as much can be observed that

— the row-wise export elasticity of exports to the Soviet Union coincides with the comparative saving which is generally characteristic of the trade with the USSR. True, a great part of the imported materials is only indirectly competitive. It could be substituted only by exporting to the West mostly agricultural products, generally not producible at home. Thus, the dynamics of Soviet relations is justified by raw-material imports acquired *in exchange for manufactured products*;

— the dynamics of exports to the GDR and Poland is in most cases not justified by comparative advantages. Other factors must be at play. In the case of the GDR the import of her relatively highly developed machines still secures a considerable advantage in adaptation for the importer. As to Poland, it is a still sufficiently large and dynamic market for machinery and other manufactured articles, which makes it worthwhile to stick to it even if the share of raw-material supply in the counter-deliveries diminishes in favour of finished goods;

— the export dynamism of the later industrializing countries (Bulgaria, Romania) does not show a uniform picture (column-wise). Bulgaria developed its exports, without accounting for momentary comparative impulses, to a number of more developed countries, in all certainty in the interest of dynamic growth, diversification of structure and in view of the adaptation advantages to be acquired. The Romanian economy developed its trade with the CMEA countries, in general, according to the comparative impulses, focussing its attention mainly on gaining adaptation advantages outside the CMEA.

The growth in the volume of trade, and the structural changes that had occurred in the meantime somewhat modified the comparative advantages and disadvantages by 1969 (see Table 14).

A *qualitative* change relative to 1960 took place only in relation to a few countries:

— The trade of the USSR with Romania began to produce advantages for the USSR instead of disadvantages, while the reverse happened in the trade of Bulgaria with the Soviet Union.

The former may be attributed above all to the fact that the share of Soviet machinery deliveries to Romania increased from 22 per cent of exports to 31 per cent, while the efficiency of engineering production increased to about 1.5-fold.

Table 14

Comparative advantages and disadvantages in 1969

Countries	USSR	GDR	Czechoslovakia	Poland	Hungary	Bulgaria	Romania
USSR	—	0.70	0.67	0.72	0.88	0.82	1.17
GDR	1.95	—	1.08	1.05	1.24	1.36	1.78
Czechoslovakia	1.95	0.98	—	1.06	1.10	1.32	1.52
Poland	1.42	1.17	0.94	—	1.03	1.09	1.11
Hungary	1.48	0.74	0.88	0.96	—	1.04	1.46
Bulgaria	0.72	0.61	0.67	0.67	0.92	—	0.72
Romania	0.75	0.79	1.04	1.00	0.96	1.11	—

At the same time, the share of basic-material supplies fell from 51 per cent to 40 per cent. (In 1969, the efficiency of Soviet raw-material deliveries to Romania was about one-third lower than the efficiency of machine production.) As against that, in imports from Romania the share of foodstuffs and chemical articles increased, which substituted for less efficient Soviet production, thus counterbalancing the increased share of machine and consumer-article imports.

The latter may be attributed clearly to the fact that Bulgaria succeeded in raising the share of machinery from 16 per cent to 29 per cent in its exports to the Soviet Union (while, in the meantime, the efficiency of its engineering productions also rose to almost twofold), and that in its imports from the USSR the share of raw materials rose from 24 to 37 per cent, substituting domestic labour which is about three times less efficient than that expended in the engineering industry.

Improvement can be observed on the other side, too. In 1960, the trade of the USSR with Romania involved palpable comparative disadvantages, and this disappeared by 1969. The trade with Bulgaria entailed comparative advantages in 1960 and this did not change by 1969.

— An opposed shift, that is, comparative advantages turning into disadvantage, took place in the trade between Czechoslovakia and Romania and between Poland and the GDR, in both cases at the expense of the first-mentioned country.

As regards the trade between Czechoslovakia and Romania, the cause of the deterioration is unequivocally the emergence of the tendency of exchanging machinery in the proportion of 1:1. The share of machines in the Romanian exports to Czechoslovakia rose from 10 to almost 23 per cent, while that of basic materials fell from 35 to 26 per cent, and that of agricultural products from 31 to 8 per cent. As a consequence, in 1969 the Romanian supplies, which in 1960 had still replaced inefficient Czechoslovak domestic labour, were made up of products of such industries whose operation at home was highly efficient. At the same time, Czechoslovakia could not attain a similar compensation by improving the export pattern, if only on account of the slowly increasing efficiency of its engineering production.

As regards the relations between Poland and the GDR, the extent of the shift towards disadvantage is by far not so great as in the case of Czechoslovakia and Romania. The small advantage of 1960 turned into a slight disadvantage by 1969. The cause of the changes may be found first of all in the fact that the increment of the GDR's machine deliveries to Poland replaces highly efficient Polish labour, while in the Polish export pattern—though the share of machinery is on the increase—an important role was played by light industry, whose efficiency indicator is by one-third smaller than that of engineering. (The computations show a turn also in the trade between Hungary and Poland, but its extent is so small that we may say that it lies between the margins of error of the computations.)

— The extent of *comparative advantages*, viewed from the aspect of the first country, is *essentially unchanged* in the trade between

the USSR and Bulgaria;
the GDR and the USSR and Hungary;
Czechoslovakia and Poland and Bulgaria;
Poland and the USSR;
Romania and Bulgaria.

— *Nor has the comparative disadvantage changed* in the trade

of the USSR with Czechoslovakia, Poland and Hungary;
of Czechoslovakia with the GDR;
of Poland with Czechoslovakia and Romania;
of Hungary with Czechoslovakia;
of Bulgaria with Czechoslovakia and Hungary;
of Romania with the GDR (to be understood in the cases listed at the expense of the first-mentioned country).

— The comparative advantage of Poland in the trade with the Soviet Union perceptibly increased.

— The *comparative advantage diminished* in the trade of

the GDR with Czechoslovakia, Bulgaria and Romania;
Czechoslovakia with the USSR and Hungary;
Poland with Hungary and Bulgaria;
Hungary with the Soviet Union, Bulgaria and Romania.

— The *comparative disadvantage became smaller* in the trade of

Bulgaria with the GDR, Poland and Romania;
Romania with Czechoslovakia and Poland, and, finally,

— the *comparative disadvantage became greater* in the trade of

the Soviet Union with the GDR;
the GDR with Poland;

Hungary with the GDR; and
Romania with Hungary.

To sum up, from among the possible 42 bilateral relations between the CMEA countries, we can speak in 17 cases about undeniable comparative advantages, in the trade of

the USSR with Bulgaria and Romania;
the GDR with the USSR, Hungary, Bulgaria and Romania;
Czechoslovakia with the USSR, Poland, Hungary and Bulgaria;
Poland with the USSR, Hungary and Bulgaria;
Hungary with the USSR and Bulgaria;
Bulgaria with the Soviet Union; and
Romania with Bulgaria.

(From among these, however, only a single one, that of Bulgaria with the USSR is *mutual.*)

— In a further 7 cases we may say that the relationships are *neutral* from the viewpoint of comparative advantages (with values between 0.95 and 1.05); these are the trade of

the GDR with Czechoslovakia;
Czechoslovakia with Romania;
Poland with the GDR and Romania;
Bulgaria with Hungary, but none of these are mutual.

— Finally, in 18 cases we may speak about *comparative disadvantages*, namely, in the trade of

the Soviet Union with the GDR, Czechoslovakia, Poland and Hungary;
the GDR with Poland;
Czechoslovakia with the GDR;
Poland with Czechoslovakia;
Hungary with the GDR and Czechoslovakia;
Bulgaria with the GDR, Czechoslovakia, Poland and Romania;
Romania with every country of the CMEA, except Bulgaria.

In the final analysis, 40 per cent of the bilateral relations was advantageous, 43 per cent disadvantageous, and 17 neutral from the viewpoint of comparative gains. It was advantageous for almost every country to continue trading with the Soviet Union (because of their efficient machinery and consumer-article deliveries and the replacement of their inefficient basic-material and agricultural production). As a reflection of this exchange pattern almost every CMEA partner caused comparative disadvantages for the Soviet economy. The situation was similar in the trade between more and less advanced countries. The neutral cases are characteristic of the exchange between countries which are on the whole on the same development level (GDR–Czechoslovakia, Poland–Hungary), or with Romania.

We may add that the Bulgarian and Romanian economies are gradually reducing their comparative disadvantages deriving from the exchange with CMEA countries, while the disadvantages of the USSR remain on the whole unchanged. In the first case the export pattern changes in favour of machinery, and this is the main factor (the change is taking place mostly at the expense of the structural importance of foodstuffs and other products of agricultural origin), but in the second case the invariably high proportion of raw materials and agricultural articles is determinative.

In the trade of *Hungary*, the Soviet and—to a lesser extent—the Bulgarian relations may be said to be advantageous, the GDR and the Czechoslovak ones disadvantageous, while the Polish and Romanian relations neutral from the viewpoint of comparative gains. The advantages diminished in the sixties, while the disadvantages towards the GDR increased.

The comparative advantage of our trade with the Soviet Union derives above all from the fact that efficient engineering labour is exchanged for labour producing mineral and agricultural raw materials, which is inefficient in Hungary. The reduction of advantages is related to the fact that the role of the export of engineering products is taken over to a considerable extent by the less efficient light industry and by the food economy which was relatively not efficient in 1969. The comparative disadvantages in the trade with the Czechoslovak and the GDR economies are due to the fact that we are net importers of machinery and net exporters of food, that is, we buy products that could be produced with more efficient labour than the domestic average, and export instead products that are produced with a productivity well below the domestic average.

Thus, the approximation of *structures* narrows down the possibilities to achieve comparative advantages. The approximation of *development levels* narrows the possibilities of gaining advantages through adaptation, if the earlier developed countries do not concentrate their development resources on a high-level development of selected areas, and if the later developing ones also rest satisfied with introducing the imported technical cultures and with multiplying them, if they do not make efforts to develop the domestic bases of innovation in selected areas which are collated on community level. The rule of "complete" technologies—the underdeveloped state of internal cooperation—that is, the lack of a network of specialized enterprises producing parts and components does not provide a favourable ground for industrial cooperation (even independently of the system of domestic control). This prevents the countries to utilize cooperation possibilities in the interest of increasing efficiency. All this, coinciding in time with the collapse of the embargo and with the gradual easing of Western discrimination, directed increased attention to East–West trade, where the possibility of additional credit resources offered itself, as well as a possibility of gains from the division of labour through importing advanced technology and gaining above all adaptation advantages. (In the trade with developed capitalist countries almost every CMEA country has considerable comparative disadvantages. Its extent—computed in a manner identical with that used in Table 14—was the following in 1969: USSR 1.09, GDR 0.94, Czechoslovakia 1.2, Poland 1.09, Hungary 1.19, Bulgaria 1.25; Romania 1.38.)

The tendency of diminishing comparative advantages in the division of labour within the CMEA was not accompanied by a sudden increase of either the adaptation or the cooperation advantages. Several factors contributed to the development of this situation. One of them was undoubtedly the seclusion from the technologically and economically most advanced countries and markets for several decades, others were the systems of economic control which absolutely preferred the demands of industrialization and quantitative growth against the adaptation to market requirements and increased efficiency of production. But this is merely a superficial explanation. The other, more important, reason is that *the CMEA*, though consisting of independently operating sovereign national economies, has behaved in the last decades in certain respect as *an integrated unit with more developed and less developed regions*—in which the less developed regions are preponderant—and the main target of its economic policy was above all *the development of backward regions.*

Apart from certain exceptions, which were made particularly in those fields where world political demands made the technological development of the economy indispensable, the CMEA has not yet succeeded in fully implementing a model of economic development which may equally promote the approximation to each other of the developed and less developed regions or countries and, simultaneously, an undisturbed development of the "peaks".

It would be very difficult to judge unequivocally to what extent the coordinated cooperation policy within the CMEA is to blame for all this, and to what extent this solution occurred under the effect of such objective factors which made it unavoidable. At any rate, the pressing circumstances had a strong effect. The seclusion from the world economy as well as from technological information channels, the relatively small ratio of the industrialized regions as compared to the whole of the region—particularly in the first decade which decisively influenced the structural transformation—were all factors influencing economic policy, whose effects cooperation could not escape.

But all this is an objectively given situation of these days. The approximation of the CMEA countries as regards their level and structure has considerably progressed according to the original objectives of economic strategy. Integration has to continue to promote this tendency also in the future, but the consequences deriving from the fact of approaching development levels and from the *particular mode* of this approximation, have to be reckoned with.

CHAPTER SEVEN

Basic features of the operation of the socialist integration

The objective historical and economic endowments, the system of realistic economic policy goals as well as the mechanism of relationships all interact in real life, but the dominating part of our active economic operations is represented by control, that is, by the regulation of the economic relationships. Finding the correct model of operation is, therefore, the cornerstone of integration, too. The model of operation has to answer, both in its details and generally, the requirements of objective endowments, and its motive force cannot surpass the possibility of forward movement allowed by the given situation. If we do not take this into account, it does not matter at all *how* wilful we are, whether we *directly* set irrealistic goals or confuse the economic processes *indirectly*, by overstimulation and disorientation.

In judging the integration processes, therefore, we have to set out from the fact that the economic mechanisms are the forms of motion of objective economic relations and the system of economic control is a deliberately established system of these mechanisms. We must separate, if only theoretically, the mechanisms working with *elementary force* in international cooperation from those *deliberately controlled*—and that in respect of both integrations, if only because the basic differences between the two integrations can be found precisely in the mechanisms working with elementary force.

From all what I have expounded it follows that the elementary forces of the economy could by themselves draw the West-European region, under the present conditions, towards some kind of integration, even if more slowly and with more contradictions than in actual reality. The position of Western Europe in the whole of the world economy also produces spontaneous cohesive forces, of course, mainly under the shadow of collective protectionism. The activity of multinational corporations seated in America but operating within the EEC, the impact of the crisis of the capitalist monetary system on the differentiation of the financial policies of the member countries, and even the resistance to the "regionalization" of East–West economic relations seem to prove that the world-economic mechanisms have a disintegrating effect on the national economies of

Western Europe. In spite of this, the West-European integration may rely within the region on selecting and *simultaneously* integrating effect of the market automatisms. Therefore, a basic condition of the upswing of integration in Western Europe was to restore the natural mechanisms of international competition *in their state prior to the 1929 world crisis*—meaning an unrestricted flow of commodities and factors of production, multilateralism and the international convertibility of currencies. This work has been complemented up to now by a few deliberate, essentially integrational steps, the creation of the *customs union*, that is, the elimination of separate national protectionisms, and the introduction of a collective protectionism in *commodity trade*. A similar step was taken to abolish the obstacles to the migration of labour within the community. Similarly to other commodities for sale, the labour-commodity is also moving freely, without major obstacles within the community. The economic "opening" within the community has created the conditions for "natural selection". Of course, the complete unification of the conditions of competition is far from having been achieved. For this the whole economic policy ought to be streamlined, including monetary policy, taxation policy, the system of non-commercial state subsidies as well as the system of economic legislation. In this book, however, we are not so much concerned with what the EEC has succeeded in attaining, but rather with the *nature* of the changes, of development. The deliberate action helping the West-European integration visibly clears the way for the spontaneous mechanisms selecting producers and structures within the region and tries to erect protective, yet not completely unsurmountable walls on the frontiers of the region. That is, it attempts to repeat in West-European dimensions the process which took place at the dawn of the development of capitalism (and somewhat later) in national dimensions.

Thus, the functional model of the integration relies on the basic premise that competition free from obstacles channels the actions of the economic units towards a technological and structural optimum within a given macro-economic framework, together with the flow and growth of factors of production and of products. Therefore, any economic unit of the community should be boldly exposed to all competitive effects *within the community*, it should be made possible for the capitals, moving freely within the community, to rearrange the production structures by following their own interests, under the impulses of the market. The community has to be defended only against external effects. But, apart from certain exceptions, this protection consists in dampening yet not eliminating the competitive effects. Up to now the experience of the functioning of the Common Market proved the viability of the operative model chosen under the given conditions. They have, however, simultaneously shown that the rearrangement of the pattern of production towards the regional optimum can be left merely to the effects of "natural selection" only if the integration is not pressed by *external* economic or political circumstances. On the other hand, the effect of the market automatisms is relatively slow, particularly if we expect them to rearrange the macro-structures. Beyond that, they influence the attaining of the optimal structure through a very long and costly approximation process. Besides, it is very difficult to subordinate the market automatisms unequivocally to the optimum conditions of the region, particularly if the region or some of its countries aspire to a dynamic impact on other sectors of the world economy. Under such conditions, the impulses of the external world unavoidably interfere with the effects of the automatisms within the region. This does not matter as long as they only promote the adaptation of the region to the external world. In this case the region may easily become a directed unit from a self-propelling one and, instead of seeking its own optimum, it will more or less adapt itself to the optimum development of some other unit. This, essentially, is a danger similar to the one we called "peripherization" when discussing the development of Eastern Europe prior to the socialist development.

In the second half of the 20th century, Western Europe is short of time. It has to take care lest it should drop behind the huge American competitive economy as regards the development level of its forces of production and its efficiency. There is every indication that the degree of integration implemented up to now —the Common Market—is not sufficient to reduce significantly the lag behind the North-American forces of production, particularly in the fields determining technical progress—as regards either the speed of effects or productive capacity. In order to avoid the position of, as François Perroux put it, an *économie dominé*, subordinated economy, the Common Market should be transformed into an *economic community*. On the one hand, this means more than what has been realized up to now—the unification of all competitive conditions—on the other hand, it also means something *different* in qualitative terms from what has been aimed at up to now. Besides following the principle of "natural selection", it is also in the interest of the West-European integration process to raise certain elements of "artificial selection" to regional level as well. As formulated by Western economists, liberalism and collective protectionism within the region should be coupled also with some kind of regional "dirigism", or at least with one coordinated on community level. Some, though not too successful, initial steps have been made in this direction. The object, contents, scope, and methods of the development programs and their relation to the armory of market regulation are different in every West-European country, which produces not negligible difficulties for coordination. Of course, the political obstacles are essentially bigger than the former ones. The medium- and long-term development programs and conceptions express in every country the national-level compromises of different capitalist circles. They are simultaneously resultants and reflections of the domestic power relations, and more or less guides to action of the national state monopoly capitalism. It is dangerous to regionalize them without strongly cutting down the freedom of action of the capitalist state—the national capital. Furthermore, giving up the last indirect tools of separate national economic protectionism or at least their subordination to compulsory coordination would put the particular governments in a position where they would be *politically responsible to their own countries for measures in taking which they have at most a right to vote.* Therefore, it may be stated with almost full certainty that the member countries are willing to "regionalize" only as big a part of their economic policies as they can counterbalance in case of need with other measures. *Thus, one of the main problems of the functional model of the West-European integration process is that it succeeded only to a restricted extent in complementing the "natural selection" with the tools of deliberate economic development.*

The functional model of East-European economic cooperation put into the centre above all the mutual aid in development. The Central and East-European socialist countries built up their internal systems of economic control along the same lines in the fifties. This system was characterized by obligatory central plans, the separation of the producer and consumer as well as of the domestic and foreign markets, all these serving as a basis for a very strict protection of industrial development. Initially, the coordination of these national economic functional models caused no particular methodological problem, especially at the then relatively rudimentary stage of cooperation. The main task of industrialization that were to be solved came to the foreground. We encounter the rudimentary elements of plan coordination already at the end of the forties, in the long-term trade contracts. By the sixties this developed into direct plan-collations of the central planning agencies.

In this functional model the *market automatisms* have but a subordinated role. The existence of the automatisms assumes, namely, that it is the economic unit (enterprise, union, etc.) that decides on the alternatives of investments, production and sales, at least in the case of simple reproduction or one not expanded at an outstanding rate. In order that the socialist state, as owner, may relegate to the economic units the decisions belonging to the scope of simple reproduction and normal expanded reproduction, together with the choice between different procurement and sales markets, the country in question must possess considerable reserves of factors of production and products, including exportable commodity funds salable at any time and on any market, and also reserves of foreign currency as well as mobilizable production funds at enterprise level. (It is a minimum requirement of planned economy to centralize in the scope of global social decisions those relating to expanded reproduction with an impact on structural changes.)

At present and foreseeably for some longer time still, the economy of the CMEA countries will develop with closely calculated minimal reserves. Particularly the shortage of those factors of production deserves attention which can be exported profitably at any time to any market (which produce, to use the professional jargon: "convertible" or "hard" goods). The "softness" of the exportable commodity fund is to be felt in the case of some CMEA countries mainly in their trade with the developed Western countries, but in the case of others also in CMEA relations. A general elimination of all restrictions, without any transition, on the present flows of commodities, investment resources, labour, and services within the CMEA would have, under such conditions, a differentiating effect on the development of the member countries, mainly through the changes in the terms of trade as well as through the dwindling CMEA markets for the products of some newly developed industries. If we organically linked this system of "natural selection" within the CMEA to the markets of the capitalist countries (e.g. through monetary channels), the traditional instruments of regional protectionism would prove to be insufficient to secure the political conditions for the industrial development of the countries. Therefore, the CMEA countries are at present not in a position to render their economies open *in the classical trade-policy meaning of the term*, neither towards third countries, nor even towards each other. (Not even those countries may be said to be really open in whose system of economic control an organic relationship has been established between the internal and external markets. Even in these, central economic policy handles the instruments connecting the external and the internal markets extremely carefully, and makes immediate changes as soon as the external market impulses do not stimulate but undermine the development objectives worked out in the economic plan. Thus, the CMEA integration develops *among national economies which are structurally more and more open* (that is, which establish ever deepening division of labour among each other), but which are, for the time being, *closed from the viewpoint of commercial policy* (that is, on micro-level they are more or less neutralized against external market impulses).

Is it not a square peg in a round hole to speak about integration among economies which are closed from the viewpoint of trade policy? If we restrict the notion of integration to its "natural selection" variant, this is indeed so. No doubt, in a group of countries whose members are market economies, and thus the bulk of decisions on the operation and development of the economies is concentrated in the economic units—where the state has but an indirect influence on these decisions by influencing the automatisms—integration remains a fiction as long as the countries are closed from the viewpoint of commercial policy. Namely, only with the methods of "natural selection" can the economies with a structure of decisions based on ownership be forced to rearrange *in their entirety* according to the requirements of a regional optimum.

But such a regional rearrangement process can be generated not only in a single manner, and the expedient method may be selected only after an examination of the circumstances. In countries with centrally planned economies, integration would be "a square peg in a round hole" only if these countries also refrained from collating their development policies. Open commercial policy is not *criterion of the functional model followed by the CMEA, which assumes, however, an opening of development policies.* Insofar as the cooperating economies coordinate their development plans, and create such conditions in their internal systems of economic control which secure a harmonious development of the forces of production, as well as the regional collective protection of the economies, this may, in the final analysis, be similar to "natural selection". From certain respects, this particular functional model also has some not negligible advantages. It produces fewer surprises in actual economic development and in the harmonious shaping of economic development levels than "natural selection". This is a viewpoint worth the attention, if we think of the characteristic "anatomy" of the setup in the CMEA region.

Two important features of the integration policy are: collective protection against the competition of third countries, and collective preference of the forces of production within the region. These may be found in both integrational groupings, but the methods applied to these ends differ considerably.

The agreements concluded within the EEC secure (though not quite efficiently) equal chances for any enterprise of any country of the Community on the market of any other member country. The CMEA secures, through plan coordination and by means of trade cooperation and other agreements, the supply of member countries with products produced in other member countries and with markets in other member countries. In the EEC the member country undertakes to open the market, in the CMEA it undertakes an obligation under interstate agreement to supply and to secure the conditions of the absorbing market as well as of cooperation. Even the socialist control system of the indirect type does not simply "open the market" for CMEA products, nor does it create simply export possibilities for other CMEA countries. It channels the autonomous sales and purchases of its economic units in a manner to meet the cooperation commitments, undertaken on national economic level. Thus, the CMEA model comprises basically the *coordinated cooperation processes,* independently of the division of the spheres of decision in the internal control systems of the individual countries between the economic units and the central economic control agencies.

In the EEC the substance of collective economic protection is the unification of the tariff system. The customs duty flows into a common purse only in the case of products affected by the agricultural treaty (though it is called "skimming", it has the effect of customs duty). In the practice of the CMEA the collective protection against third countries applies only to measures taken by third countries and expressly endangering the economic development of the member countries, like embargo or open discrimination. Apart from this exceptional case, the CMEA causes cooperation to remain within the community only by making the conditions of mutual trade and cooperation more favourable. Where the given demand for imports cannot be satisfied from regional sources for either quantitative or qualitative reasons, the CMEA "rules of the game" expressly stimulate business and division of labour relationships with third countries.

We have mentioned above that the West-European integration is not a pure "natural selection" either, and that the unfavourable conditions for a deliberate coordination of development make the whole of the integration process contradictory. The East-European socialist integration is also characterized by contradictions. In consequence of its particular historical traditions and economic–political conditions, the CMEA integration is based on the harmonization of development policies, it is mainly through this that it affects the division of labour and trade, and protects the industrial development of the member countries and stimulates the necessary rearrangements. The smaller the effect of the particular features of East-European economic development of historical origin (that is, relative backwardness, structural tensions, contrasts in development levels, the network of large-scale plants requiring protection, etc.), the more cooperation necessitates also the opening of the trade policies, i.e. the gradual easing of quotas and multilateral settlements. The CMEA integration will also reach a stage when it will be impossible to harmonize the development policies successfully without an advanced system of commercial and monetary policies. This does not mean, of course, that, as regards its functional model, the European socialist integration will become similar in time to the EEC. (Even if the active structural policy becomes stronger within the EEC, this will not make the West-European integration similar to the CMEA.) The basic difference between the two centres of integration will continue to exist. The West-European model sets out from competition and restricts, molds and regulates it as needed. The East-European model sets out from planned cooperation and attempts partly to make this regional planned character more flexible, to adapt to changing circumstances, and partly to fit it into the direct international division of labour and the economic relations existing among the economic units. It uses the market elements of cooperation not as a mechanism for "natural selection" but as elements of a signalling and helping system of the complex mechanism of planned regional development.

CHAPTER EIGHT

The building stones of the socialist integration: the national economic strategies

When speaking about the necessity of the socialist integration of the CMEA countries, we mean above all the establishment of a type of division of labour *which answers the requirements raised by the technical and scientific revolution and promotes, at the same time, the further development of the East-European societies on the road of socialism.* The desirable division of labour would differ from the present one in the following:

(a) much faster than average development of *cooperations within manufacturing* would push the exchange of raw products to the background without restricting the primary energy, basic materials and food supply of the economies;
(b) within the faster than average development of the mutual and lasting exchange of manufactured products the exchange of *intermediary products,* that is, of semi-manufactures, parts and partial units, has to grow particularly fast.

This would result in a qualitative change of the division of labour among the individual countries as regards its depth. The forms of cooperation would become much more diversified, their mechanisms more varied and the organizational and control methods more complicated.

All that sounds as a self-explanatory basic truth, but if we stop here in our reasoning and continue with the development of an adequate mechanism of cooperation, we may easily go astray. Nothing is simpler than to build up, upon the basic truth here expounded, the "rules of the game" of the international contacts of the economy. These rules may bear the imprint of the economic-theoretical position of those devising them, the imprint of the internal relations which influence their reasoning, that of the models which served as an example for the creators, etc. All this may build up into a logical system, as a matter of fact, into *as many* logical systems as many "schools" set themselves to the task. It will have only one shortcoming—and this makes it incapable of coming about, or if it comes about, *incapable of operation*—namely, it does not reckon with the realities determined by the actual daily and long-term needs of the *given* members of the given community.

This is why I believe it is *hopeless* to try to deduce the integrational mechanism to be transplanted into and to be operated in practice, from a logical construction built up independently of the conditions and efforts of the cooperating countries. Whether such a logical structure is practicable is independent of its quality, its direction and the nature of the "school" creating it. The only realistic possibility of approach is *to investigate in analytical detail the situation of the national economies making up the community*, their equilibrium and growth conditions, their foreign economic relations and their possibilities in economic policy, and to generalize these carefully, depending on space and time. That is, one has to set out not from something that is *logical in itself*, but, analysing the actual situation, *one has to arrive* at a conclusion that may result in a logical solution of the problems in the given situation. The division of labour should not be deduced from the desired functional model, it is from *a realistically formulated and highly progressive model of the division of labour that the mechanism should be derived which brings to the surface and formulates as positive partial interests the possibilities and necessities.*

It is with this definite purpose that I try to sum up the long-term development problems which may be said to be more or less *common* in the European socialist countries and which inevitably determine the system of goals of their whole economic policy, and, within it, of their foreign economic policy, together with its main constraints:

a) The most urgent problem of economic policy of the CMEA countries, and one that can be solved only in the long run and only in common, is that, under pressures of varying nature, their national economies—which were developed very fast, unevenly and burdened by contradictions from the most diverse aspects—*have to intensify production in a historically short time when they had not yet succeeded in completely eliminating the unevenness of their industrialization, or to put it in a different way, all remnants of their earlier backward state:*

— Though the whole of the population has generally shifted to the way of life demanded by modern productive activities, the general technological culture, the talent for technical innovations, as well as the organizational ability necessary for the operation of complicated production systems have not yet developed to an extent necessary for raising any productive activity to a modern level in any country and keeping on that level. Thus, as regards the *quality* of the human force of production, the socialist countries have transgressed the limit of modern society, but talents have developed unevenly, and therefore the economies are still rather rigid as regards structural changes and shifts in the technological levels in the present modern sense. Thus, for orientation in development and in foreign economic policy it is not sufficient to assess the needs, to review the cyclical situation of the world market and to make "a good resolution", because the productive population is not equally good at everything. Every country has its production traditions that were acquired or developed earlier or later. Considering their size—in a cultural medium which has *generally* improved as a result of industrialization—it is not an impossible or hopeless venture for any country to aim at the most modern "European" production level. But the traditions of this are restricted in every country. In other fields of productive activity the population is capable only of the adaptation and copying of foreign production cultures, of *following* development from some distance. Of course, this is a big achievement in itself, one of the biggest of socialist industrialization. At any rate, a *realistic assessment of the innovation and organizational talents of society, the selection of activity spheres and systems to be developed to a high degree, the establishment of the realistically attainable development degree and of the minimum distance of following in the other fields are the most important tasks of a realistic economic policy.*

— For different reasons deriving from the circumstances of industrialization, *the distribution of the productive machinery among the different productive activities* does not quite correspond either to the requirements raised by the professional skills of the population, or to the demand relations on the international (CMEA and other) markets. It follows that they have "spent", and in their national economic plans have "spent in advance", their national wealth, which had been initially relatively modest and restricted in growth by scanty sources of accumulation, partly on such productive equipment and research institutes which, in their present form, are only partially suited for innovative and productive activities of "European" standards and which can be made better suited for the purpose only with further big material sacrifices. In addition, work is organized on a social scale in a manner that further development of an internal and international division of labour of a new type requires a major reorganization, a complicated rearrangement of the spheres of authority and a regrouping of labour. Economic policy is thus extremely cautious and this considerably prolongs the time needed for a structural transformation demanded by the technical and scientific revolution.

— Finally, the *natural* conditions are also factors determining economic policy and in the case of the European CMEA countries with smaller areas the natural resources are distributed very unevenly. The possibilities for their exploitation are not too favourable either and, in addition, the distribution of productive activities is not sufficiently adapted to the possibilities of exploitation.

It follows that the CMEA countries face quantitative, qualitative and composition problems as regards all three factors of production available to them, as almost unavoidable concomitants of the dynamic industrialization process taking place under unstable physical equilibrium conditions.

b) Even if to different extent and tainted by local features, it is a similarly common problem of all CMEA countries that they are inclined to *overspend their national income.* In numerous cases this manifests itself in a tense financial equilibrium of the economies and has the following components:

— The economies are under almost equal parallel pressure by the growth of the consumption demands of the population and of the demand *for increasing production.* Since certain needs of the population (for housing, infrastructural costs related to automobilism, etc.) and also producers' need (e.g. major programs aimed at structural transformation) can be satisfied only through massive investment to be implemented in a relatively short time, it is an almost unsolvable task to eliminate the double pressure. Progress on the one side strikes back to a smaller or greater extent on the other. Lags are thus cumulating and progress is frequently not consistent.

— In respect of the allocation of development resources *within the productive sphere,* similarly parallel and almost equal pressures are exerted by the demands *for expansion* of the structures in the process of just building up, and by the claims *for modernization* of the existing capacities. Partly the restricted means of investment, partly the lack of suitable training and dexterity (discussed above) usually frustrate the building up or the radical reconstruction of complete technological vertical chains. Thus, the more advanced the process of industrialization, the greater the danger that the investments become fragmented. The investment sphere, which struggles with efficiency problems anyway on account of technological and cultural causes, is forced into a difficult situation. Sectoral problems and the choice between expansion or modernization cause constant dilemmas. All this leads easily to the "running away" of investment activity and simultaneously to an overt decline in the efficiency of productive fixed assets on an enterprise and, much more, on the national economic level. An investment "boom" comes about, whose size entails diminishing returns in terms of productivity—until it strikes against the limits of personal consumption.

Another major task of economic policies is to relieve from time to time the growing tension between the increased demands of accumulation and consumption, to solve the dilemmas between the extensive and intensive directions of investments, as well as to fight against the tendencies of fragmentation and those reducing efficiency.

c) The tensions listed exist, to some extent, in every national economy. *Their balancing may be solved by foreign trade, by fitting into the international division of labour,* insofar as the distribution of the productive activities within the economy is adapted from the outset to the requirements of external markets, and the consumption level of the population as well as the extent of accumulation keep pace with the productivity of social labour. Of course fitting to external markets either reflects passively and thus conserves the development level and structural characteristics of the economy, or tries to apply these in the interest of moving towards a given social preference. The latter is characteristic of the CMEA countries. Their foreign-trade policy is usually characterized by trying to exploit them very purposefully and in a forced manner for accelerating the implementation of the most important targets of economic policy. In the first stage of industrialization this target of economic policy was a radical transformation of the branch structure of industry. Today this is complemented by efforts to modernize the existing productive machinery. Thus, in foreign-trade policy we again meet with all the problems mentioned:

— With the mode of fitting into the international division of labour the CMEA countries wish to attain the possibility to employ their population to a growing extent in such industries which produce the attainable maximum of employment and expertise. But they wish to import the products of production processes whose level is more primitive than the "national" level of qualification, as well as such products with whose aid this level may be considerably raised. That is, every CMEA country endeavours to export products processed with qualified labour, partly in exchange for products comprising labour of low qualification and partly for investment goods and intellectual goods whose technical level exceeds *by far* that of their own products.

— The CMEA countries with narrower markets are struggling with realization problems since they maintain full employment partly by engaging (because of the extraordinary circumstances of industrialization) a considerable part of the economically active population in *quantitatively* overdeveloped productive activities. If they cannot export their surplus at a price which allows them to satisfy the material and energy needs of the big manufacturing machinery efficiently, their equilibrium inclusive of full employment cannot be maintained. Since in the first stage of industrialization their investment policies were similar, this need to export originates from identical fields in almost every CMEA country. Thus, not complementary sectors appear on the external markets but competitive ones. These being huge productive machineries, specialization relieving competitivity on a higher level can take place only slowly and gradually. At the same time these products are not competitive on the world market in respect of either quality or production costs, thus the specialization of productive activities makes sense only if linked to radical modernization, otherwise the huge transformation costs involved by specialization would never be returned. Therefore, the economic policy of the CMEA countries is facing a serious dilemma. The further development of the production of means of production (mainly these are affected) is hindered by the fact that it is obsolete and fragmented. The products can hardly be sold at all (for convertible currency) or with growing difficulties (on CMEA markets). Specialization is, however, highly investment-intensive and thus, with the present—relatively low-efficiency—investment situation it would draw off funds from the normal functioning of the existing productive machinery.

— As a consequence, another point of emphasis in the foreign-trade efforts of the CMEA countries is *to save investments* through export and import. Most of them interpret also comparative advantages in such a manner that *they prefer, among export volumes of identical price sums, that one which is least capital-intensive, and from import volumes, the most capital-intensive one.*

In the final analysis, foreign-trade efforts are motivated by the following:

— procurement of scarce materials,

— the import of equipment and intellectual products necessary for the development of the forces of production and not available under domestic conditions, as "physical" factors of equilibrium and growth; parallel to this:

— the exchange of highly qualified labour for less qualified one, and

— the exchange of fixed-capital-intensive production for labour-intensive one, as factors of growth which are called upon to ease the internal financial tensions.

d) It may be added that in an *acute* disequilibrium the countries willingly go into debt on foreign markets, since in this manner they are freed from both a radical reduction of consumption and a sudden break of their investment boom. Since tension between the created and used national income frequently emerge, the CMEA countries do not behave in a complementary manner in this respect either. None of them is induced to become a creditor, even if for a short time only. It follows that every balance of payments introduces tension into the cooperation on part of the creditor country. Deficits in the balances arise thus mainly towards the area with which trade is to be settled in convertible currencies. This increases their efforts to expand export capacities towards this area, and, as a consequence, the supply of "hard" commodities is relatively diminishing on the CMEA market.

In the final analysis, all these contradictory phenomena are almost natural concomitants of the fast growth and particular world economic situation of the CMEA countries as well as of their "adolescence", which can be at most mitigated by better suited national economic policies, even if free from subjective mistakes (by far not negligible), which cannot be eliminated.

Beside the above outlined and more or less common or similar concerns of economic policy there are a great many others which are characteristic only of one or the other of the CMEA countries. Such are: the scarcity of raw materials, the lack of food basis of their own, unfavourable conditions of transportation (lack of a seashore), or problems due to the big or small size of the country or to deficiencies in internal economic integration. Some of these strongly motivate the efforts of the leadership of the country in question, its claims on integration, or, in more concrete terms, towards the partners.

All that underlines that the "timetable" of developing the system of goals and instruments of the integration should be *compiled from* the complex summarization of the development possibilities and efforts of the countries wishing to integrate, through their synchronization, and not the other way round. From the necessities of economic development outlined it follows that in the next 15 to 20 years the economic development strategies of the CMEA countries have to be characterized by *increased selectivity in development.* But this selectivity will be of quite different nature than in the past twenty-five years. Then it meant first of all the order in which the *foundations* had to be laid for the individual industries, allowing the educational level, the living and producing conditions of the masses of village population to be raised and transformed. Now selectivity should be interpreted in a quite different way:

a) First of all those *complex technical production structures* will be selected gradually, but in a definite and planned manner, in which the population of the given country manifests the biggest creative and innovative ability.

These should be developed partly faster than average even in quantitative terms, but the nature of the development will be rather qualitative. Technological progress will accelerate in these productive activities and they will become competitive all over the world.

b) Parallel to the former, also those productive activities will be selected *for whose efficient development and maintenance there is no hope in the individual countries.* These industries will gradually fade away, whether they count as "traditional" in the given countries or were created in the course of socialist industrialization.

It is expedient, for instance, to eliminate this traditional productive activity from the structure of a small economy if competitivity today or tomorrow demands such a scale of research and development or of investment and production which anyway exceeds the stamina of the given economy. These "profiles" are taken over by bigger economies, particularly if the productive activity in question is already lagging too much behind in the small economy. The negative selection to be made in the course of structural development is a more difficult and more complicated problem than the selection of technical cultures. With the latter the most important things are: (a) to identify correctly *the most favourable* intellectual and other conditions of the national economy, and (b) to draw realistically the dividing line between the "core" of the culture and the directly or indirectly adjoining areas. In the first case, that is, with negative selection, a bold economic policy has to overcome several kinds of social and economic resistance. This is why a truly "bold" economic policy is almost an exception. The preferential development programs usually *do not replace* the unviable productive activities, but rather *settle them,* thus sentencing the program to mediocre implementation. If, however, in the smaller economy viable development and production traditions are available in the given area, the export of intellectual products or even high-level cooperation may be established. In this case the small economy will not necessarily eliminate the given productive activity from its structure, but will develop it as an integral part of the technical culture flourishing in another cooperating country. Such "fragments" of technical culture may be important and useful components of the forces of production of some smaller country. Even the latter case, namely, when a productive activity, having come about in the course of industrialization, has to be eliminated, it must not be necessarily considered as a failure of economic policy, but as a transitory stage in the history of the country which (a) helped industrialization with its products, (b) contributed to the retraining of the workers with its equipment.

c) There are activities which are neither suited to become leading technical cultures of the country, nor so "hopeless" that their elimination should be necessary from the economic structure. In some form, these will be linked to the foreign development centres, they will follow the innovative activities of the latter, reproducing their products and technologies. Except for the USSR, a considerable part of the productive activities in the CMEA countries will develop into such reproducing sectors. This is not tragic.

On the one hand, reproduction does not necessarily mean backwardness *in productivity*, only the research and development basis is not within the country. *Production* itself may be up-to-date and in a just price system the innovative basis will not earn monopolistic incomes, at the expense of the reproducing sectors, securing disproportionately greater possibilities for development.

On the other hand, *every* industrialized socialist economy should be conceived as a conglomerate of innovative and reproducing sectors. In the last resort, the structure of the whole of a smaller economy need to particularly differ, in this respect, from that of big economies. The *density* of innovative sectors need not be necessarily smaller than in big economies. The innovative sectors of the big economy are mostly related to other *domestic* reproducing sectors, while both the innovative and the reproducing sectors of smaller economies will be in more intensive relationship with foreign sectors.

Thus I conceive the structure of the smaller and the medium-sized national economies of the integrating community according to *the way* in which they are linked to the international division of labour, to be an aggregate of the following strata:

— *Innovative centres of technical cultures*, built up from complex research and development activities and the most demanding productive phases. The core may be for the most part within a national economy, complemented by close cooperation with the "fragments" of cultures in other economies, but it may be developed from the outset in the dimensions of the whole community. This may be so particularly in cases when the research, development and the production traditions are not significantly concentrated in some country (or countries) or if efficient development exceeds the resources of a country but may be concentrated for this purpose.

— *Areas outside the "core" of the cultures*, a part of which still requires demanding technology and some product development (primary reproducing sphere), while another part produces on large scale, in an up-to-date manner, and cheaply, on the basis of technical documentation originating from the "core" of the culture. Reproductive activity may extend from the production of parts or units to fitting and various contractual work, but may also include the production of end products.

— *Extracting and primary processing* (refining) industries as well as *infrastructural networks* (electric grids, oil and gas pipelines, waterways and ports, railways and motor roads, information and communication networks, environment protection and flood protection systems, etc.) which are linked to the division of labour and are partly or entirely developed jointly (bilaterally or multilaterally).

— A spectrum of products (raw, semi-finished and end products) which are produced *also* for abroad in the classical sense, but regulated in broad outlines in a planned manner and for some longer period, whose development and efficient production does not exceed the size of the available national resources.

In the structure of the big economy participating in the integrations (in the CMEA, the USSR) all these sectors will be found, with the difference that essentially more internal and less external relations will be established among the innovative cores of the particular cultures and their reproductive spheres.

In this model, the international division of labour will be established not simply *between trades or industries*, nor merely between groups of people producing different use values, but between *professional and educational levels* as well. This viewpoint must not be neglected precisely today when the wealth of an *industrialized nation* is not the consequence of having trained for manufacturing or some of its branches, but of its capability of cultivating *any* trade, on what technical level, and with what innovative and organization talents. Marx's statement regarding the value-producing ability of simple and complex labour is today much more in the forefront of world-economic processes than it has been at any time in history. *The exchange of labour of different complexity has become a basic problem of international exchange.* The national economy as a unit producing use values and specialized to a certain extent (and becoming more and more specialized) is dependent on its foreign economic relations *precisely* because it has remained simultaneously also a producer of values. The degree to which it can satisfy its own needs depends on the efficiency with which the world-economic environment *allows* it to produce what it consumes. At the same time, it also exports these products and it depends on the *quality* of realization on the external market how much it can import of the products not produced or produced in insufficient quantity. Thus a national economy fitted into the modern world economy becomes a function of the world-economic environment in respect of the equilibrium between consumption and accumulation as well as the rate of growth. The country which fits into the division of labour among nations—either under the pressure of the environment or because of its own illness—in a manner specializing in productive activities of lower complexity than its partners, will in the long run develop more slowly and will be able to accumulate and consume less than its partners. The reason is, on the one hand, that primitive labour produces less value in principle, and, on the other hand, demand for the products of primitive labour increases more slowly, and, finally, because specialization in primitive labour does not allow developing the ability for research and development and for higher organization, that is, the national technical and economic qualities which are exchanged in international trade at a premium.

It is a basic feature of the socialist international division of labour that it aims at homogeneity in development and development-ability. In the initial stage of industrialization this manifested itself in the levelling tendency of sectoral (industrial) and trade structures. Today—without denying the justification for the sectoral "viewpoints" in the division of labour—the interest of the individual national economies to secure for the innovative ability of the population a growing role in the international division of labour breaks way with elementary force. This is a new point of view which is asserted, for the time being, parallel and in complicated and many-sided interrelation with the sectoral viewpoint.

CHAPTER NINE

Harmonization of national economic policies: the basic mechanism of socialist integration

Relying on the model of division of labour outlined in the preceding chapters, I shall attempt in the following to sketch the problems that have to be faced in working out the mechanism of integration of the socialist countries united in the CMEA.

Above all, it is necessary to harmonize the development strategies of the national economies. That is, the innovative cores of technical cultures have to be allocated among the different national units in a planned manner. It is similarly indispensable to link the fragments of cultures in a planned way to the innovative cores. It is also necessary to establish the primary and secondary sectors around these cores. Beyond that, arrangements have to be made to establish the material bases, transportation, communications and environment protection networks necessary for the coordinated working of these cultures over wide geographical areas. The first condition of being able to speak of an *integrated* regional economy is a complex and unified development of the technical cultures in the national economies of the region, a proportionate distribution of the innovative and reproductive activities in the economic region homogeneous in respect of development level and ability to develop. If these technical cultures are not established, or develop in isolation from each other, in divergent directions, we cannot speak of integration. Insofar as the distribution of the innovative cores in the area tends not towards homogeneity, but towards an unequal distribution among the national economies, we can by no means speak about an integration of *socialist* type, the integration process itself will become full of internal tensions and thus unstable. The regional community which is unable to bring about and realize an economic strategy working towards a homogeneous field of force from the viewpoint of technological levels, will sooner or later become the victim of its own growing internal contradictions. For a revival of the economic integration of the CMEA countries, it is above all necessary that each country should possess a 12 to 20 years longer horizon for its development strategy unified in respect of its fundamental viewpoints. This has to comprise not only the development ideas about particular productive activities or industries, but also—in view of realistic possibilities—the technical cultures in the development of which they can participate, to a planned extent and in a planned capacity.

These strategies should not be confronted at the end points, but have to be worked out in an iterative manner, in a process of constant collation. Thus, the idea which emerges from the Comprehensive Program in connection with consultations about economic policy is not *one* of the methodological instruments of integration, not even one of the major methods, but a *conditio sine qua non* of the integration. It would be expedient to develop further the Comprehensive Program mainly in this respect. First of all, it should be clear that not consultations are needed but coordination, more exactly: *synchronization.* Secondly, it is not simply the synchronization of economic policies that should be aimed at—it would be futile to aim at the synchronization of short- and medium-term economic policies in the case of independent national economies—but that of *strategies.* Finally, also the key points should be exactly identified where strategies must by all means be collated. In my view such are the problems related to the decisions of the division of labour to be made in the future years, regarding the *technical cultures and the development of their innovative cores*, and to the joint establishment of the *basic materials, energy* and infrastructural systems.

The coordination of medium-term economic cooperation must be based on this strategic synchronization. I deliberately use here the term coordination which means a looser collation than synchronization. At the same time, as regards its nature and scope, this coordination would considerably differ from the present practice of medium-term plan-coordination. Coordination would not be focussed on contractual formulation of more or less operative activities, but on the mutual deliveries and regrouping of assets related to the strategic points, the basis of their commercial conditions, and those blocs of the national economic control systems whose collation is a condition of the functioning of the division of labour, the guide-lines for the organizational and legal solutions of joint actions, and, finally, the guidelines related to the policy of the whole community towards other sectors of the world economy. This does not exclude five-year commodity delivery contracts, cooperation or other agreements. But all these cannot replace the political coordination of development and cooperation over the five years, and cannot push the concentration on the most important problems claiming common interest into the background. One can only agree that the Comprehensive Program has been accorded an important place in the coordination of five-year plans within the mechanism of integration. But this central place does not determine in itself the extent contents and nature of the changes in coordination that have to organize not cooperation in general, but a coordination that entails integration. As a matter of fact, it became clear from the preceding that coordination, instead of trying to cover everything, should be reoriented towards a strong selection of problems to be coordinated, from the collation of mutual deliveries to problems of investment and technological development, from the sectoral approach towards complex technical cultures, extracting and infrastructural systems, from the collation of plan data in the closer sense towards development and coordination of policies and conceptions.

Further, the reduction of the category of plan-coordination to a simple collation in the central planning bodies must be done away with. If development is grouped in CMEA dimensions around internationally harmonized technical cultures, then, particularly in manufacturing, we shall meet several vertical productive complexes, medium level administrative organs, main contractors, etc., needing in their own special areas bilateral and multilateral—at least five-year—coordination in order to be able to fulfill their tasks. *Thus, medium-term cooperation in planning means at the same time the coordination of plans of the cooperating key units of the economies.* This has to be acknowledged and promoted if we do not want to drown the actual and purposeful intertwining of technical cultures in the swamp of bureaucracy, incompetence and dead slowness. Cooperation in planning cannot thus be by far restricted to the coordinating activities of central planning agencies or of ministries. From what has been said it follows that it should be extended to the coordination of development, investment, production and trade programs of those participating in the division of labour, and to their joint elaboration, as well as to the cooperation of producers and users in different countries.

At this point *the most important internal contradiction of the international integration process is revealed.* If it is true that the contradictory nature of commodity production is met in the international division of labour on macro-economic level as the contradiction of national economies specializing in the production of use values but remaining independent in respect of the production of values, then the consequences of this emerging in the model of integration also have to be reckoned with. A national economy which is an autonomous producer of values—that is, which consumes and accumulates on a level secured by the efficiency of *national* labour—will naturally aim in its economic development plans to maximize the efficiency of various national productive activities and, through this, to attain a structural and efficiency optimum of the national production. It will put the system of goals and instruments of its economic policy above all at the service of attaining this optimum, and will endeavour to direct its foreign-trade policy to fit into the international division of labour to approach this optimum.

Parallel to that, *international production structures* develop, located in several countries but closely cooperating with each other, consisting of enterprises, unions of enterprises, whose development requirements become independent in certain respects. In an internationalized agricultural engineering culture it will be established on the basis of intrinsic criteria where to produce, say, tools and where the development and production of prime movers should take place. An internationalized petrochemical culture will judge by its own criteria where it will be optimal to locate the most capital-intensive, the most research-intensive or the least qualified labour-intensive technological processes. All these "international" criteria will not necessarily coincide with the particular optimum criteria of the national economies, they may partly or entirely become alienated from or conflict with the latter. The optimum criteria emerging in various cross sections may fight with each other and it may be feared that the efficiency of production will be the loser.

In the capitalist system this contradiction is usually solved in a drastic manner. The capitalist interests which are most powerful technically and financially will internationalize production under their own control and try to push into the background the particular viewpoints of the national economies affected. The national economies either adapt themselves or try to influence with various economic policy measures (taxes, restriction of capital flows, foreign-exchange policy) the optimizing behaviour of the multinational corporations, detrimental to them.

Obviously, this "solution" is not an example to be followed in a socialist integration. We are in the particular objective situation that we cannot solve the former contradictions at the expense of the national optimum criteria, nor can we dispense with a strong internationalization of the productive processes. It follows that we also have to accept the optimum criteria of the technical cultures appearing on an international level.

If this contradiction appears on a "micro-economic" level in the closer sense, that is, if its effects become accentuated in a great many minor cooperative actions, an adequately "calibrated" (national and international) market-regulating system may provide, as a matter of fact, a tolerable framework for its movements. International cooperation produces major or minor positive and negative effects on a mass scale, and these can be satisfactorily compensated by an international "pool" or fund of the national budgets of the member countries set aside for the purpose. Insofar as such cooperation develops among CMEA countries in the future, their regulating mechanism will be in any case of a market character, and the outstandingly positive and negative effects of individual transactions must be neutralized through compensation.

But today we have not yet reached the stage where cooperation within the CMEA massively extends to the micro-sphere in the closer sense. But there are several tasks of cooperation which, as regards their size, are of decisive importance for the development of a smaller or a medium-sized economy. Let us only remember the programs covering computer techniques, the production of equipment for atomic power plants, or the container program, or the introduction of the automatic railway wagon-coupling devices. These all represent such technological cultures in respect of which the decision of a national enterprise or industry may sensitively affect the operation of the entire national economy in question and also the international culture. In the next decade we cannot escape the "challenge" of this contradiction: a socialist alternative must be found for the solution.

It must be clearly understood that cooperation in planning also means the direct contacts of planning agencies and productive organizations, since the problem cannot be solved on the levels of either the planning organs or the productive organizations alone. Coordination among the planning organs unavoidably puts into the fore the "optima" of the particular national economies, and optimum can figure here only in quotation marks, since for the development possibilities of the culture that can be developed only through international cooperation, the narrow resources of a small or a medium-sized country can be only a bed of Procrustes, and it may confront through the actual cooperation problem to be solved the well or less well-conceived interests of the economies. A cooperation reduced to the possibilities of establishing business contacts moves between the limits of the general scope of movement of the enterprises of the country in question. This is either too narrow—then cooperation cannot come about—and the international development of the culture becomes impossible; or it is too wide and then the future fate of cooperation will be decided by the power relations of the enterprises of different nationality and the activated national resources behind them, but not by the perspectivic possibilities. The nature of cooperation would tend towards a situation which has been just excluded from the socialist alternatives.

The solution might be based not on the alternative of "either–or", but on that of "also"; its outline may be the following one:

— *Collation of economic strategies on state level* has to decide on the development of the international culture, on the size of the resources the individual countries use for the purpose, on the areas the individual countries undertake in this division of labour, as well as on the time schedule of development. It has to be decided on the same level in what depth and in what organizational framework the participating research and productive organs, investments and commercial activities should be coordinated *with each other*. For example where is it enough to link the affected enterprises with long-term contracts and where an international economic organization should also be brought about, and if so, to what extent this organization should decide on the management of the member enterprises and how it should coordinate its decisions with the national planning agencies.

— Similarly, government level *economic policy coordination* is needed to establish the principles of comparison for research, productive and service activities participating in the joint activity and belonging to different national economies (meaning the pricing and costing principles, those of currency conversion, the norms of profitability, etc.). Furthermore, decisions have to be made also on the extent and form of the flow of net social income realized by the whole international culture among the productive units working in the culture and on the gain due to the national budget of the country where the activity is located. Agreement has to be reached, on the same economic policy level, about the extent and terms under which the international enterprise may avail itself of the credits, convertible currency and rouble resources of the individual member countries. Finally, interstate negotiations are needed in order to fit the enterprise into the national legal systems. It will be expedient to include all this in interstate contracts.

On problems of the actual technological division of labour, cost normatives, plans for research and release of new products, price conditions of mutual deliveries, their time schedule, raising of credit, etc., that is, on all technical and economic as well as organizational conditions of operative cooperation, decisions must be reached in the framework of coordinative relations between the *productive* units affected, of course within the framework of the interstate contract.

The points listed above do not claim to be a concrete proposal, they are merely called upon to exemplify that cooperation contracts, international unions, joint enterprises are organic parts of economic coordination activities in the wider sense (in the wording of the Comprehensive Program: of cooperation in planning). Long-, medium- and short-term state-level coordination, in respect of the jointly developed technical cultures, all necessarily develop into direct enterprise coordination. These two levels of coordination imply each other. Both assume the existence of reliable measuring and stimulating instruments of the national labour, that is, purposeful systems of prices and currencies, compensation funds and credits. I emphasize that this completely intergrown form of macro- and micro-coordination, as well as coordination as such, and the monetary and price mechanisms are needed for the development and operation of *big common ventures*. (Above all for the development and operation of complex technical cultures and their innovative cores, further for the raw-material bases and infrastructural networks serving the whole of the integration.) *They are, therefore, indispensable for realizing the synchronized development strategies so that the contradiction between the national economic optimum and that of the "culture" may find an acceptable form of notion.*

Separate consideration is needed for the "sector" of integration which lies outside the scope of the decisive "innovative cores" as well as the big material supply bases and the infrastructural networks. These are the cooperation matters which are slight by themselves, but which *in their aggregate*, may yield extraordinary additional efficiency for the national economies. Here belong the "traditional" foreign trade, the cooperations of smaller volume, exchange of assortments, tourism, etc. As a matter of fact, the contractual relations of the innovative cores with their technological environment also belong here.

I believe it is important to stress that it is expedient to handle separately, *as regards approach and principles*, the mechanisms serving the development of cooperation implemented in these "cultures" and those outside them. Not because in some marginal cases it might cause hesitation under what type a cooperation in question should be classified: obviously, here we have to face debates, and at times take upon ourselves even the risk of incorrect choice. But we would take upon ourselves a much greater burden, if we tried to squeeze into the Procrustes-bed of a uniform mechanism two types of cooperation which differ from each other in principle, either the one into that of the other, or both into some mixed mechanism born out of some compromise.

The basic difference between the two kinds of cooperation may be found in the quantity and quality of their effect on the national economies. Each of the integrations realized in the "cultures" is important enough to have in itself an important effect on the technical development and world-market competitivity of all participating national economies, in the final analysis, on their internal growth and equilibrium through the external factors of economic growth. As a consequence, these demand individual, state-level control, collation and financing. The latter, the cooperations "outside the cultures" have such effect only in their aggregate. It follows that their individual control is impossible—or would demand such unsurmountable organizational tasks from central organs they cannot cope with. *Here the only realistic possibility attainable for economic policy collations is to create the norms and frameworks for cooperation.*

CHAPTER TEN

Market systems at the service of economic policy coordination

Insofar as we accept that the harmonization of the "decisive" planned economic processes is a corner-stone of cooperation (for the time being, and at least for one or two decades, we do not reckon with the emergence of direct cooperation between small and medium-sized enterprises on a mass scale), we also have to take into account that the *value relations regulating the profitability of international exchange will have an active influence first of all on long-term development decisions, either on central state level or on that of the productive enterprises.* This determines the scope in which we have to look, already now, for the ways of strengthening the effects of commodity (market) and money relations. Furthermore, we also have to be aware that the assertion of the principle of profit motive takes place in the framework of the deliberate collation of development preferences, as a system of criteria for economic policy, for choosing variants in respect of development and the division of labour—but not necessarily the only system. The relative rouble prices, their deviations from the relative prices expressed in convertible currencies, the parities between the rouble and the Western key currencies, as well as the rouble and key-currency parities of the other CMEA currencies, the terms of delivery and payment, the multilateral transferability of surpluses in the balances of payment, etc., will influence the national, sectoral and corporation decisions first of all in respect of the limits of "decisive" cooperation volumes, and the ways of realization. Thus, the elements of the price and monetary mechanisms influence above all a *relatively small number of decisions which are of major portent.* They attain these effects first of all on such levels where (a) decisions are taken on the long-term or long-term implications are of decisive importance also in the short-term decisions, (b) the effects of efficiency impulses are weighed together with other comprehensive circumstances of economic and general policy.

As a consequence, the price and monetary mechanisms to be worked out in the socialist cooperation cannot be conceived of as being independent of, as if only *assigned to*, the economic strategy coordination. It has to be an instrument of control orientating cooperation in economic strategy and its practical implementation. Therefore, investigating the correct developments of the elements of the mechanism in its interrelated blocs is not an expedient method in itself, it may lead astray the measures aimed at promoting the integration. The CMEA countries are in such a phase of development and of developing cooperation when *progress comes about only with the aid of complex action systems oriented towards very definite objectives.* From among them, three systems will be separately investigated: the system of *economic protection,* the system of *compensating risks and gains,* and finally, the system of *financing.*

a) The system of economic protection

I deliberately avoid using the expression "protectionism", though etymologically it would be correct. But economic theory has appropriated this word for denoting the aggregate of such direct or indicative measures which generally protect the "domestic" (national or regional) activities, and support their expansion on external markets, that is, which work in *autarkic* or *"mercantilist"* directions. It does not make sense to speak about such protectionism in respect of the CMEA member countries, nor the CMEA as a whole. On the other hand, in the heads of economists the word protectionism is linked to the "educative" tariff as a "mild" form, and to quantitative restriction of imports as a "rough" form. The task of both is to restrict foreign competition on the domestic market. The system of economic protection of the socialist community *must not* work in the direction of either autarky or mercantilism, as regards either the member countries or the community as a whole. Furthermore, this system of protection is functioning in a quite different medium than the protectionism in capitalist countries. It is not called upon to forestall the attacks of the competitive (or potentially competitive) environment, but to secure an adequate market for realization and a supply basis for the export-oriented national productive activities which have come about in consequence of the collation of economic strategies and for the sectors depending on imports. From this aspect the socialist system of international economic protection means the extension of necessary development and market security, deriving from planned economy, to the whole of the community.

In economic contacts with third countries the state monopoly of foreign trade is at work. It is called upon to promote economic cooperation in the cases when equal rights and the conditions of mutual advantages are given, and to prevent the assertion of effects hindering development from outside the Community. Insofar as the need arises, the elimination of undesirable effects emanating from some CMEA countries to other areas of the Community belongs to the scope of economic policy coordination. Similarly, in this framework any CMEA country may look for an alternative solution within the CMEA, whenever the solution of some economic problem with third countries would involve unfavourable consequences. In this sense, the protective function *on the scale of the CMEA community* is restricted to warding off the destructive impulses through joint help, and does not include actions against solutions with third countries in favour of an alternative within the CMEA, if this is favourable for the economies.

Protection of the individual countries within the CMEA, however, must be, necessarily, of a double purpose and a double edge. On the one hand, the *producer* (the exporting country or enterprise) depending on the buyers market within the community has to be protected, insofar as its specialization develops in the course of cooperation, in consequence of its requirements. The system has to secure the possibility for the specializing producer to "run in" in respect of quantity and quality (waiting time), as well as the possibilities of realization after "running in", together with a fair profit and accumulation possibility. On the other hand, the system of protection has to protect the *user* (importing country or enterprise) depending on the supply base, similarly if the dependence has come about in consequence of decisions on cooperation or traditions in respect of the division of labour. In this case the system has to secure imports in terms of quantity and quality (technical parameters) and time schedule, guaranty has to be provided against unjustified price fluctuations, neglect of services and supply of parts.

As can be seen, the system of protection within the CMEA is a qualitatively different category from, say, the collective tariff system of the Common Market. It is less, since it does not work at any price towards alternatives to be implemented within the CMEA, and more, as it provides the security guaranteed by planned economy both for producers and users in the whole community.

For building up such a system of protection it is not enough to set up one or two market or monetary mechanisms carefully, the tariffs, the rouble-dollar parity, or the parities between the rouble and the national currencies. The system of protection *starts* to operate through the collation of economic strategies and plans, but it covers, in a complex manner, the prices, the types of contracts and of unions, credits and their conditions, and, of course, the elements of the mechanism of monetary nature as well, all related to each other.

As a consequence, when developing the mechanism of CMEA cooperation it will be expedient to harmonize and complement all regulating elements and institutions in a complex manner from the viewpoint whether, *in their aggregate*, they secure a protection of the right direction and extent, a favourable national economic and enterprise environment for the implementation of the most important and collated tasks of economic strategy.

b) The system of compensation

As has been mentioned in the foregoing, equal gain can be derived for each participant in the cooperation only by chance. At the same time, it is in the interest of all those participating that phases of work which yielding relatively low profits, should be also performed. Obviously, the solution lies in approximation, and in certain cases compensating the larger or smaller risks and results. The differences in gains to be derived from the division of labour may be, in general, traced back to two kinds of reasons:

— Either those participating in the cooperation cannot produce with equal productivity, as a consequence of the different degree of their economic development level, organization or labour intensity. This I shall not take into account in connection with the system of compensation. Namely, insofar as this difference in efficiency derives from backwardness owing to *historical* development, it should not be compensated for, but complex help should be provided in order to eliminate the causes. Insofar as the disproportionately small gain derives from bad work organization, loose discipline in technology, or is perhaps the consequence of other national or local deficiencies in economic management, it would be unfair to raise low productivity to the rank of "socially necessary labour".

— It may derive from the fact that in the course of the division of labour some participants are allocated phases of work which reckon with their capabilities to maximum extent, while others are compelled to rest satisfied with more primitive or less efficient work they are capable of performing. Such cases may occur, e.g., when mineral deposits are exploited under unfavourable conditions of extraction or with the export of agricultural products; or when specialization covers such phase of work in whose product the valid foreign-trade price system comprises only a small part of value to be accumulated. In these cases compensation for the efficiency between the cooperating countries is not only justified but it is an elementary condition of the division of labour as well. Of course, it is difficult to separate the two kinds in practice. The odium of debates and negotiations must be undertaken even if a legion of actual cases has to be faced. We should be also aware that the system of compensation cannot be reduced to the creation of an international fund or to the harmonization of the national systems of subsidies. The system of compensation also begins with the coordination of economic policies and continues with the systems of prices and credit, exchange rates, cost accounting methods and their approximation. It is only in the course of their complex harmonization and "grinding" that the conditions will mature for the creation of international compensation funds and their smooth functioning—but these are only important, though not exclusive elements. That is, for being able to bring about the system of compensating for gains and risks, the available (existing or possible) elements of regulation should be rethought and adjusted to each other in their whole complexity also from this special point of view.

c) The system of financing

The specialized roles undertaken within the division of labour differ not only in respect of current costs and the possibilities of price receipts, but also in respect of the *absolute or relative* volumes of *capital* to be advanced. Whether the absolute volume of the assets to be advanced exceeds the capacity of the country, or the specific capital requirements are too high or slower returned than the country is able to bear the capital factor may become a serious obstacle to a given and technically and economically otherwise well-founded and necessary integrational cooperation. In such cases the necessity of joint financing of the venture by several countries to be implemented in cooperation comes to the fore (investment, creation of foreign affiliation or capital participation, breaking into markets, service network, development loan to third countries, etc.).

In the current practice of the CMEA, cooperation in financing comes about partly through bilateral intergovernmental credits or investment contributions, and partly through the credits of the International Investment Bank. In this field we can thus start from a point well above zero. But it cannot be said that the existing credit constructions have become organic parts of the mechanism of the integration. There is no organic relationship as yet between the economic development policies, the collation process of plans and the credit system of the IIB. Nor is the commodity cover of credits, raised in transferable roubles from the IIB clear. The condition system of investment credits granted with the aim of extracting raw materials has not yet developed, the rouble flowing through this channel from country to country is not organically related to the whole of the international money circulation. Interest does not fulfil its function of re-allocating gains. That is, the joint financing of major joint ventures is just emerging within the CMEA, but its elements have not yet amalgamated into a *system* with whose existence, criteria and conditions the member countries could safely reckon and to which they could adapt their internal financing systems and development programs.

I believe it needs no special proof that the international financing system affects all elements of the mechanism and superstructure, beginning with the collation of economic policies and plans through the price systems and rates of exchange to the institutional framework of cooperation.

In working out the system of instruments of the integration it would be a mistake to judge the role, scope and intensity of effect of the individual regulatory elements in isolation. For a correct approach it is necessary to fit these into those complex systems of mechanisms which are themselves called upon to create a favourable medium for clearsight, interests and institutions, for the collation and implementation of economic policy objectives.

PART FOUR

The Basic Conditions of the Hungarian Economic Development Strategy

CHAPTER ONE

The basic conditions of the Hungarian foreign-trade strategy

Because of its small size, its development level and structure, Hungarian economy is strongly dependent on world economic relations. The value of the volume of commodities yearly exchanged in foreign trade approximates half of our national income. More than one-third of total trade is transacted with the Soviet Union, about one-third with other European socialist countries, less than one quarter with the advanced capitalist countries, and about 6 to 8 per cent with the developing world. Thus, the foreign economic relations of Hungary have most intensively developed with the socialist world and about four-fifths of the trade are transacted with European countries. *The primary foreign economic medium of the Hungarian economy is the community of countries united in the CMEA, and our scope of movement in the wider sense is essentially Europe.*

The fact itself that our dependence on foreign economic relations is particularly strong demand that in working out the national policy of economic development the movements, developments and changes in the power relations of the external economic environment should be followed with increased attention. It is no exaggeration to state that the development possibilities of the Hungarian economy and its equilibrium in the external economic environment are at least as much determined by the conditions of the latter as by those deriving from the economy itself.

a) The physical determination of the Hungarian economy in the world-economic situation

By the physical determination of our world-economic situation I mean the *dependence on imports and exports of the employment of the economically active population, of the living circumstances proportionate to the quality and quantity of the labour performed, as well as of the maintenance of the normal growth rate of the economy.* More exactly it depends on the extent to which the national economy has to rely on imports of primary energy, basic materials and foodstuffs, as well as of the tools of labour necessary for the maintenance and development of the productive machinery, furthermore, the portion of the output that has to be produced under the conditions of the given structure for foreign users, in order to secure the functioning of the domestic productive machinery.

According to 1971 statistics, about 14 per cent of all sources of the economy came from imports (23 per cent in industry and 4 per cent in agriculture), while 0.28 Ft exports stand against 1.00 Ft of domestic utilization, the corresponding values being 0.56 in industry and 0.30 in agriculture. Of course, these values show wide dispersion in the economy according to various fields of production (see Table 15). The fact in itself that one-fourth of agricultural end products and more than one-third of those in industry are produced from the outset with the aim of being exported, while almost one-third of the machinery and chemical products used in the economy are imported, are highly meaningful. It is worthwhile to analyse these data in some greater detail.

Table 15

Role of exports and imports in various branches

Branches, industries	Complementary imports as percentage of all sources	Exports per Ft 1 of domestic utilization
National economy, total	13.6	0.28
Agriculture	4.3	0.30
Industry	23.1	0.56
of which: Electric energy	11.8	0.05
Mining	28.0	0.20
Metallurgy	23.8	4.68
Engineering	30.6	0.61
Chemical industry	30.5	1.47
Light industry	18.3	0.44
Food industry	10.6	0.34

The input-output data show surprisingly low ratios in mining and metallurgy. But the dependence on imports immediately becomes more marked, if we think of the basic materials of key importance. Namely, their effect on the ability of the economy to function is not of the magnitude shown by the sums in the I/O table.

According to the data of the Statistical Yearbook for 1971, three-fourths of the crude oil used were imported. Essentially the whole of our needs for copper, zinc, lead, tin, sulphur, rubber and cotton are covered from imports. Similarly, 70 per cent of coking coal and soft sawnwood are imported, as well as 40 per cent of the cement and paper used, and two-thirds of cow hides. The ratio of imports is of about the same magnitude in the supply of iron (in Fe-contents, up to the metallurgical phase). Thus, in respect of the materials and primary energy influencing the operation of the whole of the economy the most, the impact of imports is much deeper than shown by the average figures.

In engineering the use of parts of foreign origin is growing. In 1971 somewhat more than one-fourth of all parts were imported, while in the same year parts for exports constituted one-tenth of the total output of engineering.

The dependence of Hungarian production is not less in some key areas of realizing exports. From among the products of the aluminium industry about one-fourth of bauxite and nine-tenths of alumina are exported (the latter is smelted in its bulk in the framework of the Hungarian–Soviet and the Hungarian–Polish agreements). And the aluminium blocks produced are practically also exported. As regards the products of the machine-tool industry, one-fourth of the milling machines and almost 100 per cent of the planing machines are exported.

The bus industry, the pharmaceutical industry, the industries producing medical and industrial X-ray apparatuses, and the crane industry produce 80 to 100 per cent of their output for export, but the volume of exports exceeds two-thirds in such productive activities as coffee-making equipment for restaurants, aluminium kitchenware, electric bulbs and tubes, photochemical papers, dressed poultry, canned fruits and vegetables, tomato pulp and red pepper. About half of the railway passenger wagons, electronic tubes, shoes, salami, sausage, and eggs produced are exported annually. The ratio of exports is considerable in the electric and electronic instruments industry, in telecommunication equipments. That is, some key industries and agricultural branches depend to a much greater extent and more concentratedly on export markets than this appears from average indicators.

Considering the physical determination on both the export and the import side, the nature of the Hungarian economy may be outlined. With some exaggeration one might say that the Hungarian economy is a "sub-contracting unit". According to my estimates, from the economically active 5 million people only about 800 thousand are engaged in extracting activities and 2.6 million are directly engaged in the transformation of the domestic and imported products. In the productive sphere we find more than three manufacturers for one engaged in extraction. Almost nine-tenths of those engaged in extraction are plant producers and only 130 thousand are miners (90 thousand of these coal miners). Thus, the basic materials and energy procured through imports are transformed in the hands of three-fourths of the active Hungarian population and are mostly exported. The domestic labour added to the value of the raw materials must be of a quantity, quality and qualification sufficient for covering the material consumption of the domestic productive sphere and of the consumption of the population and also for allowing the exchange of a part of manufacturing labour for foreign one. Thus, in the basic formula of the functioning of the Hungarian economy the independent variables are industry, organization and skill.

This is why it can be stated that the most important natural resource of the Hungarian economy is brains, more important than bauxite, coal, hydrocarbons, and even than the favourable natural conditions for agriculture. From this aspect, the nature of the Hungarian economy resembles that of every densely populated, industrialized country short of raw materials, like Switzerland, Austria, Denmark, Japan, Bulgaria, etc.

It follows that though Hungarian economy is highly dependent on the international division of labour, that is, in the sense of the I/O table it may be considered as a very open economy, it should not, however, be forgotten that only such division of labour can serve a balanced fast development in which the industry and skills of the population can be realized, that is, where the country may *receive extractive activity in exchange for manufacturing activity*, and that in such ratio that the extracting activity remaining in the country may satisfy the realistic equilibrium and development requirements of the economy.

Beyond what has been said, because of the necessarily oversize manufacturing apparatus—relative to the needs of the domestic market—the Hungarian economy is naturally attracted by a *division of labour that is safe in the long run.* In the order of preferences of the Hungarian economic strategy stability of international economic relations should always precede the relations promising big but uncertain profit. This is particularly justified also by the fact that our manufacturing started to develop with a time lag of almost a hundred years relative to the advanced, earlier industrialized countries. Therefore it needs, for the time being, protection from competition, and because of the small size of the economy, national protection seems to be ineffective and unpromising from the very outset.

Finally, the fact that the main "natural" resource of the Hungarian economy is the diligence and skills of the population, determines from the outset the main direction and basic character of "internal" economic strategy. On the one hand, production policy has to reckon increasingly with the development possibilities deriving from skills, and, on the other hand, economic policy has to manage the quality of living labour very carefully. The most important instrument of developing the forces of production of the economy is vocational training, as well as raising the general level of education. *Public education and vocational training are at least as important sectors of investment as construction or machine building*. In a country which has to live almost exclusively from the labour capacity of its population, an outstanding feature of economic policy as a whole is its *being centred on man.* This can secure the generally favourable social atmosphere which, as a medium, promotes the widest development of industry and skills as well as their smooth functioning.

Thus, despite all appearances, the ultimate problem to be solved in the Hungarian economy is not the supply of raw materials or market realization. Insofar as we do not recognize that the only factor of our forces of production that can be rendered dynamic is—even on a world scale—the mass of educated, competent, disciplined and satisfied people, the working population itself, then our efforts to supply material and energy and to secure markets might become a hasty chase after short-term advantages. This may only impair our world-economic position in the future and together with it also the conditions of our internal equilibrium and growth will deteriorate. If, however, we are aware of these, we can find the common points where the human-centred economic policy will not be a "social burden", but accelerate economic development and gain such a place for us in the division of labour of the world—above all in the CMEA integration—in which our efforts will simultaneously meet with the long-term development concepts of our partners in cooperation. As a result of such policy, the external market realization possibilities will increase and the supply of energy and raw material will be secured in the long run.

b) Possibilities of the Hungarian economy to fit into the division of labour

It is, of course, not sufficient to state the well-known fact that the Hungarian economy is a manufacturing character and, as a developed country, it can be fitted only as such into the division of labour of the developed world. The purpose of foreign economic relations is not only to import articles in short supply, but also to acquire advantages. In the preceding chapters it has been explained that through the international division of labour not only comparative advantages may be attained, but also advantages deriving from dynamism, from adaptation of imported technologies and from cooperation which cannot be fitted into the Ricardian theory.

It is also unequivocal that every advantage realizable for the economy depends partly on the domestic social-labour productivity it induces, and partly also on the terms of trade in which domestic labour is exchanged through foreign-trade relations. Thus, the national economic gain derived from the division of labour has a production and a turnover component. The production factor may be structural—this is the comparative advantage in the purest sense of the word—but the dynamic advantage is also near to it, and it may be linked to a definite productive activity (such may be, e.g., the advantages from cooperation or adaptation). The gain emerging in turnover may derive from favourable changes in prices, in exchange relations, from improved terms of credit, etc. From the viewpoint of the present reasoning, the latter should be taken into account only insofar as they influence the long-term (at least fifteen-year) structural transformation, the strategy of international cooperation.

What objectively determined efforts may the Hungarian national economy take as regards the different advantages realizable through international cooperation?

In respect of the *comparative* advantages, our possibilities are as follows:

— *Comparative advantages may be gained everywhere, where the natural conditions of production are favourable in Hungary.* This may be found in some agricultural branches, at some points of the vertical chain of the aluminium industry, in tourism related to spas, in transit transportation, etc. *In these fields the most important element of comparative advantage is the differential land (and mine) rent incomes.* It means that the relation between the forint and the foreign currency may remain favourable for some longer time, and also additional investments may earn foreign currency at favourable terms. But three factors have to be taken into consideration.

One is the relation between the productivity of labour on national level and the cost of labour. If—overestimating the importance of favourable natural conditions—we do not try to develop and maintain highly effective cultures in these areas, after some time the favourable "foreign currency earning" conditions will no longer reflect the advantageous natural conditions, but merely the *relatively low wage* of domestic labour. In reality the tendency should be precisely the reverse. A favourable cost of earning foreign currency should reflect *less and less* the differences in wages and more markedly the comparative advantage similar to differential land rent. If the labour productivity determined by the technology is low, then the maintenance of the activity either becomes inefficient, at least for export purposes, or it can be maintained only at the expense of the level of consumption of the population.

The other factor is *prices*. There may be such activities whose foreign exchange returns are today favourable, but become increasingly difficult to maintain, in consequence of the unfavourable long-term development of the terms of trade. This may occur also because other producers, too, turn towards the same product (e.g. with a lower wage level, say, in fruits and vegetables production or in low-quality wine), but this may also happen if world consumption turns away from product. In vain do we have perhaps outstandingly favourable natural conditions, in vain do we equip labour with excellent skills and technology, the terms of trade do not allow realizing the comparative advantage of the differential rent. Ever more has to be exported in order to import less. Conversely, if we can select from among our existing natural advantages those whose development coincides with the changes in future world demand, the rise in prices will make the latent comparative advantages realizable. This is generally true for structural transformation, yet I underline it in this place. It requires big advances in investment and the productive and service capacities created are, as a matter of fact, inconvertible. A bauxite mine opened cannot be converted into a corn-producing system, and a sanatorium built at Zalakaros spa cannot be converted into a lock on the Danube, particularly not if the depreciation of the not quite well-founded projects is not properly secured.

— In the long run such development may also bring comparative advantages, which *concentrates* the available labour *on the most promising points of "domestic industry and skill"*, beginning with the research centres up to the productive and service sectors. In such a case, the comparative advantage does not possess the nature of land rent, there is no such guaranty for the realization of additional efficiency. Yet we may reckon with a comparative advantage in the long run, since what we have in mind are such special areas for the expression of particular domestic skills and production experience, in respect of which it is difficult for the foreign partners to make up for Hungary's advantage.

Again, we have to be aware of two dangers. Since these are highly research and development intensive areas of production, that is, areas where the conditions for concentration are much more favourable in the bigger and more advanced countries, it cannot be expected that we can advance along a broad front. Not even if the personal conditions of progress were otherwise given, since this would lead to a fragmentation of our restricted assets, which, again, would result in a declining rate of innovative activities, and the comparative advantages would soon vanish. In this case, we would be compelled to use the fragmented and technologically backward research and development capacity as auxiliary workshops of foreign innovative bases. Maybe, for some time this would secure favourable foreign-currency earning possibilities in the export of intellectual products, but, again, *this would only reflect the relative cheapness of domestic intellectual labour*, and not the size of intellectual value created. Thus, the lack of selectivity or inconsiderate implementation may conflict after some time with the basic motive of our socialist economic policy. We have to select and several factors should be taken into account in selection. The first such factor is *the existence, development possibility and reproducibility of the domestic innovative bases*. We must be in a position to select such activities, in which vocational training is also on a high level, where the research bases are already available and also the core of the productive basis is ready for a simultaneous implementation of expansion and deepening (extensive and intensive development). Insofar as foreign intellectual import has to be added or equipment has to be bought, these should be of a complementary character, their use should not mean only adaptation, but also further development. The other is the *high-level further development of the world surrounding us*. From the range of choice offered by domestic possibilities those have to be selected which aim at the satisfaction of social needs that are emergent and developing, and not only on a domestic but even on a world scale. In vain did the Hungarian industry produce for decades solid steam engines, it would be a folly to concentrate the available resources on the further maintenance of a *dead* technology. This is nonsense, as it would be nonsense to try to revive the production of helicopters which broke off in an experimental stage in the thirties—in spite of the fact that the first helicopter was constructed in Hungary and the industry is not among the degrading ones. In such cases we have to put up with the fact that erstwhile Hungarian achievements can no longer be exploited, they are lost forever. Someone else has adopted and further improved them. The costs of reintroduction would exceed our risk-taking and load-bearing capacity.

— Finally, we can acquire advantages from cooperation also if we *produce certain products in such lots* which extremely press down the costs relative to other products which are not mass-producible. In an economy with a narrow internal market, as ours, it is very risky to *base* the acquisition of comparative advantages on mass production, first of all because in this respect a small country has considerable initial disadvantages relative to a bigger economy. Insofar as a small economy wishes to introduce efficient modern technology in the mass production of end products or parts, it has to install special automated machinery and to write it off at a rate at which similar machinery becomes obsolete and is replaced by new. This is an investment-intensive activity and entails big risk. If the country does not undertake this cost of investment and risk and wants to realize mass production with universal machines—in the interest of the easier convertibility of products—this may be detrimental to productivity. Under such conditions the cost of earning foreign currency will again depend on the depressed wage level.

Thus, the policy aimed at deriving comparative advantages from large series is again *a problem of selection.* The first viewpoint of selection is the *acquirability, introduction possibility and investment cost of the technology.* The second is the convertibility of the technology of mass production and the *costs of conversion,* finally, the *price* that can be prognosticated in the long run. The less capital-intensive the technology needed for mass production, the less it is linked to the production of a given product (likely to become obsolete), the more promising its introduction in a small country will be. The more difficult the technology to learn, that is, the bigger skills and organization it requires, the longer its life cycle and the higher the attainable foreign-trade price. But this contradicts the requirements raised against capital intensity and convertibility. It is very difficult to find a solution in this dilemma. Therefore, to acquire comparative advantages through large series is a relatively difficult task to tackle for a small country which is not in the front line of development. This may be somewhat alleviated by being linked to a market secured for some longer time, or by renouncing on a considerable part of the profit in the interest of supply with machinery (foreign investment, leasing).

The possibilities of the Hungarian economy to acquire comparative advantages are thus restricted to a part of the *extracting sector* of relatively small volume. Here belong coarse grain, quality wines and red pepper from plant cultivation, bauxite from mining and tourism related to spas and transit transportation from services. From the *manufacturing sector some mass producing industries linked to big, secured markets* may earn comparative advantages, e.g. vehicle parts, as well as the *Hungarian innovative cores* around which the quickly developing production cultures attaining the European technological and cost level may be built. All three fields have to be handled as development-intensive ones if in the future we want to rely to a decreasing extent on the favourable possibilities of earning foreign currency through the relatively low costs of domestic living labour, that is, in the last resort, on the consequences of our relative technological backwardness on the living standard.

As regards the advantages of *dynamism*, the Hungarian economic strategy has to develop such a selective production policy which links the productive activities developing more or less on independent intellectual and material bases to the quickly developing market needs, and undertakes "sub-contracting" roles in fast-developing foreign productive activities. In the case of productive activities which require little capital, the capacities of which can be quickly converted and which can be quickly learnt, it is enough to make a medium-term estimate of the foreign demand and the foreign sub-contracting base. But in the case of products which constitute the basis of the economy and which are highly capital-intensive, the long-term tendencies of the world economy should be taken for basis, even if the given assets could be invested into industries with a shorter cycle at a faster return and higher profit. This self-restraint is demanded first of all by the small size of the economy. It would be a mistake to believe that the small economy has to move by all means in the "gaps" of the structural changes in the world economy; either by adopting the structural elements already discarded by the "big" in order to wring the meagre gains of the last hours of the boom, or by adopting smaller ideas satisfying marginal needs and earn the "demi-mondain" profits of short-lived fashion waves. This behaviour is very characteristic of a part of small capital pushed to the periphery of the developed big economies, as well as of certain—not negligible—sectors of countries on the periphery of the world economy.

The socialist economic policy is in a position to channel also the structural and technological development of small countries into such dynamic world-economic trends which allow stable development also in the long run—not least because of the possibilities provided by socialist integration. I regard as such trends, among other things, the solution of the food problem, public health, telecommunications, water control, education, all of them problems embracing mankind which offer for decades fast expanding development and selling chances for the Hungarian economy.

An economy like Hungary's, which has to struggle simultaneously with two initial difficulties, namely, of being "undersized" and "medium-developed", must think twice before deciding on the development of the areas where it will concentrate its narrowly limited resources. From this viewpoint the role of technology developed abroad may be to *stimulate and complement* the independent Hungarian technological development, or it may help *synchronous development* with the partner or partners, or it may *replace* domestic development. In any case, we expect an economic-policy gain from the import of technology, as is the case in general with the development of the forces of production. This gain is partly measurable (to be felt), it manifests itself in increased efficiency, either where the imported technology is implanted, or through secondary effects in other areas. Of course, the import of technology has side effects difficult to measure which can be felt also only after many years. Such are the increased demands on labour performance, the demanding nature of the workplace, weariness of work. If we truly believe that our almost only natural resources are the five million brains and ten million hands, this cannot be left out from any calculation of economic strategy, even if it is difficult to quantify exactly. This is why the necessity of importing technologies cannot be sufficiently underlined, always adding, of course, that it must not be allowed that imports should *replace* independent innovative activities at pivotal points of the national economy, they should only refresh them. The economy that puts up with one-sided imports of technology in the long run, will inescapably slide down to the periphery of development. The possibility of adaptation does not make it superfluous for society to contribute by its efforts to the development of human culture.

What advantages may the Hungarian economy attain through adaptation? I deem it necessary to stress again that this advantage derives from the division of labour, not from foreign trade. Its result is not an improvement of the indicator showing the costs of earning foreign exchange, but increased productivity of labour, as in the case when forces of production are developing from any source. It is related to the foreign trade relations insofar as (a) imported technology has a price, (b) its countervalue has to be produced at home, and (c) exchanged for money on external markets. An evaluation of the transaction from the viewpoint of foreign trade *in the closer sense* cannot transgress the world of comparative costs. Only a third factor is added: the *future* increase in national economic efficiency released by the operation of new technology. I believe it is necessary to underline the latter precisely because I am a citizen of a moderately developed small country depending on the import of technology. I understand that we can appear on the markets of countries with advanced technology with a domestic labour input 40 to 60 per cent higher than what is needed if we trade with countries on a development level similar to ours. That is, a moderately developed country wishing to develop fast—not only to grow—pays a very high price for the imports of technology accelerating the development of the forces of production. This prompts me to press for a highly *disciplined policy regarding imports of technology, a policy subjected to the considerations of long-term development.*

This policy must find a *way to concentrate a considerable part of the available foreign currency on "refreshing" imports.* I consider, namely, the comparative loss to more developed countries as an additional investment whose returns is secured through the additional efficiency derived from the technology imported in exchange. I believe that the most stable and most effective investments are made at those places where the imported technology does not replace but accelerates the operation of the domestic brains. At these points I would suggest mainly the imports of research, licences and major equipment and, insofar as this is possible, I would avoid importing ready technical solutions.

The remaining sum has to serve the purposes of adaptive connections to foreign technical cultures. There is place for the adoption of foreign licences providing ready technical solutions, particularly if the seller is willing to hand over continually the products of its own development activity, and also for cooperation constructions involving additional imports as well as for the purchase of equipment. The money spent on such purposes need not be used in so concentrated a way as in the case of the "refreshing" imports, but we should refrain from total fragmentation, because the degree of concentration of imports is, in a sense, inversely proportionate to the attainable "follow-up distance" and also to the terms of imports.

Finally, the Hungarian economy has to take great efforts to attain advantages through cooperation, the small size of the country is, in a sense, a predestination in this respect. These advantages may derive first of all from the increased scale of production. In the last resort this is realized in cost reductions relative to the price attainable on the world market, whether specialization in end products, parts or partial units is meant.

In shaping long-term production policies both technical progress (development of production and products) and the shaping of the macro- and micro-structure have to be channelled in a direction to strike a sound balance between the possibilities of acquiring comparative advantages *today and tomorrow.* In the meantime, it is indispensable to secure a fast-rate development of the economy, partly through increasing the domestic research and development potential and partly through a quick adoption of foreign technological achievements.

All these are of equal importance. *If economic policy one-sidedly commits itself to gaining comparative advantages of the moment,* the foreign market effects will, almost unequivocally, "dissuade" the economic leadership from increasing the domestic bases of research and development. This is natural: every economy which is a "latecomer" in development, finds itself facing the foreign development cores on the foreign markets. Let us assume that it bends under the pressure. In this case it may always have *some* gain from the adaptation with a certain time-lag of foreign research and development results. I stress: *some* gain, since the big gain has already been "skimmed" by the innovating society. From this small gain a relatively fast development can be produced if the growth of mass consumption is very strongly restricted. A smaller part of the higher-quality products of the cultures adopted will be consumed by narrow domestic strata with high incomes, the bigger part must be sold abroad. It follows that in the innovative economies these are no longer novelties or luxury items. Their prices tend to fall. It depends on the velocity of adaptation *how long and on what level* we can acquire foreign currency in order to cover the deficit of the economy in intellectual products and raw materials. Thus, an economic policy which is unequivocally directed towards gaining comparative advantages implies unequivocally a policy of adaptation, particularly in small half-backward countries short of raw materials, which also implies that the necessary growth rate can be secured only *at the price of polarizing internal standards of living*. The model is typically one of economies at the periphery of the developed world. It produces a development which does not curb mass consumption for a future high development level, but attains welfare for a narrow social stratum, without producing any guaranty for the future to discontinue this trend. This model of foreign trade —which might be called the *model of missing foreign-trade strategy*—pushes the economy towards dependence on the innovative cores, on business cycles, and in respect of domestic policy towards frustration of the demands of a socialist society as regards the living standard of the masses. Politics tends anyway towards developing schizophrenic phenomena. Either it is forced to a daily practice which is opposed to its own foreign-trade ideas, e.g. autarky, or it is compelled to distort the socialist principles related to the way of life of the population under the pressure of the tendencies asserting themselves. It can by no means escape the gradual deterioration of the position of the economy, nor the emergence of internal social and economic tension. Clearly, a socialist economic policy cannot venture to enter this swamp.

Let us assume another extreme. *Economic policy commits itself one-sidedly to an independent development of the forces of production*, suffering all economic and social consequences in its stride as long as it does not overtake the more developed environment. This model does not exclude efforts to gain advantages through adaptation, but this is not an action preparatory to comparative advantages to be measured and enjoyed already today, but serves unequivocally technical progress and world market competitivity *in the long run*. The economy which chooses this way must have by all means a developed internal research, development and productive machinery, and must feed the imported technical know-how into the domestic intellectual trends in order to be able to serve acceleration of the development of the innovative base. If a country does not possess such base, the massive import of technology will be utilized with a very low degree of efficiency: frequently it will not attain the necessary efficiency of an economy arranging for adaptation from the very outset. At the same time, this kind of development puts the accumulation efforts of the economy very much to the test. The growth rate is frequently imposingly high, but for a long time the consumption fund is lagging. The difference is that, in the hope of a future high development level, wide strata of the population have to restrict their consumption, and that, in consequence of the strong orientation of development towards major projects, luxury items are produced (or imported) in small quantities and thus do not require domestic markets and do not irritate the masses with low earnings. The final effect is, of course, again a shortage of consumer goods—perhaps linked with an increasing deficit in the balance of payments, that is, in a socialist sense, an unstable economic and social equilibrium. The bigger a country and the bigger its self-sufficiency in respect of basic materials, primary energy and food, the greater the expected success with which it can build the elements of this model into its foreign-trade strategy. The greater the dependence of an economy on foreign raw material and realization markets, the smaller the hope it may cherish to make this policy a basic component of its foreign-trade strategy. Neither its internal nor its external economic equilibrium, nor its social relations can bear the pressure for long, and the attainment of its final objective, i.e. raising the forces of production to the world level, is also highly doubtful. A sound socialist foreign-trade strategy cannot risk either of these extremes.

We are thus left with *mixed solutions*. When planning the development of relatively backward small socialist economies, the short- and the long-term development and the viewpoints of gaining advantages on the world market have to be reconciled. This is what usually happens now in practical economic policy in the CMEA countries. Even under conditions forced by world policy events, as was the cold war—or, in the case of Yugoslavia, the situation which developed after the 1949 resolution of the Information Bureau—attempts were made to reconcile the development requirements and the international division of labour of *today and tomorrow*. This was so in spite of the fact that the logic of the events—not always completely understood—pushed the strategy of the economies united in the CMEA, among them that of Hungary, towards the second solution in the fifties, and that of Yugoslavia towards the first one.

But even the search for the mixed solutions mentioned is a road full of pitfalls. The compromise working towards the optimal solution is frequently separated only by a hair's breadth from ill-matched solutions. The difference between the two is immense. While a sound compromise produces a hybrid solution from the extremes by minimizing the effects which are unfavourable for development and for the population, in the wake of an ill-matched solution the unfavourable effects of the extremes might cumulate. Figuratively we may fare like a clumsy biologist who succeeds in selecting a kind of wheat with low yield and also sensitive to frost.

Such solutions come about usually when the economy shifts towards some extreme and the correction becomes urgently necessary. The resulting haste produces inconsequent corrections. In what form does this become manifest?

Let us assume that—for one reason or another—the economic policy overaccentuated the elements of the *second* model. It staked too much on foreign-trade advantages to be realized in the far future, and these either have not come true (the direction of technical progress, the demand, etc. were wrongly prognosticated), or the planned level could not be attained (e.g. on account of the insufficient domestic innovative base or the too wide field covered by the system of goals). The result is accumulating foreign debts without the means of repayment having been created, unsatisfactory results of high cost investments, shortages on the consumer market, perhaps inflation—all that coupled with a gradual technical lag of the economy relative to world-market requirements. The momentary urgent need breeds three dangers. In order to avoid them, either the over-dimensioned rate of investment has to be radically braked or consumption has to be curbed—even in absolute terms—or a further grave deterioration in the balance of payments has to be reckoned with, e.g. a shift in the structure of credits towards short-term ones. Economic leadership will increase first of all exports in order to avoid measures affecting consumption and to minimize the brake on the rate of investment. Since it has no export commodity fund that could be increased elastically, it will start exporting "at any price". This strongly raises the pressure for subsidies and increases the deficit of the budget. A selective process will start which pushes the demand of foreign trade towards the *momentarily most profitable and best salable products in relative terms.* Through this (either under the effect of the market or by resorting to operative planning) the pattern of production is also shifted in the same direction. Thus, the demand impulses of a foreign economic environment that is more advanced than the country, produce panic and counteract the whole previous economic strategy. Of course, the established structure cannot be changed radically in a few month. Therefore, the "traditional" structure will remain unfinished and uncompleted, it may even develop somewhat, but by far not at the original rate or in the original mode, that is, it will be *distorted.* It becomes a greater burden on the economy than its creation had *seemed* to be. The new structure will constitute a layer which is not organically linked to the basic structure. Its development will constantly run against shortage of money, its adaptation capacity will not come up to the expectations raised by the external market. An *ill-matched* solution will come about, and one that carries a series of subjective tensions as well, besides objective difficulties. The braking of the development of the basic structure justly evokes the dissatisfaction of a part of economic experts, while if continued, investment and foreign-exchange demands are felt to be a heavy burden by those who advocate the new structure. The new structural elements do not come up to expectation as regards either a faster acquisition of foreign exchange or the general acceleration of development, but the new sector's dependence on, and sensitivity to, business fluctuations become conspicuous. This opens the door for attacks against structural changes. Delays may end up again in hasty actions. In the last resort, the economy becomes increasingly difficult to plan, and its attraction towards foreigners becomes weaker in all fields where it would be capable of innovative activities, and where it should cleverly adapt and reproduce the foreign results of innovation. In such a situation it is difficult to find a single factor to be blamed. The difficulties are also due to the former strategy, inclined to extremes and also to the inconsiderate corrective steps.

A similar situation may develop also in the case of development in the opposite direction. Let us assume that an economy made efforts for years or even decades to gain short-term comparative advantages, neglecting the development of domestic innovative cores, say, it had essentially no strategy for economic development and international division of labour worth mentioning. The results of one-sided development cumulate. The comparative advantages of the given structure diminish because the positional advantages of production are either overcompensated—in lack of domestic development—by the disadvantages of absolute backwardness, or a growing part of profit will be pumped into the foreign innovative centres on which the technical progress of the area depends. The economy is dependent on imports in several dimensions, thus it is continually struggling with balance-of-payments problems. The reason is partly that its export supply is less dynamic than its import needs, and partly that the minimum of necessary exports can be maintained only with deteriorating terms of trade, delivery against credit, etc. This situation will slowly affect all factors in the national equilibrium, although it is rooted in the lack of a policy aimed at finding an active place for the country in the world economic environment. When this becomes conscious, great care must be taken again that the corrective measures should be sound, moderate, or else the strategy worked out will necessarily fail. The innovative centres called into being, among other things, with the aim of gaining long-term advantages will be unable to become consolidated, mainly because of weaknesses in preparation and because of fragmentation, their results will lag behind the expectations. At the same time also the reproductive sectors will be short of assets, particularly in respect of foreign exchange, and the distance between them and the foreign innovative centres will be growing. In the last resort, this, too, leads to an *ill-matched* solution, with all its drawbacks.

I believe it needs no particular proof that socialist economic strategy has to beware not only of extreme models, but also of letting the economy drift towards such ill-matched solutions, "disadvantageous hybrids", in the wake of unfounded corrective steps. Of course, this does not mean that certain fluctuations in economic policy can or should be avoided by all means around a domestic or foreign-trade optimum—which is anyway difficult to determine and changes over time as well. Thus I do not state that a small socialist economy, which has to make up for many things relative to its more advanced environment, must either possess a *perfect* economic strategy or get ruined. I only mean that *a series of typical errors can be avoided, which extremely hamper economic policy*. Such are:

— *A mechanical projection of the momentary changes in the world economic environment*, and the basing of structural policy on these fictitious development trends.

This might happen if we cannot successfully separate the temporary factors and the forces bringing about long-term changes. If we repeatedly build up strategic theories on short-term business trends, the ill-matched solutions will abound. If we regard the short-term zig-zags of the world economy as fate and renounce a strategy, we shall be forced to ill-matched solutions from the other end.

— *One-sided over- or underestimation of the possibilities of the country to cooperate* (to appear on the world market), more exactly, an unjustified generalization for the whole economy of certain phenomena observable in the economy and judged as favourable or unfavourable for foreign trade. This may apply to an irrealistic judgment of our performance capacity in *certain* production lines (technical, market or investment potential), but also to the capability of adaptation of the whole economy, whether we compare ourselves to the requirements of the world economy in general, or to some of its regions, or to partner countries in our narrower environment.

— Finally, from time to time we have to find the sound middle—both within the narrower area of experts and towards public opinion—between the pragmatic approach to our own concepts and an all too ideological relationship. In respect of a strategy, the economic leadership cannot take the unprincipled standpoint that the value of well-founded and sound conceptions should be reduced to nil at the first sign of changes in circumstances. Such an "easy-going" attitude in respect of principles creates the most favourable subjective medium for ill-matched and hasty solutions. At the same time, even if we possess a well-founded strategy, it might be very harmful if we rigidly insist on every detail of the original conception. A strategy must never be so tense as to exclude any change or modification in its major or less important elements. Therefore, in the professional and mass propaganda following the taking of the strategic decision it is not expedient to commit politically the economic leadership to every detail of some solution. It is much more worthwhile to call attention to the changes in internal or external conditions that may warrant a modification of the strategy.

If we can manage to avoid these "typical mistakes", we have satisfactory guarantee for a sound weighing of the conditions of development and "fitting in", and also our commitments to a line of reasoning or a complexity of measures becomes clearer.

Under the present Hungarian conditions it would be very difficult to tell unequivocally which of the "typical mistakes" is the most dangerous. At any rate, since 1957 Hungarian economic policy has been moving in a zone *between* the extremes outlined. The impulses of individual comprehensive decisions of economic policy (the medium-term plans, major development programs, the reform of the economic mechanism, etc.) worked in the majority of cases in a direction *deflecting us from extremes* while their *strength* usually carried the economy over the dead point towards the other extreme. In the final analysis, foreign economic policy has been mixed—sometimes even ill-matched; its strategic elements did not constitute a consistent and flexible system. But it cannot be stated either that the policy helping our joining the international division of labour was lacking in actively and steadily working solutions, which were based on a sound assessment of the internal and international assessment of the Hungarian economy and which were viable also in the long run. Without a claim to completeness, I will list some for illustration:

1. The Hungarian economic leadership recognized and made it conscious (not only for itself, but also for professionals and public opinion) that Hungary, being a moderately developed small economy, cannot join the world economy successfully in any way other than by consistently, flexibly and actively adapting itself to it. It cannot claim an initiating role in all fields of economic life, but it cannot isolate itself either, nor can it choose passive dependence. This means essentially that for the viability of a small country and for its *catching up* in respect of development and attainable welfare to the presently more advanced countries, *it is necessary not only to be industrious, but also clever.* Searching for the possibilities of a flexible and clever adaptation to the world economic environment, and their assertion in the control methods of foreign trade have been one of the principles of Hungarian foreign-trade policy.

2. The fact that the domestic production of basic primary energy and raw materials, necessary for maintaining a modern industry, are restricted, forced the country to *rely on human knowledge as the most important condition of development.* Another principle of Hungarian foreign-trade policy has been an endeavour to realize the industry and talent of the working population through international economic relations.

3. The recognition has also become a self-evident principle of foreign economic policy that the first two principles can be implemented in a more developed world-economic environment only *if our relations are built out mainly in the framework of a community which, by its nature, is capable of providing meritory help in our efforts.* This community could not—and cannot even in the future—be any association of developed capitalist countries. Beyond political circumstances, the capitalist world-economic relations release impulses which are opposed to our national efforts. They make, from the outset, the development of productive activities seem uneconomical and hopeless without which our gradual catching up with the forces of production of the developed world would be impossible. On the other hand, they implant into our economy such way of life, such technical and organization systems which, besides becoming possible hotbeds of tendencies opposed to our social order, may also lead our economic development efforts into a blind alley. All these considerations have not produced an isolation from economic relations with the developed capitalist countries, but have only underlined the strategic principle that *the Western relations must also be based on CMEA cooperation as a firm foundation.*

In addition to the principles mentioned above, many important and lasting elements of economic policy could be listed whose correctness has stood the test of time. But this would exceed the purpose and the limits of this book. My purpose was only to prove that for the creation of a flexible and yet consistent *system* of Hungarian foreign-trade strategy the foundations and the building stones of economic strategy are at our disposal.

CHAPTER TWO

Possible innovative cores of the Hungarian economy

The innovative cores to be developed in the small economies and to be maintained on world level at any time have to be linked above all to domestic traditions. These traditions are alive mainly in the ability of the working population to produce and build up a system. Thus, when determining the possible innovative centres we have to look for advice not only to the history of technology and economy, but also to the knowledge of the living society. I shall try to outline the two in parallel.

The present pattern of the Hungarian economy has emerged as a result of development in several stages since the middle of the last century. In the development of *agriculture* essentially three stages may be distinguished. The first period lasted till the land reform of 1945. It was characterized on the one hand by the development of the commodity-producing large estates, which attained good results above all in some branches of plant cultivation, and some estates in the raising of cattle and pigs. On the other hand, this era was characterized by the decline of peasant farming, which the small-holders tried to counter by labour-intensive cultures. For the processing of agricultural products an important, highly concentrated food industry developed which brought to the market a number of world-famous specialities.

What kind of human knowledge and talents can be brought under the heading of "tradition"? Above all the Hungarian food and *agrarian science*, which has a great past and can claim several new results as well, from plant-improvement through agro-biological research to veterinary science and food chemistry. Furthermore, the *organization and agrotechnical practice*, emerging in the large estates, which could develop, of course, first of all in the organization of work processes requiring much live labour and in the agrotechniques of extensive farming. The same holds for organization and technical knowledge in the food industry. *The great historical wealth of the Hungarian food economy is the constant organic link among the scientific and the practical experts of the productive areas related to nutrition.* This was not only the consequence of the wide horizon of the scientists working in these disciplines, but also of the circumstances, i.e., of the facts that the bulk of agriculture and the food industry were functioning in large-scale organizations, that there were wide personal connections and intertwinings of capital, etc.

The second stage in the development of the Hungarian food economy lasted from the land reform to the completion of mass collectivization, to the consolidation of the agricultural cooperatives. This was characterized by the *large-scale spreading of agricultural expertise*, partly because of the distribution of land, partly under the forced effect of the needs of self-management following the formation of the cooperatives, partly because of the sudden increase in vocational training, and under the effect of the agricultural research base and the state farms which were trial fields of the new technologies. The development of agricultural knowledge never turned in Hungary towards small-scale work organization and technology. Small-scale farming of erstwhile day-labourers provided the basis for their skills, which later bore fruit in the socialist large-scale farms, after the consolidation of the cooperatives. It was in the same period that the flow of industrial technology and approach into agricultural production started, partly through mechanization, the use of fertilizers, large-scale methods of transportation and partly because of the fact that a growing number of workers and engineers participated in directing the life in the countryside. It was in this period that the mechanization and large-scale organization of producing some plant cultures started, together with the start of manufacture-like animal husbandry and its mechanization, as well as the shifting to a large-scale basis of some branches which had been earlier cultivated only on small farms (horticulture, poultry-raising), at first also on manufacture level, but later with some elements of mechanization.

How was the century-old tradition enriched? Above all in *breadth*. Instead of a few model large estates it extended to a considerable part of the socialist large-scale farm. Furthermore, it helped to develop and spread methods of industrial work organization and industrial production methods in both the traditional large-scale cultures and in animal husbandry as well as in horticulture. With this, Hungarian agriculture built up the basic pillars of industrialization, both in the brains and in equipment and also as regards farm size. True, in the meantime the relationship with the food-processing industry became weaker, but this was not of an extent to make the reintegration of the two complementary productive activities, which in fact belong together, impossible.

The third stage, as a matter of fact, is just evolving, when, based on the century-old tradition expanding and deepening after the socialist reorganization of agriculture, a radical transformation started, relying on the full integration of traditional agriculture, the food industry and the engineering and chemical industries supplying their means of production. In its course food production becomes more and more a complex bio-industrial structure. Hungarian economic strategy, more closely the strategy of foreign trade cannot leave this process out of account.

In the development of industry several stages involving qualitative changes may be distinguished. Each of them is characterized by the introduction of new industries and their becoming leading ones. It is also characteristic that from among the new cultures *always those succeeded in attaining the level of the European vanguard whose development was related to some major domestic social program.* Finally, it is characteristic that *the productive activities having lost their dynamism did not die away,* but, after a long and painful search for a way out, took their place among the industries lagging behind the European vanguard and maintaining average standards.

For example, one of the big national programs which boosted industrial development was that the capital Budapest became a big town and the other that in the last decades of the last century the *railway system* was built out. Some industries were similarly affected by the development of the *health service network.* The postal services also belonged to the big ordering parties of industry and at times also the army. In the past the *pattern of industrial development was determined to at least half not so much by the consumption of the population and the domestic productive consumption, but by the orders of the public bodies.* The main line of production of the industries turning out producer goods was to supply equipment for infrastructural projects, thus for transportation, communications, water conduits and sewerage, the health service and education. But the Hungarian industry has thus become receptive to both technical progress—equally in innovative and adaptive capacities—and to close cooperation with the users in the interest of building up a complex system.

It was under such historical conditions that at that time the Csepel, Diósgyőr, Győr, Ganz and the MÁVAG, later the Chinoin, the Richter and several other plants became important factors not only for Hungary, but for the whole Austro-Hungarian Monarchy. With their new products and inventions these factories brought the sector into the vanguard of Europe.

Another part of the industry developed as affiliates of known foreign firms. These turned out products which were competitive on both the domestic and the foreign markets, using usually little domestic research and development activity. Their foreign centre supplied them with the documentation for production and frequently also with highly qualified specialists.

There were also such sectors of the Hungarian industry, particularly in light industry, which substituted for modern technology the cheap Hungarian labour and secured their supply with means of production not infrequently by purchasing and importing completely obsolete machinery from the developed countries. Finally, in engineering, chemical industry and light industry there were important sectors working more or less with artisans' methods, but these were not subcontractors of the big factories, or producing parts, but were rather engaged in producing individual end products.

In the Hungarian industry prior to the liberation of the country there were great traditions of modern complex production on orders by public bodies, of supplying equipment for complex systems, of modern mass production based on foreign documentation, of the competitive utilization of cheap labour with outdated equipment, and of the production of individual machines. At the moment of the liberation, this structure on the whole corresponded to that of the traditional industrial countries at the beginning of the century, even if the equipments were in their bulk more up-to-date and a great part of the products turned out was such which was missing from the range of the Belgian or German products in the 1910s.

In the years following the war, the further development of the Hungarian industry was characterized by the following:

— A part of the modern "copying" sector which had come about between the two wars in the wake of foreign capital penetration (the war industries), was converted into something else (thus from an aeroplane factory a spinnery was made, from another one a truck factory), and the rest, having lost contacts with the centre abroad, were compelled to work on their own (Standard—Beloiannis factory). Then, the nationalizations and the introduction of planned economy washed away and even made seemingly unreasonable the maintenance of the direct contacts the classical Hungarian heavy industry had had with the public bodies as ordering parties.

— At the same time, with the emergence of the sectoral ministries, and within them of the directorates, a large-scale, partly vertical and partly horizontal centralization of the industry took place which *relied mainly on common technical features*, and left little room for development determined by the purpose of the user. This organizational concept had its realistic bases. A grandiose industrialization started in the country with the primary aim of radically transforming the pattern of employment of the population, and bringing a revolutionary change in the way of life. This was a basic condition of starting later the all-embracing modernization. Figuratively speaking—and somewhat exaggeratedly—the first phase of industrialization should be conceived—this means in Hungary the years between 1948 and 1960—*as a huge program of "vocational training" extending to the whole country*, in the course of which every industrially trained person became a "pedagogue" and every new factory a "training workshop"; and the organs of industrial administration were organized as "overseers" of the huge network of technological training. I stress that all this is rather a poetical metaphor. Of course, during this "vocational training" we had to live, to produce and to export. In the minds of the economic leaders all this appeared in a combined way, not simply as a by-product of "vocational training". Still I do not deem it superfluous to stress ulteriorly what radical social and intellectual changes were produced by industrialization in the knowledge, views and way of life of the population. I believe this is the most valuable product of industrialization, more lasting than what the factories created, since the latter becomes worn out and obsolete. However, the new consciousness and way of life of the population is capable of lending further impetus and thus to reproduce the technological machinery at a higher level. This "training workshop" of an area of 93 thousand square kilometres could hardly have been arranged in any other way than on the basis of the industrial ministries and the subordinated hierarchy built out. I may also add that this form of organization possesses lasting elements which are valid in the long run, too. *One aspect* of the development of the forces of production is always the development of the technologies, and the organs of industrial administration may direct for a long time the national development of production technologies.

— The traditional branches of Hungarian large-scale industry which had attained European standards prior to the war, i.e. which had been competitive, now multiplied their capacities in the course of industrialization. Although this "increase through division" consumed a considerable part of the energies of the country and thus—particularly in the first decade of industrialization—there remained no sufficient means for technological development that would have sufficed for "keeping pace" with European standards. At the same time, several new industries were born, started to function or just stepped out from the basements into large factory halls. What we have in mind: a considerable part of the chemical industry, the machine tools industry, the production of vehicles, etc. *The technological and economic standards of the industry started to show some levelling tendency.* The technological superiority of the pre-war leading industries began to fade away, partly because of their unsatisfactory technical progress, partly because structural policy spent more than average on the hitherto backward or neglected industries. This corresponded to the basic aim that employment relations of the population should be radically changed, and a preference toward increasing the number of workplaces not demanding too much skill, requiring relatively small investment, as against capital-intensive development demanding high technical qualification.

At the same time, the industry began to lose its characteristics from a certain aspect. In the early sixties we already possessed fewer production lines taken in either the broader or narrower sense, in which we could appear with novelties or at least with products competitive on every market, manufactured with Hungarian intellectual and productive capacities. This was particularly evident in respect of the complex product systems, whose development and production frequently became separated as regards administration and the requirements of the users could not be asserted, partly on account of their scattered state, and partly because of the shortage economy. In these years "simple reproduction" was going on in various big complex systems, as transportation, education, the health service, water control, trade and households or their completion or expansion on almost the same technical level. The traditions of the Hungarian industry for creating complex systems could survive at most as embers glowing under the ashes. Unfortunately, in some fields also history transgressed these traditions.

— Parallel to industry, expansion and diversification and, similarly, the lack of concentration was characteristic also of *research in natural sciences and technological research and development*. It has always been characteristic of Hungarian technological and natural sciences that they are ahead of production. This is quite natural, since in a country moving on the periphery of the developed world the *intellectual* currents of the developed environment always penetrate more easily and fertilize the talents than capital, and mass education, which can develop only in a developed environment, is also deficient. The "density" of talents in natural sciences and technology, of innovations and inventions could not have been much less in Hungary than in the neighbouring more developed countries. But these research and development activities were mostly not utilized at home. The excellent experts either made carreers abroad or at least tried to assert themselves through relations with foreign research and productive centres. *A considerable part of Hungarian science constituted thus in pre-war times not part of domestic concentration, but of some foreign current. We inherited a fragmented research capacity from the capitalist system.* Later, in the fifties, this scientific structure had to face the demands of industry of those times. Many research and development bases were built out, which frequently operated parallel to those in other countries, and that with a considerable time lag; in lack of a satisfactory number of experts, instruments and other financial assets, not infrequently without the minimum information. This fragmentation would not have developed so easily and would have been easier to eliminate, had it not been born from the meeting of these two factors.

In the sixties, particularly in the second half of the decade, important attempts were already made at reshaping the particular features of Hungarian industry. Important successes can be registered: let us remember the upswing in the production of vehicles, communications equipment, instruments, machinery for the food industry, and of many other sectors. The results of the resolute initial steps could be "reaped", as a matter of fact, in the seventies if we could couple the structural emphasis on the "carrier" areas of the Hungarian industry with a fast development of the forces of production.

The particular features of the Hungarian industry which, particularly in certain highly important fields of infrastructure, are capable of creating complex systems and equipment are still present. Though this character has somewhat faded, and the level of technological and organizational performance has not kept pace with world development, it may be revived and maintained at a high level allowed by the capacity of today's Hungarian economy.

In the following I shall attempt to quote some examples for technical cultures based on technologies and systems of products on which the foreign-trade strategy may be based in Hungary, which may become the foundations of the Hungarian innovative centres that might be reckoned with even on a European scale, and for such fragments of cultures which might become parts of foreign innovative centres. The purpose of the list is not to draw up some long-term program. Although the selection is not without foundations, with their aid I wish to present mainly the methodology of selecting the innovative cores.

a) Export-oriented complex system of products related to the health service

When, with the participation of outstanding health and industrial experts we started working on the plans of developing a complex system of products, we set out from the following considerations:[15]

Health service has great traditions in Hungary. *Important elements of the system were highly developed even prior to socialism.*

The training of doctors already looks back upon a hundred years, together with clinical research, the system of medical officers, the network of hospitals and social insurance.

For about 60 or 70 years Hungary has been an important producer of pharmaceutical products and has also been regarded as a research base for such products.

Between the two world wars the production of medical instruments and appliances started to develop quickly. There are considerable traditions of balneology, spas and related tourism.

Thus, the health culture has had many-sided traditions for several generations, extending to a very wide domain of production and services, from scientific and educational activities through production to various branches of the public health service.

In the three decades after the war we have made use of these traditions basically well, but—for various objective and (partly) subjective reasons—in a contradictory manner.

As regards the health service, positive features of the development were the

[15] The main work was done by István Martos, György Csákány, György Csákvári, Tamás Sugár and Gyula Vajda.

considerable quantitative increase of the training of *cadres*, the expansion of *social insurance* and, as its function, of medical supply to the whole population. Relatively well-organized national networks have developed (ambulance service, public health and epidemic control stations, multi-stage treatment of patients, care for mothers and infants, factory dispensaries, blood banks, X-ray screening stations, etc.).

The positive developments were accompanied by negative phenomena as well. The development of hospitals and outpatients' clinics was unsatisfactory, which led to crowdedness; the workplaces were poorly equipped with instruments, the workload of the staff was heavy and all that worked in the final analysis towards low standards. The exaggerated decentralization of investment funds, the lack of a systematic approach and the constant last-minute rush stimulated the creation of workplaces which were *inefficient and secured a relatively low level of supply* instead of the necessary concentration of investments. The rigid separation of industry along lines of industrial branches, as well as the chronic schortage of funds in the health network *prevented the development of an organic relationship between the health industry and the health service network.* The domestic system of health protection could not become a sufficiently wide and demanding market for the industry, nor could it satisfactorily play the role of a development background; also the culture of medicinal baths declined.

Thus the symptoms of the "illness" of our health-service system are similar to the general ones of the economy, namely, to the dominance of extensive development at the expense of intensification. The situation is all the graver since *a culture of European standards and looking back upon several generations got into a dangerous situation*, and such a culture at that which is a basic pillar of both the socialist social policy and of the development of the economy, and potentially also of improving our world economic position.

Nor were the investment sums spent during the different five-year plans on the development of the health service sufficient for a "dynamic maintenance of standards". The development level of the Hungarian health service shows, year by year, signs of an even more palpable lag not only relative to the industrialized capitalist countries, but it even starts to lose its lead over those socialist countries which have much less historical traditions than Hungary. We have reached now the last decade when this process is still reversible.

As regards *the production of goods to be used in the health service*, here extensive development was less dominating at the expense of technical progress.

Both the pharmaceutical industry and the production of medical instruments and appliances are developing *at an outstanding rate* even by European standards, and the development of their exports to the world market exceeds by far the general importance of Hungarian export products, since a considerable part of their export products stands competition on any market.

Production is *concentrated* in large-scale plants outstanding even by European standards, which is particularly favourable for research and development in respect of both the *products* to be released and the *technology* to be applied.

The Hungarian producers have established fast expanding foreign relations. Through them they have in principle (and partly also in practice) the possibility to obtain intellectual products, equipment, parts, cooperation possibilities and markets.

Domestic production has reached a stage of development where the enterprises themselves believe it is necessary *to coordinate technological development and appearance on external markets,* both among the various factories turning out products to be used in the health service and among the production bases and the domestic health-service networks.

At the same time, the emergence of a modern health-industrial system faces a whole series of problems.

The quality and the development of *products* is hampered—particularly in the industry turning out medical instruments and appliances—by the lack of high-quality structural materials, as well as by the underdeveloped state of the plants producing parts.

The enterprises belonging to different ministries have no practice in coordinating research, development and investment as well as production programs, nor have they any direct incentive for doing so.

Joint appearance on *foreign markets* is greatly impeded by the underdeveloped state of the form of general contracting which would involve complex commitments, as well as the difficulties of financing and the division of profits.

Finally, the development of the health industry sensitively feels the weaknesses of the Hungarian health service.

The above sketchy list shows that at present there are two weak points hindering the development of a complex system. One is the "poverty" of the domestic health-service network and its ensuing gradual lag, the other the underdevelopment of the forms, practice and stimulation of coordinated productive and commercial activities.

— The industrial and service activities related to the protection of human health are a field that will be required and dynamically growing also in a longer perspective.

About two-thirds of the earth's population are living under conditions of a health service that does not satisfy even the minimum requirements. At the same time, the demands steeply increase as a result of breaking with the primitive forms of life, in consequence of urbanization and joining the world's "blood circulation". Since the protection of human health is an *elementary need*—and its importance is similar to nutrition—the demand of the population for health service is such a direct political force in every country which cannot be neglected by either the local power or the international organizations. That is, *we have here a huge demand of the masses which will grow like an explosion in the next decades and will continue to increase even thereafter.* These are needs whose satisfaction will be mostly covered *from state and integrational sources of money,* that is, they are *concentrated and relatively safe markets.*

This relates first of all to the *developing* countries, but its importance will be great also in the developed capitalist and the socialist countries. The failure of the "consumer society" releases the necessity of improving social policies with elementary force, and includes the improvement of the health conditions of the masses. In the latter countries, depending on economic development, more and more means can be used for improving the living circumstances of the population and in this policy a very distinguished place will be taken by the improvement of the health-service system.

In the 1980s this tendency will expectably accelerate. The country that becomes aware of this tendency in time and takes the necessary measures needed for development serves simultaneously its own material welfare and the cause of the whole of mankind.

The system that may be developed in Hungary with great requirements includes the sectors bringing about products and services for prophylaxis, diagnosis, healing and rehabilitation, scientific and technological research related to health, vocational training, the budget as well as systems organization and other services.

In Hungary, the organizational elements of the system are as follows:

The research–production–service core of the system:

— Vocational training (vocational secondary schools, medical universities, post-graduate training).

— Medical research institutes.

— Research and development bases of the pharmaceutical industry.

— Research and development bases for medical instruments and appliances.

— Systems technical research and development concerning the health service.

— Pharmaceutical industry.

— Medical instruments and appliances industry.

— Production of therapeutical equipment.

— Capacities for designing and building health institutions.

— The service sector related to spas (sanatoria, spa-hotels, baths, rehabilitation and aftercare institutions, special hospitals and the related communal establishments).

Related areas of the system:

— Biological and chemical research.
— Electronics and precision engineering research and development.
— The industry producing machinery, instruments and appliances for analytical chemistry.
— The industry producing machinery and equipment for the precision engineering industry.
— Production of plastics, fine metallurgy.
— Health institutions:
  — the network of hospitals, outpatient clinics, district dispensaries, screening stations (TB, oncology, etc.);
  — the network of maternity and infant care;
  — factory health service (industrial hygiene);
  — the network of epidemic control stations;
  — the system of medical officers.

Adjoining areas of the system:

— Production of chemicals, cosmetics.
— Production of medicaments for veterinary use, plant protectives, victuals.
— Production of instruments for veterinary use.
— Precision mechanics, precision engineering, electronics.
— Construction and fitting industry, production of lifts.
— Production of laboratory equipment, glassware production.
— Production of catering equipment, furniture industry.
— Agriculture and the food industry.
— Tourism.

The first circle, the sector producing goods for use in the health service, employs 5.1 per cent of the total Hungarian industrial labour force, or 31,500 people. Two-thirds of them produce pharmaceuticals, one-fourth medical instruments, less than one-tenth therapeutical equipment. About 3.5 per cent of the secondary-school capacities (meaning 12,400 pupils) and about 6 per cent of the capacity in higher education (5,200 students) serve the training of cadres for the health service. About 10 per cent of the Hungarian research capacity available for basic research (in academic and university institutions) specialize in subjects related to health (medical, medical—biological, health organization, etc. research), this means not much less than 3,000 researchers. (Every tenth physician has a job requiring additional scientific qualification.) To this can be added about 2,500 researchers in industry (in the pharmaceutical industry and in the production of medical equipment). The products destined for use in the health service constituted 6.5 per cent of Hungarian exports in 1972. There are no statistical data available for separating the second and the third circles. According to my estimates, the second similarly means about 30,000 to 40,000 industrial employees and a further 1,500 to 2,000 researchers, as well as an army of 33,000 employees in the health institutions. The third circle—again approximatively—affects the activities of about 80,000 to 85,000 people in the whole economy. This means 150,000 workers altogether, amounting to 5 per cent of total employment in the fields concerned (industry, construction and other activities).

In the final analysis, the three circles of culture are in direct or indirect relationship with a rather considerable part of the Hungarian economy. Therefore, an acceleration of its technological and economic development will make its effect felt in a rather wide domain. *As regards its size and its indirect "radiation", the complex health system is of national economic importance.*

Because of limitations deriving from the size and development level of the Hungarian national economy, it would be unrealistic to develop the totality of research, production and services related to the protection of human health to a "world level", and to maintain it on this level. What we must achieve is that those system *elements* we produce should be competitive on any market as regards quality and price. A further objective is that—where our research conditions are extremely good—the industry should attain an *initiating role*, and also the stimulative domestic investment background should be secured. It is not to be neglected to yield to the health industry should a possibility for *joint ventures* in development in complex domestic and foreign undertakings, and the relevant organizational and stimulative conditions have to be provided for this. It is essential that the domestic network of the health service should have closer relations with the health industry.

Turning the whole health service towards exports serves several objectives of foreign trade policy: 1. The *foreign markets* of domestic products destined for use in the health service have to be stabilized and expanded, particularly those of medical instruments and pharmaceutical products. 2. Sales and per unit returns in foreign exchange have to be increased with the aid of *new complex business constructions*. Such are:

— supply of complete health institutions[16] (designing, construction, equipment, continuous supply with instruments and pharmaceutical products);

— supply of complete equipment for health institutions;

— supply of equipment for certain special sections of health institutions;

[16] Hospitals, outpatient clinics, district dispensaries, screening stations, epidemic stations and laboratories, institutions for maternity and infant care, etc.

— creation of training and research centres for the health service, their operation, and training of the importing country's own staff;

— organization and establishment of national health systems (including the training of staff, communications techniques, car park, the system of documentation and recording, as well as the designing and equipment of individual institutions).[17]

3. Performance of work processes requiring less demanding qualification abroad through *cooperation* relying on Hungarian innovative bases, allowing thereby the domestic labour to be engaged in work processes requiring higher qualifications. 4. With the aid of *research licences* to be imported from the foreign innovative centres and by purchasing product and production licences with high technological content, as well as through cooperations with advanced firms, the development of the Hungarian innovative base should be accelerated within the system, but also in the related and adjoining fields ("refreshing" imports of technology). 5. With the aid of specialization and cooperation the scope, volume and range of production made abroad based on the Hungarian health culture should be increased, and, simultaneously, by narrowing the scope of domestic production, the possibilities of power concentration should be increased. 6. Through Hungarian general contractors of international size and through Hungarian participation in foreign general contracting the volume of business activities should be increased and our relations with the partner countries and with enterprises should be stabilized.

In my opinion, the application of a systems approach in development should not suffer any delay.[18] It has to be reckoned with that not only Hungary has favourable traditions in health matters, either among the industrialized countries or even the CMEA countries. *We have no monopoly position whatsoever.* The "health business" brings profit to the country which first discovers it.

We have an undoubted edge over the capitalist countries because

— we can regroup and concentrate our assets according to plan,

— we can coordinate the various productive and service activities more easily,

— the systems approach in the health service strongly coincides with the social policy objectives of our system.

All these are, of course, not advantages which cannot be made up for or counterbalanced, but *positional* advantages, which we have to make use of.

It must also be reckoned with that the détente in the world's political situation releases ordnance capacities (in the USA and the USSR, but also in Western

[17] Differentiated medical-care service, systems for the distribution of medicaments, systems for screening the population, epidemic control systems, blood donor service, ambulance service, maternity and infant care services, etc.

[18] Since the writing of these lines a union of general contractors for the export of complex health equipment has come about. (Author's note.)

Europe), which can be easily converted for the purposes of pharmaceuticals and medical instruments production. If we are quick enough in our own development and in penetrating the markets, this development will take place—at least in the USSR and in some Western European countries—*not without us or against us, but with our active participation,* that is, we can join the development and remain on the markets.

Without developing the domestic network of the health service, an export-oriented development of the health system would be based on quicksand. We have here a uniform process, whose "first push" under domestic conditions should be given from the side of external relations. But a very close mutual relationship has to emerge from this. If we are late with this first push, in a few years we shall lose the existing background and any trial at the foreign front will be inopportune.

b) Export-oriented complex culture of staple food

Food economy is a field where high-standard domestic production traditions are linked with the singular natural endowment of flatland which is remarkable for its *size* also on a European scale. If we think about the selection of export-oriented complex technical cultures to be established in Hungary, we are undoubtedly on the right track if we find one of these in the production of food. The biggest problem of the working panel engaged in this field[19] is to delimit the scope within productive and service activities related to food, whose development as an innovative core does not exceed the investment and intellectual power-concentration potentials of the country, which is based on the domestic climatic, soil, etc. conditions and, finally, which fits in with the realistic demands of the partners abroad. It is the *corn-based production of meat* that neets simultaneously these three requirements.

A considerable portion of the agriculturally cultivable area of the country belongs to the European corn belt which reaches from Southern France through Northern Italy and Hungary, the Voivodina and Wallachia to the Kuban river. The Hungarian corn-growing area is somewhat more than 8 per cent of the total area of this belt. The Hungarian output of corn was 2 per cent of the world's output and 15.4 per cent of that of the CMEA countries in 1972. The average per hectare yield exceeded the European average already in the late sixties, and in 1972 it closely approached the West-European average. Per capita meat production (122 kg in 1972) was one and a half to twofold of that in the other

[19] The details of the ideas related to the food culture are being worked out in the Research Institute for Agrarian Economy, by a working panel led by János Marton.

CMEA countries. Its volume was (excluding the data of Mongolia and Cuba) 6 per cent of the total CMEA meat production.

Thus, the Hungarian economy can export in the long run both corn and meat. If we take the corn-producing area for unchanged, when the yield of 6 tons/ha has been attained (the present US level) we shall be able to reap 8.4 million tons of corn. This allows raising our output of meat to 1.9 million tons, even if we do not succeed in reducing the feed necessary for producing one kg of meat. If the area sown is also increased to somewhat more than 1.5 million hectares, by 1990 an output of 10 million tons may be attained and meat production may also exceed 2.1 or 2.2 million tons. This offers increasing export possibilities, even if in the meantime the domestic consumption of food increases by half. Export revenues and efficiency may be considerably increased by the export of *chemicals* to be derived from a complex industrial processing of corn (oil, starch, medicaments, etc.), and, on the other hand, by the exports of highly processed *meatware*. Also the export of eggs and dairy products may be increased.

The efficient export of foodstuffs, meat and by-products of processing may be a palpable result of the complex utilization of domestic knowledge and the favourable natural endowments. Considering the significant increase of the world population, staple foodstuffs become more and more *scarce goods* on the world market, all the more so as in the developing countries neither the technical nor the economic conditions are present for an increase of food production that would keep pace with needs. In a considerable part of the *developing* world the supply with staple foodstuffs will in one or two decades exceed the scope of problems that can be solved within the framework of the foreign-trade policies of the individual countries. It may be expected that a worldwide cooperation will become necessary to solve the problem of basic nutrition (grain, meat, milk), or at least to ease the hunger to a considerable extent.

Thus the market of staple foodstuffs is heading toward a dynamic development and international funds will obtain a growing role in paying for the purchases. But, even if this factor is left out of account and we restrict the prognosis merely to the CMEA, an important expansion of the market may be reckoned with. In 1972 per capita meat production was below 60 kg in the USSR and Romania, between 60 and 80 kg in Bulgaria and Poland, and between 80 and 90 kg in the GDR and Czechoslovakia. If the Soviet Union wishes to increase its domestic consumption by 1990 to the 1972 level of the GDR and Czechoslovakia, it has to raise its output of meat by 3.3 or 3.4 per cent annually, that is 1.7-fold in fifteen years, meaning in 1990 almost 9 million tons of additional meat production annually. This requires extreme efforts. But the targets may be reduced if regular imports are provided from such socialist countries which can undertake considerable deliveries of meat in the framework of an international specialization agreement, as well as by considerably expanding the area of cattle fattening to the north, beyond the area of fodder growing, relying on imported fodder, similarly on the basis of long-term specialization agreements. Both variants promise big and safe markets for the export of Hungarian corn and meat, particularly if in exchange the basic materials necessary for the Hungarian economy can be procured. Similar, though smaller, possibilities can be found in the northern CMEA countries which are already outside the corn belt.

Although the *developed* European capitalist countries are important purchasers of meat, it is not likely that meat exports to them may be increased by orders of magnitude in the foreseeable future—except in years of business boom.

Thus, in the final analysis we may expect that the biggest absorptive market of the exportable feedstock and meat surplus coming about after the full development of the system will be the CMEA, to be followed perhaps, at some later date, by the "third world", depending on the increase of its foreign-exchange revenues, partly from growing exports of raw materials and partly from international resources. A deliberate development at home (e.g. the solution of producing lamb on an industrial scale) would allow utilizing the advantages of the food boom expectable for the last decade of the millennium.

But this is only one aspect of nutrition culture—though, as regards its importance, not the last one. As the productivity of domestic labour in the agrarian sector approaches that in the advanced countries, and as the dynamism of the international market for agricultural products as well as the prices of foodstuffs approach those of industrial raw and manufactured goods, the comparative advantages potentially given in Hungary's natural endowments and its production traditions will come more and more to the fore. Even with their maximum utilization we cannot renounce the possibilities deriving from the *export of technical culture* related to the production of fodder and meat. In my opinion, *in the perspective of ten years foreign trade in complete corn–meat–meat products production systems under Hungarian general contracting may attain a bigger volume, both to the socialist and to the developing countries, than the exports of either fodder and meat or meat products.*

The complete vertical chain of meat production cannot be fully built out in our country. It is hindered by the lack of two decisive links in the chain: the production of corn and its system of machines. The two factors can be brought about only through division of labour with the CMEA partners. In the development of the *machine system* the Hungarian industry can participate partly with designing and development capacities, partly with the production of certain machines, as well as of parts and units. The building out of the protein base requires, however, such a huge biochemical research apparatus whose creation and maintenance exceeds the possibilities of the country.

When speaking about an export-oriented complex meat culture as a possible characteristic Hungarian innovative centre, we mean above all the following:

(a) supply, under general contracting, of corn-producing and complex processing systems adaptable to various conditions, (b) export of stock-breeding stations, (c) export of complete, industrialized poultry, eggs, pigs, sheep and cattle raising stations, (d) export of complete meat-producing plants, (e) export of research results, professional training, (f) continuous supply of the cooperating partners with improved corn seed, breeding stock, plant protective agents, veterinary articles, training personnel, information, (g) working out and making available software necessary for the programming of corn and meat production, as well as systems organization methods.

I should like to stress repeatedly that the innovative centre need not and must not strive after a monopoly position, not even in areas where it has concentrated its intellectual and material forces. It is not a tragedy if also the fodder and meat production of other countries, belonging to the corn belt, closes up gradually to the high Hungarian standards to be attained. On the contrary, this will facilitate the expansion of cooperation possibilities in respect of both the improvement of species and the production of machinery and equipment. The innovative centre will expand and specialize, while becoming simultaneously integrated on a higher level. But one must not *lag behind.* We should direct our intellectual and material powers so that they should always further the production of food in the most revolutionary direction. To this end it is expedient to concentrate gradually the sums destined for developing the food economy on the areas selected as innovative centres, even if this happens at the expense of the domestic development of other cultures.

This applies also to investments, *but particularly to science policy.* Food economy in Hungary has a relatively big vocational training and research base. About 9 per cent of skilled-worker training, 5 per cent of secondary and 8 per cent of higher education produce experts for the agrarian sector. Of those having secondary and higher qualifications, 8.2 per cent possess agricultural degrees and almost 10 per cent of the research capacity is engaged in agricultural research. This means that the development of the food economy relies on a potential base of about twenty thousand cadres with higher qualifications, of whom about 2.6 thousand are professional researchers. There are no separate data available on chemists, engineers or biologists working on themes related to the development of the food economy, but their number should be added to the above figures. If we consider that this sizable staff of specialists and researchers is now engaged in the exploration of theoretical and technological problems emerging over the whole spectrum of agriculture and the food industry, the research capacity should be judged by all means as insufficient for a *breakthrough* in the development of the key areas described in the preceding. But with proper concentration, with the proper education and direction of replacement a breakthrough may be attained in a few years already.

As regards the *domestic* development of complex production systems, we are long past the initial steps. There are closed corn-production systems and complex fodder and meat combines operating, not only in state farms, but in agricultural cooperatives as well. The vertical integration of the food economy has also started, and for some years already the unified state control of agriculture, the food industry and the agricultural machinery industry has been operating. The food sector has vivid relations with foreign cooperating partners, both Western and socialist machines have been used as bases, but also exported. The pattern of agriculture is well suited for a relatively fast spread of the industrial forms of production. About one-third of the cultivable area, 1.7 million hectares are concentrated in farms bigger than 4,000 hectares. The Hungarian food industry traditionally developed as a large-scale industry. The Hungarian fodder-grain and meat, as well as meat products do not require to be introduced on foreign markets and also the goodwill of production systems has started to be established. Therefore, beyond developing and operating the system of general contracting for the export of complete systems through creating the proper domestic conditions, I believe that the key problem of the coming years is to concentrate the *research basis* related to the food economy.

Knowing all that, we are justified to ask the question whether other traditional and developed, sometimes world-famous, Hungarian food cultures can rank *beside* the corn-based meat system (or, perhaps, as an alternative, *instead of it*). Such may be, e.g., the production of apples, peaches, grapes and wine, tomato and paprika (red pepper). Maybe we have to renounce, in the interest of the culture selected as an innovative centre, the development of other traditional branches of production?

The concern is justified from several aspects. Not every hectare of the agriculturally cultivable area of the country is suited for producing corn, but perhaps high-quality and efficiently exportable products can be produced on it. For the latter, even the research base is available for the improvement of species, plant organization, mechanization and *in many cases these are not convertible bases* at all (apple-improving specialists cannot be retrained into pig-breeders). This is why we would not agree with any kind of exaggeration. The corn-based meat culture does not have to exceed the area of one and a half million hectares in order to develop on world level, to supply the domestic market easily and to secure exports, *as well as to become a domestic background of adequate size for the industrial service branches developing the system itself.* It is enough if half of the domestic food-research capacity works on the development of the elements of the system. In the interest of the necessary concentration it is not the other traditional branches of the food economy that ought to be thrown overboard, but those for whose cultivation either our domestic natural endowments are not favourable or the development apparatus is not strong enough. Owing to our favourable climatic and soil conditions it is possible to produce melon or lucerne also on the basis of foreign species. But, owing to unfavourable climatic and soil conditions it is not worthwhile to employ a big staff of talented researchers in order to raise the hectare yield of potato from 120 q to 130 q, when almost the double has been attained in Poland.

The situation is different with the food products for the production of which we have *unique natural conditions*. Such are red pepper, winter apples, peaches, wines of the historical regions, seeds for peas, lentil, etc. These can remain and develop as special *domestic* production cultures and excellent export articles. It would be in vain to try to export the technological culture of the Tokay wines, say, to Georgia, or to the winegrowers in Beaujolais. Our efforts would be lost. I have underlined the importance of the corn-based meat culture as a Hungarian innovative centre because we have excellent—*though not unique*—natural and intellectual conditions for its development. This is why we cannot only learn from others, but also successfully pass the results of our talent and knowledge to our partners in cooperation. This is a foreign-trade activity whose rate of exchange will rapidly rise on the world market.

c) Export-oriented complex water management know-how[20]

Hungary as a country in the middle of the Carpathian basin and with a mostly continental climate had to realize rather early that a planned and comprehensive management of water stocks is necessary. The best pages of the history of Hungarian technology were written on the subjects of river control, establishment of canals, irrigation projects, water-prospecting, planning and creating projects for the utilization of water, flood control, etc. This is one of those technical cultures where we have a rich past and a productive present. The development level is of European standards, undisputable not only in respect of underwater construction and geology, but also as regards the production of the necessary machinery. The drilling machines, pumps, aggregates, complete irrigation equipment and other machinery produced in Hungary are appreciated both at home and abroad. Expeditions engaged in the prospecting and utilization of water are successfully operating in several countries of Africa and Asia. The intellectual base of the "industry" is rather wide.

[20] A valuable study has been undertaken on the subject by the National Water-Control Trust.

The powerful development in one direction of technology and economic activities has a great future. The nationwide planned organization of water management, rational utilization of surface waters, exploration of water deposits below the surface and their rational feeding into the economic life, flood control, supply with healthy drinking water, purification of water, the fight against water pollution, the expansion of transportation on the waterways, etc., are all prime tasks of every country. The shortage of water and the lack of a water-management culture is a particularly grave problem in such developing countries which are situated in the continental highlands (Mongolia, Iran, Ethiopia), and in the desert or half-desert areas (the Sahara region, the Middle East, Mexico, etc.). The millions of people living there are endangered in their very existence by the regularly recurring shortage of water which has even become permanent in recent years. The possibilities of the world for food production are considerably restricted by draught and floods. The health of mankind is continuously menaced by water pollution and contaminated water. We again have here a complexity of products and services suited for satisfying social needs, which will come to the fore in a few years or decades and whose development promises safe sales possibilities. The guaranty is that the financing of these systems and projects will be solved from state budgets or international funds.

Water-control culture covers a rather broad area—similarly to the one treated above. At any rate, four closely interrelated, yet distinguishable branches can be separated from each other: 1. water-energy where water is a *working tool*, 2. river control, which partly uses water as a *transportation route*, partly subjugates its power as a dangerous element, 3. the supply of industry, agriculture and the population with water, handling thus water as a *raw material to be exploited*, and 4. finally, the cleansing of live and used waters, which creates a technology similar to the recuperation (recycling) of industrial waste. Hungarian technical culture can show results mainly in the area of medium-sized river control, water supply and water cleansing. From the imagined innovative centre of the development, production and large-scale export of big hydro-electric equipment as well as the designing and construction of hydro-electric power stations have to be excluded from the outset. But, since most hydro-electric stations are utilized for two or even three purposes, it is expedient if the domestic development establishes cooperation with the designing bodies of such countries—e.g. with the Soviet designers—which plan domestic or foreign power plants and efforts are made to participate as subcontractors in the planning of water supply, river control, and in the establishment of the necessary lifting, distributing and cleansing plants as well as in waterworks and irrigation systems. The basic condition of such tenders is a high technical standard of the equipments, competitive price and the high quality of the intellectual labour input. We can appear independently or as general contractors in complex water research, water supply and irrigation systems, prospecting for thermal waters and their utilization, drainage, etc. Hungarian ventures may have a future also in designing and carrying out complex river control, but it should be reckoned with that this is a work requiring much machinery and the background for the necessary earth moving machines is missing, and very probably cannot be created either.

d) Other possibilities

We cannot avoid discussing the lines of production which, either traditionally or in consequence of some major industrial development program implemented over the last decades, have become characteristic of the Hungarian industry and of exports as well. Such are the communications and vacuum-technical industries, the production of railway vehicles, buses, the aluminium processing industry, the industry turning out chemicals for households, etc.

If the complex planning approach setting out from the aspect of social needs breaks its way—and we can hope for that in the socialist countries—it will sooner or later become impossible to develop the means of transportation in separate technical cultures. The demands of the population for transportation will be satisfied by a network *built out on the basis of a unified conception*, and its organic parts will be long-distance and suburban railways, urban fast railways, urban and inter-city buses, as well as electric buses and, besides them, also private cars. Both the buses and the suburban as well as the medium-distance railcars now produced will fit into the system. The working out of the system itself, the development of the basic technological and economic conditions will not occur in the medium-sized or the small countries. There can be no doubt that the innovative core of transportation will, in a few decades, be finally transferred into the large economies—in our community into the Soviet Union. Beyond systems-theoretical considerations, this is required by the development and production costs, as well as by the economies of scale. The small and the medium-sized economies either undertake relatively independent lines of production, in the development of special vehicles needed in relatively small series (fire-engines, dispensaries or screening stations mounted in buses, repair vehicles, etc.), or arrange for the production of parts and partial units. Thus the Hungarian vehicle industry looking back on great traditions should further specialize in the future. Insofar as we can raise the production of buses (in respect of engines and other parts) to such high technological standards which secure continually and justifiedly the first place within the CMEA, and a competitive level also in terms of prices in Western Europe, it is conceivable that the production of buses becomes final as a "Hungarian profile". It then becomes possible for it to become the carrier of development-intensive profiles, such as the vehicles for the health service (moving dispensaries, etc.). But the lion's share of the industry producing vehicles will be made up even in this case by the production of parts and partial units, as the main domestic cover for meeting the Hungarian needs for transportation through imports. If the bus industry cannot keep pace, we shall be forced sooner or later to abandon it as an industry releasing independent end products. This situation is similar with the industry producing suburban and medium-range railcars and perhaps with the machine-tools industry as well. As regards these, the production in series of a good, standard quality may carry the overhead of special or individually designed types. If this cannot be realized, the Hungarian industry will continue to operate in cooperation as subcontractor. In whatever manner the Hungarian vehicle industry develops, it has to be reckoned with that it will gradually become an organic part of the transportation system establishing itself within the socialist community. The question is whether it can become a part of the integrated innovative centre established in the Soviet Union as a "fragment of culture" or whether it rests satisfied with the role of a reproductive sector. I do not consider the first alternative to be the only guaranty of national progress, but neither do I believe that the second one would be a national disaster. The choice between the two—the production of road and railway vehicles separately—should be based on economic efficiency computations. But the decision should be influenced by a basic constraining factor, namely that it is not expedient to push to the foreground either solution at the expense of developing or delaying the Hungarian innovative centres marked out by economic strategy. This is all the more so, as in the vehicle industry even the investment demand of a practical solution may be more than what is demanded for raising the *whole* of the productive machinery of the health culture to the most modern level, or for *fully developing* some decisive link of the food culture—e.g. the complex industrial processing of corn.

The situation is somewhat different in communications techniques, the precision engineering and the vacuum-technological industries. All three are points of emphasis in the Hungarian industry not only in production, but also in development. At the same time, it is a problem common to all three industries that the domestic base of parts is underdeveloped and that the range of end-products is all too wide. The road of development may be a double one. The range of end-products should be narrowed by all means, either in the direction of groups of products related from the point of view of *research and development*, or by focusing on the equipment with instruments of the Hungarian *centres of innovation*. In the first case, the fastest developing parts of the instruments and electronic component industries would approach the development of a new innovative centre (e.g. in producing and exporting transmission technical, electro-acoustic complex equipment, complex vacuum-technical plants), while in the latter case the fast modernizing plants of the industry would become organic parts of the innovative centres to be established. It depends on the load-bearing capacity of the economy whether the two can be implemented *simultaneously*.

I believe that if Hungarian economic strategy commits itself to the consistent development of a few export-oriented complex technical cultures, the linking up of a considerable part of the electronic component and the high precision industries will be not only unavoidable but even expedient. The production of medical equipment is an organic part of the health system from the outset. It depends on the explored external market and integrational possibilities whether this industry remains in the present framework or also other precision engineering and electronic factories have to be converted for the technological needs of the health complex. The same holds for the production of instruments needed in agriculture. Also it should be reckoned with that in developing the computer industry we have to prefer the production of machines and peripheries as well as of independent special software helping programming, data storage and control in the health service (e.g. screening examinations) and in the food economy. It is the *transmission-techniques* industry that seems best suited and prepared for developing an independent system of products. This industry relies on an important research base and also has rich experience.

The export-oriented development of the Hungarian *aluminium industry* presents a separate problem. The industry attained its present order of magnitude in the course of the Hungarian–Soviet and Hungarian–Polish alumina–aluminium cooperation. At present 28 per cent of the bauxite output and 94 per cent of the alumina output is exported, 65 per cent of the domestically available aluminium metal derives from imports in the framework of the cooperation, and 38 per cent of it is exported in the form of blocks. Thus, beside the mining of bauxite also the production of alumina and the processing of aluminium are important, of which, for the time being, alumina production may be said to possess developed traditions. It is unlikely that *in the near future* we can realistically set the aim of developing an independent domestic technical culture of aluminium processing that would be significant on a European scale. It would have to be examined whether it would not be expedient to specialize in the development of aluminium processing as part of the innovative centre to be established (e.g. in packaging techniques, building components, parts, etc.), and to increase the export orientation of the industry partly linked to the centres.

CHAPTER THREE

Some conclusions

Reasoning has to end with linking the different strands. Up to now I have tried to disentangle three factors: (a) the general world development, (b) the European integration process and, within it, the particular features of the socialist integration of the CMEA member countries and, finally, (c) some key points of the long-term development of the Hungarian economy.

Two important conclusions follow from disentangling the first line, both for the Hungarian national economy and for the whole of the CMEA community. The first is that the development of the capitalist world economy—including the technological and scientific revolution evolving in the capitalist world—cannot serve as an example for the socialist societies in respect of either the way of life, or the model of organizing society and technology. In the process of our development we cannot copy even the advanced capitalist forces of production *as a system*. We have to develop our own technological basis corresponding to our own way of life and adapt to these the fragments adopted from the forces of production of the capitalist countries independently. The second conclusion is that, however important and mutual interests are related to the development of "East–West" economic relations, in consequence of objectively working factors they will always occupy a *secondary place* in our foreign economic relations, and we can exploit them in the interest of our development only if we link the East–West cooperation closely to the cooperation with the socialist countries.

A series of conclusions follow also from disentangling the second line of reasoning. The most important one is that the process of socialist integration started within the CMEA—its rate, forms of appearance, the quality of its system of goals and instruments—is determined, in general, by the objective historical, geographical, political, social and economic conditions. These bring about the particular "space of gravitation" whose power lines assume a palpable form in the economic policy efforts of the CMEA member countries. Integrational development and the prognostication of how to fit into it cannot neglect the analysis of the development of economic policies in the CMEA countries, it rather has to be based on this analysis. There exists no "good" or "perfect" integration model or mechanism that would be independent of the strivings of the member countries. On the contrary, the "time-schedule" of integration should be synthesized from the conditions of economic development, from conceptions and realities as well as from their subjective reflections as motivating factors.

This is at the same time the process in which the economic strategies of the member countries united in the community are adjusted to each other. Under the actual historical relations of the CMEA I cannot conceive of any other model of the integration than a synchronized development policy. The conditions of flexible communication—that is, the solution of the difficulties of adjustment, of the contradictions between actual development and the possibilities of synchronization—are secured by strongly controlled market mechanisms. The recurring crisis phenomena of the Common Market are also caused by the fact that they do not attempt to *compose* the integration from the economic efforts of the individual countries, but wish to *derive* it from some mythical supranational efforts and interests quasi-automatically constructed from demands and supplies, more exactly with the help of the Brussels Centre. Thus, in actual development, the biggest, most powerful capitalist partial interests have a greater say (among them also those which are expressive of exogenous efforts, as the multinational corporations) than the objectively derivable development interests of the West-European region.

The CMEA integration has to avoid this danger by all means, and also the confrontation of the economic policy strivings of the member countries which *paralyse* or reduce to a minimum the common area of the cooperation. This is why it is unavoidable to concentrate our efforts in the development of the cooperation mechanism on economic protection, on the compensation of the risks undertaken and the advantages to be realized, and on building out the financing system which distributes the investment burdens. In this manner we may expand the scope of common interests to maximum while synchronizing the national economic policies—above all in the sphere of major undertakings of vital importance for the development of the Community as a whole.

Figuratively, and with some simplification, the integration of the CMEA countries amounts to a transformation of the character of *their division of labour*, according to the requirements of a stage of history when the demands for the intensification of economic life are dominating, but the needs of industrialization have not yet died away, and the economies are still struggling with the consequences of structural imbalances owing to fast industrialization. The mechanism of the integration consists, on the one hand, of a workshop of national organs preparing and making decisions, where the synchronism of decisions is forged, and, on the other hand, of a huge "insurance company" which compensates for the risks and burdens (inputs) related to the division of labour. *The integration of socialist national economies cannot be based on the possibility that the weaker or those whose business choice was unfortunate, perhaps those who undertook greater burdens, should lose or lag behind.* The socialist countries in economic cooperation are not linked to each other by superficial business interests.

The success of the integration depends first of all on the quality of the division of labour. Of course, such objective realities have to be reckoned with that determine a considerable part of the division of labour. Such are, e.g., the places where the population is concentrated, the geographical location of manufacturing capacities, raw-material deposits, food-production centres, as well as the lines of transportation and the national frontiers. Supply with materials, energy and food remains one of the basic elements in the CMEA division of labour also in the future. Their percentual share in turnover will diminish, but their importance will not. It will be a condition of deepening the division of labour in manufacturing, whether the supply with materials and food can be solved, whether the interests of the exploiters and the users can be secured. This is also true conversely. The material and food circulation in the CMEA cannot be satisfactorily solved but with a parallel industrial division of labour in manufacturing, satisfying high-quality needs—otherwise it would be a futile undertaking.

This is why I deem the development of division of labour in manufacturing, and also a simultaneous radical revaluation of our related concepts to be crucial problems. *It is a basic and strategically important requirement of the CMEA division of labour that the innovative centres and the reproducing machinery should be evenly distributed among the countries and peoples of the Community.* This division of labour results in the strategically measurable and socially palpable gradual approximation of the development levels and, in the final analysis, in their levelling not only between countries, but also between regions within a country.

For an intensive and planned relationship to come about and function between the innovative activities and those adapting their results, *the plan-collating activity of the CMEA community has to become a comprehensive mode of existence of the whole economic life.* Plan-collation has to extend to the enterprise sphere as well. The volume of technical and economic *information exchanged* between industries and enterprises has to grow by orders of magnitude, the uniformization of *standards* has to be accelerated, the *cost-accounting methods* have to be known mutually, etc. On these bases it has to be attained that every economy should become *open* within the Community.

This does not mean that the enterprises should openly compete with each other, but that they should have the opportunity to link their development ideas, and to use a common technical and economic language in their contacts. From this a greater economic effect may be expected than from the liquidation of obstacles to competition, particularly in respect of the production of investment goods.

While disentangling the *third* line, I tried to answer the question how a small national economy, in actual terms the *Hungarian* national economy, can find its proper place in the foreign economic medium which surrounds it. Above all, I interpreted this medium so that this is fundamentally the socialist integration. It was not at all the purpose of my line of reasoning to become a pamphlet in favour of our participation in the socialist integration, since I might have shared the same fate as the talented "genius" who became the laughing-stock of the whole country with his poster: "Buy shoes in the shoeshop!" It need not be separately proven that the Hungarian economy cannot live outside the socialist community, it is superfluous to make propaganda along this line. The history of the last twenty-five years proved this, much more palpably than any series of data or line of reasoning. My problem is *how* this should be attained.

No country can participate in the integrating community by separately choosing for itself the most favourable conditions in the division of labour, in respect of commercial credit terms, etc., unless it aspires to the founding of a new Commonwealth whose centre it will be. Nor can it be expected to monopolize the position of the technological research centre of the CMEA as a fruit of a uniquely favourable intellectual capital. We have never had such a monopolistic situation and shall never have one. Nor can we expect to shape the terms of trade so cleverly as to attain exceptional advantages from trade for the Hungarian economy. Even if we had exceptionally favourable extracting possibilities from important basic materials, a hundred per cent exploitation of this monopoly situation for our own gain would contradict the iron laws of the community of which we are a member and which secures our existence. However, we have no such possibilities at all.

Thus we have to revert to sober reality, to exploiting our industry and talents by linking them to the industry and talents of eight fraternal countries, by fitting into the CMEA-sized network of innovative and adaptive production units which are more and more evenly distributed.

Of course, this fitting in may also happen so that the Hungarian economy will maintain exclusively copying sectors. Both our CMEA and Western partners will consider conceivable an alternative in which in the Hungarian foreign trade and production cooperation the import of products having lost their dynamism, technically undemanding work phases and parts will be preponderant. For *us* this would mean that for a long time we would be pushed off the road of development to the side or into the ditch. Socialist international cooperation does not know the distinction between "dominating" and "dominated" economies as the mode of asserting the will of the bigger and more developed partners over the weaker ones, but if a smaller and less developed economy cannot or does not endeavour to develop of its innovative centres, then, even if it will not be subjugated, it will be pushed to the periphery. That is, we have to search very consistently for the points where the Hungarian knowledge and industry can push to the front line of innovation.

If we examine the national traditions of our forces of production, we find several points where this breakthrough into the frontline might become a reality with proper investment and research policy, and in the wake of measures aimed at international cooperation, in a foreseeable time. I may add that these are areas almost without exception which provide an answer to cardinal problems of the mankind of tomorrow: nutrition, health, water control, telecommunications, etc. It is not the inflated fashionable industries of the West of today that we are really good at, but those which will remain viable also when mankind looks back wondering on what the West of the second half of the twentieth century called "consumer society" and "technical-scientific revolution". If one of the starting points of this line of reasoning was that the socialist society has to develop an adequate way of life, and adapt the technological development to it, its most important conclusion is that the Hungarian society is capable of creating a part of the material conditions of this form of life on a high level by relying on the socialist international division of labour.